PRAISE FOR *ADVERSITY QUOTIENT: TURNING OBSTACLES INTO OPPORTUNITIES*

"Solid truth, well-packaged. Dr. Stoltz has built a highly usable model that creates significant and sustainable change in people's lives. This is a breakthrough application that provides people a healthy and effective approach to building personal resiliency."

Phil Styrlund, Divisional Vice President, ADC Telecommunications

"Every person on earth should apply these principles. Paul Stoltz has found the missing ingredient for improving and succeeding in the workplace and at home. I will live by the wisdom in this book and teach it to my children."

Niel Campbell, Principal Hardware Engineer, Microsoft Corporation

"Paul Stoltz has written the enduring guidebook for the twenty-first century. In it he provides exceptional wisdom for personal and professional success. I place this book on par with *Seven Habits of Highly Effective People.*"

Stephen Burrill, Partner with Deloitte & Touche LLP

"In an era of uncontrollable, unforecastable change, we at Mott's believe that speed in managing change can give us a sustainable competitive advantage in the marketplace. Paul Stoltz and his AQ theory have allowed us to adopt the position with our managers that "not managing change is considered failure of duty!" Finally this scientific practice process shows us how to help people understand and, more importantly, cope with change and adversity."

Jeff Black, Vice President of Sales and Consumer Marketing, Mott's

"There is an urgent need for this book. The fresh information, grounded research, and practical tools within its pages are essential to anyone wishing to raise his or her effectiveness. Read this book to become undaunted in the face of adveristy big or small."

Jim Williams, President, Options for Organizational Effectiveness

"An unusual insight into how to jump start yourself and your organization."

Edwin Russell, President and CEO of Minnesota Power

"It's time to test your AQ—and Paul Stoltz's timely and important book will show you how."

> Dr. Eric Soares, Chair, Department of Marketing, California State University, Hayward

"Beyond climbing through adversity, AQ is about how we can live better lives. Full of wisdom, common sense, and insight, this book should be available in the seat back pocket of every airplane today."

> Richard J. Leider, Partner, The Inventure Group, Author of The Power of Purpose and Repacking Your Bags

"The expanding global economy, combined with the "do-more-with-less" thinking in today's right-sized corporations, makes AQ one of the best leadership instruments available to your management team. I recommend the AQ philosophy when you are in search of (and in need of predictors of success for) those who are at their best navigating the rough seas of today's matrix organizations."

> R. Todd Rossel, National Director, Human Resources Management Solutions and Services, Deloitte & Touche LLP

"In AQ, Paul Stoltz presents a compelling argument for the need to redefine what it takes to succeed. AQ is both a measure and a philosophy. As a measure it brings together research of cognitive psychology, psychoneuroimmunology, and neurophysiology to form a composite picture of how we approach adversity and why. As a philosophy, AQ represents a way of reframing our lives. AQ is a logic for moving forward, for becoming more than we are, and for taking control of where we are going."

> Dr. Gerald Pepper, Professor, Department of Communication, University of Minnesota

"A valuable, much-needed book! A real contribution to the field of leadership and change. The book provides a creative, fresh approach to overcoming adversity through well-grounded, tightly-organized, and current research, as well as inspiring stories and information."

> Dr. Margaret Hatcher, Director, Northern Arizona Leadership Institute, Northern Arizona University

"AQ is a must read for anyone interested in raising their own performance potential and should be mandatory reading for all professionals, managers, and all motivators of teams, institutions, and corporations."

> R. Martin Kenney, President Emeritus, Notre Dame College, Canada

"AQ provides a practical, easily learned, and highly effective tool to change self-defeating thought patterns. AQ gave me a sense of perspective and control over what's important to me. My leadership team is better able to work through barriers and move rapidly to solve problems. The result is increased productivity and satisfaction."

> Conny Frish, Forest Supervisor, Kaibab National Forest

"Dr. Stoltz's approach addresses the critical element in dealing with the problems of the inner city."

> Rod Hohl, CFO, Southwest Leadership Institute

"Dr. Paul G. Stoltz is a "Climber" whose work on raising one's AQ has given me a most valued gift toward achieving my personal and professional goals. I consider Paul Stoltz a leader in his field with a message and a method that really works!"

> Daniel S. Dubrava, Regional Manager, Raynor Manufacturing

"This seminal book should be of interest to managers, executives, educators, and scholars. Dr. Stoltz shows us how a person can thrive in spite of the adversity of our ever-changing environment."

> Dr. Alfred Raisters, Honorary Consul, Consulate of Latvia

"In a world preoccupied with quick fixes, Paul Stoltz offers paths and payoffs for facing and surmounting adversity. In AQ, 'turning lemons into lemonade' is not a cliche, but rather a recipe for a rich and rewarding life. Paul's work is a creative application of hard science to the soft science of individual and societal potential."

> Joel Hodroff, Founder, Commonweal, Inc.

"Paul Stoltz grabbed my attention and wouldn't let go. You don't read this book; it reads you. You don't pick this book up; it picks you up. AQ is a work of breadth and depth, one of the rare examples of psychological research transformed into practical wisdom."

> Dale Dauten, columnist, nationally syndicated by King Features

"IQ may have been a way to get the job, but AQ will keep you there. Stoltz shows us what, why, and how to sustain and succeed in this downsized decade and the next century. I have worked with leaders, managers, and staff in corporations on six continents. Regardless of country or culture, I have found AQ to be a better indicator of personal balance and business success than anything else."

Bailey Allard, President, Allard Associates, Inc.

ADVERSITY QUOTIENT

ADVERSITY QUOTIENT

TURNING OBSTACLES INTO OPPORTUNITIES

PAUL G. STOLTZ, PhD

JOHN WILEY & SONS, INC.

New York • Chichester • Weinheim • Brisbane • Singapore • Toronto

Copyright © 1997 by Paul G. Stoltz, Ph.D.
Published by John Wiley & Sons, Inc.

Library of Congress Cataloging-in-Publication Data:

Stoltz, Paul Gordon.
    Adversity quotient : turning obstacles into opportunities / by
Paul G. Stoltz.
       p.   cm.
    Includes bibliographical references.
    ISBN 0-471-17892-6 (cloth : alk. paper)
    1. Success—Psychological aspects.   2. Self-management
(Psychology)   I. Title.
BF637.S8S696   1997
158.1—dc21   96-51989

Printed in the United States of America

10 9 8

*To my bride, the true talent in the family,
without whom this book would not exist,
for elevating the human spirit and
providing a daily example of the Ascent.*

FOREWORD

For too many, hopelessness is defined very early in life. Too frequently, what might have been never gets a chance. What determines our ambition over time? What is the unique factor in each of our lives that will determine where we set our sights? And what forces will cause us to move closer or further from their realization? What can we do to alter the outcome? Dr. Stoltz's work helps us to seize control of our destinies, to understand and permanently improve our own ambition and motivation, and to lead a meaningful life.

Now more than ever there is an urgent need to identify, grow, and become full contributors in work and in life. This book provides the long awaited answer to the question, "What does it take to make an extraordinary contribution over a lifetime?" It pinpoints and teaches the behaviors and characteristics that differentiate extraordinary people from those who settle for less, or do not participate at all. No message could be more timely.

Paradox rules the day. On the one hand is the promise of technology to improve our lives. On the other hand is the disheartening societal discord, a growing economic gap between the classes, relentless competition, and largely unmet human needs.

For some of us, technological advances offer improvements. But for many of us, it just doesn't work out that way. Despite the gains in information technology, the burden of striving in modern society and assimilating increasing levels of information has become overwhelming to a large portion of our population. A pervasive sense of hopelessness is too often the result. Old cures fall short.

Adversity Quotient, or AQ, is at once a powerful theory, a meaningful measure, and a honed set of tools for persevering through challenging times. It will provoke you to rethink your current formula of success. Yet, current challenges require more than new thoughts. Graspable, useable, and effective methods are a must.

What determines your drive to live and contribute purposefully? Consider ambition and volition to be plotted on a bell curve. The implications of where you are on the curve are profound. On the low end are those who show little if any effort. In the middle bulge ride the majority who do enough to get by, but fall short of their full potential. On the high end are the 10 percent of people who pioneer change and advancement for the remaining 90 percent. For the first time, AQ unravels this mystery of human motivation and empowerment, infusing us with the fundamental hope, principles, and methods for a rarefied life and career on the front of the curve.

The thoughtful, systematic improvement process contained in these pages pertains as essentially to organizations as it does to teams, families, communities, and individuals. Each will benefit from the three-point process of discovering, measuring, and improving their individual and collective AQs.

Organizational leaders are given a new way of defining, pinpointing, and developing top performers. They are provided with a sustainable path, map, and compass for pursuing a culture of perseverance and achievement, and with it a new notion of managing change.

Teams are given a refreshing and essential understanding of participation, contribution, and interpersonal dynamics. AQ quickly becomes an integral part of any high-performance team's vocabulary and norms. Through the AQ model and methods, families and communities learn practical approaches for turning hopelessness around while fortifying their members with enduring strategies for greater purpose and fulfillment.

Ultimately, this book is about hope for human (one) and humanity (all). With that hope comes the doing and the ability to *aspire*. I believe this work represents the clearest and most succinctly expressed hope any of us has, individually and collectively, to live more fully, starting today.

DAVID PULATIE
Senior Vice President
Motorola, Inc.

CONTENTS

ix

PART ONE

THRIVING IN THE
AGE OF ADVERSITY

A New View of Success

Deep within humans dwell those slumbering powers; powers that would astonish them, that they never dreamed of possessing; forces that would revolutionize their lives if aroused and put into action.

Orison Marden

It is an area about the size of a garage, a rugged throne of rock and ice jutting nearly six miles up toward the heavens. Above the jet-stream itself and higher than most airliners fly is the pinnacle of Mt. Everest, the mountain of all mountains.

As the place on earth that is closest to the stars, climbers are lured by its magnificence and the sheer challenge. Yet, there are no guarantees. Only one in seven who attempt the summit ever make it. Close to the summit storms blow through at 100 miles per hour pounding their victims with triple-digit wind chills, and zero visibility. Every climber dies a little, fighting a losing battle against cachexia. Above 18,000 feet, cuts never heal, the body depletes, and the air is so dry a cough literally fractures ribs. To climb through such adverse conditions is the ultimate test of a human being.

On Friday, May 10, 1996, 31 climbers from five expeditions reached the summit. Suddenly, a ferocious storm took hold, stranding many of the climbers. Within hours, some of them would live, others would die. Among them was Doug Hanson, a postal worker from Renton, Washington. When the storm hit, Hanson laid down. It is extremely dangerous to lie down on your descent. Few ever get back up. Some time during that frozen night, Hanson submitted and died.

Hanson was not alone in facing the harsh conditions of the mountain. Elsewhere on the route to the summit another climber, Beck Weathers lay unconscious in the snow. During the night, a rescue team found Weathers and determined it was impossible to save him. It was too dark, the trail too treacherous, and Weathers was too far gone.

However, a few hours later, Weathers stirred something deep inside himself that saved him from his icy doom and awakened him to his grim situation. According to *Newsweek,* Weathers reported, "I was on my back on the ice. It was colder than anything you can believe. My right glove was gone, my hand looked like it was molded of plastic."

Weathers had every reason to give up. He had taken on the mountain and lost. He lacked supplies, his team, shelter, and any probability of survival. But, confronted with his end, Weathers somehow triggered the inner resolve to take on a mountain bigger than he had ever climbed before. Frozen, exhausted, alone, and barely alive, Weathers would have to somehow move, stand, and navigate the treacherous journey back to Base Camp, a speck in a wilderness of white. A deep sense of purpose spurred him to action. Lying there in the snow, he said, "I could see the faces of my wife and children pretty clearly. I figured I had three or four hours to live, so I started walking." To Weathers, the next few hours seemed like centuries. Knowing rest meant certain death, he somehow kept moving.

It became light and Weathers stumbled upon what looked like a blue rock. Fortunately, it was a tent. His team hauled Weathers inside; his clothes were so stiff with ice they had to cut them away. They put a hot water bottle to his chest and gave him oxygen. No one expected Weathers to survive. Due to the unexpected adversity brought on by the storm, others with greater skill, even world-famous mountaineering guides such as Scott Fischer, would die.

In fact, Weathers' wife had already received a message that her husband had died, only to find out hours later that he had somehow lived. None had accounted for that element inside Beck Weathers that enabled him to survive against such insurmountable odds while so many others perished. *Would you have survived?*

THE ASCENT—REDEFINING SUCCESS

Life is like mountain climbing. Fulfillment is achieved by relentless dedication to the ascent, sometimes slow, painful step, by slow, painful step.

Scaling the mountain is an indescribable experience, one only fellow climbers can understand and share. Amid the relief, satisfaction, and exhaustion is a sense of joy and peace as rarefied as the mountain air. Only the Climber tastes this sweet success. Those who stay encamped may be justified, as well as warmer and safer, but never will they feel "on purpose," as alive, as proud and as joyful.

Success can be defined as the degree to which one moves forward and upward, progressing in one's lifelong mission, despite all obstacles or other forms of *adversity*.

THE FUNDAMENTAL QUESTION OF
HUMAN EFFECTIVENESS

Why do some people persist, while others fall short or even quit? Drawing from scientific research, this book answers the most fundamental question of human and organizational effectiveness. The question takes many forms:

- Why do some organizations thrive on competition, while others are crushed?
- Why does one entrepreneur beat unfathomable odds, while others give up?
- Why do some parents rear children who are good citizens in neighborhoods riddled with violence and drugs?
- Why does an individual beat the odds, overcoming an abusive childhood when most do not?

- Why does one inner-city teacher positively impact students' lives, while the rest of the faculty barely get by?

- Why does one laid-off aerospace manager spring to action and reshape her destiny, while her counterparts fall into fear and depression?

- Why do so many gifted or high IQ people fall far short of their potential?

Every day we see people like Beck Weathers, who, despite seemingly insurmountable odds, somehow keep going. While others are pounded down by an incessant avalanche of change, these individuals are able to consistently rise up and break through, becoming more skilled and empowered as they go. Adversity doesn't create insurmountable barriers. Each hardship is a challenge, each challenge an opportunity, and each opportunity embraced. Change is a welcome part of the journey.

If, like Beck Weathers, you are the kind of person who would fight back and somehow find a way to continue where no possibility of success appears to exist, *this book explains why.* It is a vital resource to fuel even greater success and substantially strengthen you as a leader.

Unfortunately, when faced with life's challenges, *most people stop short* before they have tested their limits and contributed their utmost. If you have stopped short, this book explains why. More importantly, this book explains how to gain the power necessary to permanently improve your ability to climb through adversity.

Some individuals simply quit. If you feel you are in this category, this book is also for you. It will provide you with new insights and tools for strengthening your fortitude and resuming the climb.

> *It is far more important to know how to deal with the negative than to be "positive."*
>
> Martin Seligman, *Learned Optimism*

WHAT IS AQ?

This work builds upon the landmark research of dozens of top scholars and more than 500 studies from around the world. Drawing from three major sciences: cognitive psychology, psychoneuroimmunology, and neurophysiology, Adversity Quotient embodies two essential components of any practical concept—scientific theory and real-world application. The concepts and tools presented here have been honed over years of application with thousands of people from organizations around the world. You will read about their challenges and successes.

The result of 19 years of research and 10 years of application is a major breakthrough in our understanding of what it takes to succeed. Your success in your work and in life is largely determined by your *Adversity Quotient* (AQ):

- AQ tells you how well you withstand adversity and your ability to surmount it.
- AQ predicts who will overcome adversity and who will be crushed.
- AQ predicts who will exceed expectations of their performance and potential and who will fall short.
- AQ predicts who gives up and who prevails.

AQ takes three forms. First, *AQ is a new conceptual framework for understanding and enhancing all facets of success.* It builds upon a substantial base of landmark research, offering a practical, new combination of knowledge that redefines what it takes to succeed. This new knowledge is explained in Chapter 3.

Second, *AQ is a measure of how you respond to adversity.* Unchecked, these subconscious patterns are yours for life. Now, for the first time, they can be measured, understood, and changed. You will calculate and interpret your AQ in Chapters 4 and 5.

Finally, *AQ is a scientifically-grounded set of tools for improving how you respond to adversity,* and, as a result, your overall personal and professional effectiveness. You will learn and apply these skills to yourself, others, and your organizations in Chapters 6 through 9.

The combination of these three elements—new knowledge, the measure, and practical tools—is a complete package for understanding and improving a fundamental component of your daily and lifelong ascent (see Figure 1–1).

FIGURE 1–1 AQ Defined

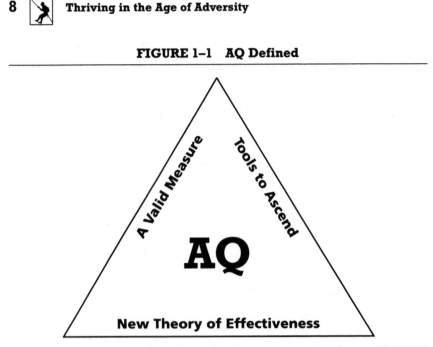

Beyond the Individual

AQ begins with, but goes *beyond* the individual. You will discover that the theory, measure, and tools presented in this book can be used to enhance the effectiveness of:

- Teams.
- Relationships.
- Families.
- Organizations.
- Communities.
- Cultures.
- Societies.

As you will discover, AQ can be used readily in your family, relationships, and organization. Chapter 9 provides knowledge and tools for creating a high AQ organization or climbing culture. AQ

AQ Predicts

- Performance.
- Motivation.
- Empowerment.
- Creativity.
- Productivity.
- Learning.
- Energy.
- Hope.
- Happiness, vitality, and joy.
- Emotional health.
- Physical health.
- Persistence.
- Resilience.
- Improvement over time.
- Attitude.
- Longevity.
- Response to change.

---

will strengthen your effectiveness as a leader while enhancing the effectiveness of those you lead. In a time where entitlement is at an all time high and responsibility an all time low, AQ redefines accountability and how to take take ownership for a situation.

AQ in Organizations

Your AQ underlies all other facets of success. At dozens of organizations in a variety of industries including Abbott Labs, Kaibab National Forest, Boehringer Ingelheim, W. L. Gore & Associates (makers of Gore-Tex), Deloitte & Touche LLP, Minnesota Power, ADC Telecommunications, and U.S. West, my clients and I have demonstrated that those with higher AQs enjoy a host of benefits including greater performance, productivity, creativity, health, persistence, resilience, and vitality than their low AQ counterparts.

Leaders at Mott's discovered that AQ predicts how people respond to change. At First Data Corporation, a group of leaders and I found that AQ predicts who will overcome adversity and who will be crushed. At Deloitte & Touche LLP, AQ predicts who will exceed expectations of their performance and who will fall short. AQ is used to develop professionals capable of rising to the ever-increasing demands of their clients. At Minnesota Power, AQ is used to help leaders break through the adversity of change, reducing the costly transition stage, and speeding the change cycle. Facing the volatility of their industry, ADC Telecommunications uses AQ for competitive advantage, using it to help their top sales executives persevere on an ambitious track of nonstop, double-digit growth. In a growing school district, AQ was used to help teachers develop the resilience and fortitude to teach with meaning and purpose. Within the Kaibab National Forest, AQ is used to ready the workforce and its leaders for the rigors of fulfilling their ambitious vision. Maricopa Community College used AQ to develop staff who thrive under the "do more with less" demands of the workplace. At a high altitude Olympic training complex, AQ was used to predict a swimmer's ability to spring back from any setback or defeat. Regularly, AQ is used to help individuals strengthen their ability to persevere through life's daily challenges, remaining true to their principles and dreams, no matter what occurs.

The Role of AQ in Leading Self and Others

Leadership begins with an inward journey. In the following pages, you will further your journey as you gain new knowledge for surviving and thriving through adversity. But leaders need followers.

In the current times of chaos and change, it is not enough to lead. As a leader, it is your responsibility to make sure people have the *capacity* to follow through challenging times. The following chapters will provide essential information, tools, and strategies for measuring and strengthening this capacity in others.

You will also learn to create a more resilient, agile, and high performance organization. Chapter 10 will coach you on how to create and lead a high AQ climbing culture.

Accountability and Responsiblity

Parents, leaders, and team members alike constantly struggle with two questions:

1. Why won't some people take responsibility for solving problems and for their actions?
2. How do I instill this sense of ownership in others?

If you struggle with these issues within yourself or with others, this book will provide you with a new theory for enhancing ownership and accountability.

A Global Predictor of Success: AQ versus IQ and EQ

The standard predictors fail. Without a doubt, some people are more gifted in life than others. Some are blessed with superior intellects, specialized aptitudes, considerable physical strength, caring families, strong communities, and unlimited resources while others are severely lacking in these areas. Yet despite these blatant advantages, why is it that so many obviously gifted individuals fall short of their potential while others, with a small fraction of the same resources and opportunities, rise above their circumstances and exceed all expectations? This is a central question of success.

IQ isn't enough to succeed. Consider the outdated thinking about the traditional measure, IQ, or Intelligence Quotient. This genetically-influenced, scientifically-measured aptitude was long thought by parents, teachers, and employers to be the definitive predictor of success. However, the world is rife with examples of people with high IQs who do not fulfill their potential. We've all known brilliant people who have contributed far less than others who have more moderate intellectual endowments.

Take the extreme case of Ted Kaczynski, under investigation as the alleged "Unabomber." Kaczynski had all the indications of a high IQ. He was standout smart from youth. He sprinted through high school, not bothering with his junior year. A *wunderkind*, he entered Harvard at age 16 and graduated at 20. He went on to complete his master's and Ph.D. in math at the University of Michigan, then to teach at the world's premiere math department at the the University of California at Berkeley. Teaching was the closest Kaczynski came to making a meaningful contribution to society. Yet, he quit his teaching position after two years.

Raised to develop his mind, Kaczynski never developed his social skills or emotional intelligence. All the way through school he was virtually invisible, socializing with no one and forming no enduring bonds. "Ted had a special talent for avoiding relationships by moving quickly past groups of people and slamming the door behind him," says Patrick McIntosh, one of Kaczynski's suite mates in college. Townspeople in Montana described him as socially removed. In college, he earned the nickname "the Hermit of Harvard."

Although Kaczynski demonstrated great ingenuity in allegedly creating and planting his bombs while evading the law, he was socially inept. Rather than contributing to the betterment of the world, he may have used his one strength—his intelligence—to kill three people and injure 22. IQ clearly falls short as a predictor of success.

Intelligence is redefined. In his bestselling book, *Emotional Intelligence,* Daniel Goleman insightfully explains why some people with high IQs flounder while many with modest IQs flourish. Goleman introduces a scientifically grounded, expanded notion of intelligence, providing strong evidence for the concept that, in addition to an IQ, we each have an EQ, or Emotional Quotient. Your EQ, which remains a *hypothetical* measure, reflects your ability to empathize with others, postpone gratification, control your impulses, be self-aware, persist, and interact effectively with others. Citing several examples, Goleman argues convincingly that, in life, EQ is more important than IQ. As with IQ, however, not everyone takes full advantage of their EQ, stopping short of their potential despite their valuable skills. Because it lacks a valid measure and a definitive method of learning it, emotional intelligence remains elusive.

FIGURE 1-2 AQ—The Global Predictor of Success

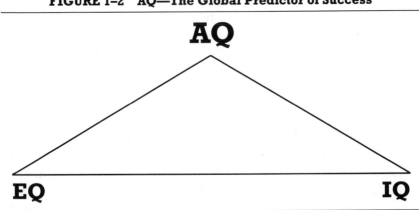

Some people possess a high IQ and all the aspects of emotional intelligence, yet fall tragically short of their potential. Neither IQ nor EQ appear to determine one's success. Nonetheless, both play a role. The question remains, however, why do some people persist while others—perhaps equally brilliant and well-adjusted—fall short and still others quit? AQ answers this question (see Figure 1–2).

To understand the role of AQ in continuing to climb where others quit, we must first define the mountain and the three categories of response to its challenge more precisely.

THE MOUNTAIN—ASCENDING TOWARD SUCCESS

Never measure the height of a mountain, until you have reached the top. Then you will see how low it was.

Dag Hammarskjold

We are born with the core human drive to *Ascend*. By Ascend I do not mean floating in a lotus position into the clouds while methodically chanting your mantra. Nor do I mean simply moving up the corporate ladder, buying a house on the hill, or accumulating wealth. Although, these may be rewards for your Ascent. I use the term Ascend in the broadest sense—moving your *purpose* in your life forward no matter what your goals. Whether your Ascent is about gaining market share, getting better grades, improving your relationships, becoming better at what you do, completing an education, raising stellar children, growing closer to God, or making a meaningful contribution during your brief stint on the planet, the drive is imperative. Successful people share the profound urge to strive, to make progress, to achieve their goals and fulfill their dreams.

The core human drive to Ascend is our instinctual race against the clock to accomplish as much of our mission, written or implicit, as we can in the little time we're given. Whether or not you have a formal statement of purpose, you feel this drive. If you don't believe me, just watch what happens to people who experience an unexpected remission in their cancer or who narrowly escape death. Their instant reevaluation of their lives and "what really matters" often results in profound changes in behavior.

These individuals dedicate newfound energy toward the *important* things in life—things related to their purpose.

The Ascent is not just limited to the individual. Every organization and work team tries to move forward and upward. Total quality programs, growth initiatives, reengineering, restructuring, tapping the power of a diverse workforce, reducing cycle time, eliminating waste, and enhancing innovation are all efforts to ascend a mountain plagued by avalanches, inclement weather, and unforeseen crevasses.

If we share this core human drive to Ascend, why then, do we not see the mountaintop overcrowded with peak achievers and the base of the mountain unpopulated? Why is just the reverse true?

To answer this question, we need to examine what occurs in three types of people whom we encounter along our journey up the mountain. These individuals have different responses to the Ascent and, as result, enjoy varying levels of success and joy in their lives. We can readily spot these people in our organizations, in our relationships, at high school reunions, in our children's schools, on the news—in all walks of life.

The Quitter

Without a doubt, there are plenty of people who choose to opt out, cop out, back out, and drop out. These are the *Quitters*. Quitters abandon the climb. They refuse the opportunity the mountain presents. They ignore, mask, or desert their core human drive to Ascend and with it much of what life offers.

The Camper

The second group of individuals are *Campers*. These people go only so far, and then say, "This is as far as I can (or want to) go." Weary of the climb, they terminate their Ascent and find a smooth, comfortable plateau on which to hide from adversity. And there, they choose to sit out their remaining years.

Campers, unlike Quitters, have at least taken on the challenge of the Ascent. They have gained some ground. Their journey may have been easy, or they may have sacrificed much and worked diligently to get as far as they have. Their partial Ascent may be viewed by some as "success" in the final, conclusive sense of the word. This is a common misperception among people who view success as a specific destination, as opposed to a journey. However, although Campers may have been successful in reaching the campground, they cannot maintain success without continuing to Ascend. It is the lifelong growth and improvement of one's self that *defines* the Ascent.

> *To strive, to seek, to find, and not to yield.*
> Tennyson

The Climber

I call the people who are dedicated to the lifelong Ascent *Climbers*. Regardless of background, advantages or disadvantages, misfortune or good fortune, they continue the Ascent. They are the Energizer™ Bunnies of the mountain. Climbers are possibility thinkers, never allowing age, gender, race, physical or mental disability, or any other obstacle to get in the way of the Ascent.

Quitter, Camper, and Climber Lifestyles

Quitters, by definition, lead compromised lives. They have abandoned their dreams and have selected what they perceive to be a flatter, easier path. The irony, of course, is that as life wears on, the Quitter suffers far greater pain than that which they attempted to avoid by not climbing. Without a doubt, one of the most gut-wrenching, agonizing moments a person could face is looking back on a life poorly lived. This is the Quitter's fate.

> *For of all sad words of tongue or pen,*
> *The saddest are these, "It might have been!"*
> John Greenleaf Whittier, *Maud Muller*, 1856, Stanza 53

As a result, Quitters are often bitter, depressed, and emotionally numb. Alternatively, they may be mad and frustrated, striking out at the world around them, resentful of those who Ascend.

Quitters often are heavily into substance abuse. Be it alcohol, drugs, or junk TV, Quitters are looking for a mind-altering, numbing escape.

Stephen Covey, Roger and Rebecca Merrill, authors of *First Things First* explain how effective people spend their time—usually, on areas important (that is, related to their purpose) to them, but not urgent. Ineffective people live in a world of meaningless but seductive time wasters. This is where we can find a disproportionate number of Quitters. Subconsciously or consciously, Quitters are escaping the climb while ignoring their full potential in life.

You need not wait until the end of life to learn that the people most afraid to die are the ones who know they never really lived.

Ah, to come to the end of one's life and realize one has never lived.
Henry David Thoreau

Like Quitters, Campers lead compromised lives. The difference is in the *degree*. Weary of the climb, they say, "This is good enough," unaware of the price they will pay. Campers may feel quite content with the apparent trade-off between sacrificing *what could be* in order to hang onto the illusion of keeping *what is*. They generally feel quite justified in ceasing the Ascent in order to enjoy the fruits of their labor, or, more accurately, whatever view and comforts they have earned through their partial Ascent.

As they set up camp, Campers often refocus their energy on filling their tents with material goods that make them as comfortable as possible. By dedicating their energy and resources to the comforts of the campground, the Camper foregoes the progress such energy and resources could create, if properly directed.

While we never hear someone define success as comfort, we meet so many who *believe* as if it were their ultimate goal. These are the Campers. Campers create a "comfortable prison"—a place too cushy to risk leaving. Here life is not everything it could be, but it is just good enough. I meet an awful lot of Campers and see daily examples of comfortable prisons in the organizations in which I have consulted. Campers have decent jobs with good pay and benefits. However, their days of excitement, learning, growth, and creative energy are long gone. Life appears easy; they know what to expect, and the moments of anguishing over anything are long gone—except for the gnawing realizations that many of their dreams have passed out of existence unfulfilled and that constant change threatens the campground.

Campers are *satis-ficers*. They are satisfied with sufficing, rather than striving. Think back to psychologist Abraham Maslow's Hierarchy of Needs (Figure 1–3). Campers have succeeded at achieving their basic needs—food, water, security, shelter, even a sense of belonging. They have traversed the base of the mountain. By camping, they have sacrificed the top of Maslow's Hierarchy—

FIGURE 1-3   Maslow's Hierarchy of Needs

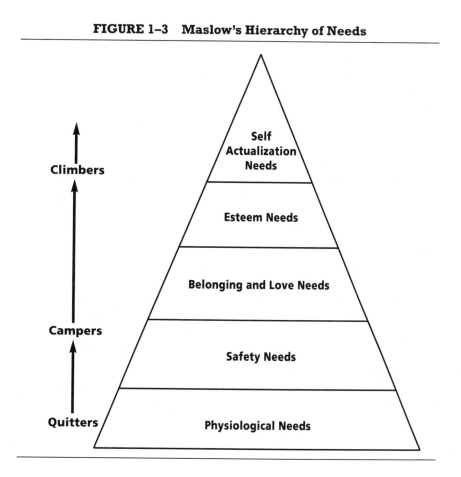

self actualization, the peak—in order to hang onto what they have. As a result, Campers become strongly motivated by comfort and fear. They fear losing ground, and they seek the comfort of their cozy little campground.

Of these three types of people, *only Climbers live life fully.* They feel a deep sense of purpose and passion for what they do. They know how to experience joy, recognizing it as a gift and reward for the Climb. Knowing that the peak may be elusive, Climbers never forget the power of the journey over the destination.

Climbers know that many of the rewards come in the form of long-term benefits and that small steps now can lead to sizable advances further up the mountain later. Climbers embrace the challenges they inevitably face.

The famous story of Thomas Edison, who took more than 20 years and 50,000 experiments to invent a light, durable, efficient battery for use as an independent power supply, tells of someone questioning his route. "Mr. Edison, you have failed 50,000 times. What makes you think you will ever get results?" To which Edison replied, "Results? Why I've gotten a lot of results. I know 50,000 things that won't work!" Edison, too, was a Climber, who shed light on the true meaning of persistence.

Climbers often have strong faith in something bigger than themselves. This faith buoys them when the mountain is overwhelming and intimidating, and any hope of advancing is fiercely challenged. It is the Climber's faith that somehow things can and will be done despite the negativism of others who have determined that a certain route is impossible. I'm sure the Wright Brothers would have had a few words to say about believing in the impossible.

Like Beck Weathers on Mt. Everest, Climbers are persistent, tenacious, and resilient. They keep plugging away at the Ascent. When they reach a formidable overhang or a deadend, they simply reroute. When they tire and cannot go another step, they reach deep inside and press on. The word *quit* is not in Climbers' vocabularies. They have the maturity and wisdom to understand that sometimes you need to go backward in order to move forward. Setbacks are a natural part of the Ascent. As a result, Climbers brave life's hardships with genuine courage and discipline.

Climbers are also human. They sometimes grow weary of the climb. They may have doubts, or feel lonely and bruised. They may question their struggles. Sometimes, you can find them hanging out with the Campers. The difference is that the Climbers are there to rejuvenate, refuel, reenergize for the Climb ahead, while the Campers are there to stay. To Climbers, the campground is a base camp. To Campers, it is home.

Quitters, Campers, and Climbers at Work

By definition, Quitters do just enough to get by. They demonstrate little ambition, minimal drive, and sub-par quality. They take few risks and are rarely creative, except when it comes to avoiding big challenges. Minimally invested in their work, Quitters are the dead weight of any organization.

As a result of their partial Ascent, Campers, unlike Quitters, show *some* initiative, *some* drive, and put forth *some* effort. They will work hard on anything that helps them better secure what they already have. They do what is required. Most Campers will not knowingly risk being fired for their performance. This is part of what is so difficult and costly about being a Camper. If you know one, he or she probably falls short of his or her true abilities, yet does enough to stay safely employed. However, in a day and age when performance capacity and degrees of perfection mean everything and organizations strive to become "best in class," anything less than one's best detracts from the results, if not survival, of the whole organization. It is that baseline of satisfactory performance that keeps the Camper employed and the visionaries who are striving to create ultimate performance frustrated.

Campers can show moderate creativity and take some calculated risks but usually they play it safe, demonstrating creativity and risk taking only in areas that pose a minimal threat. Camping, by definition, precludes taking the kind of wholesale leaps of faith that can bring about significant change. In an era when thinking out of the box has gone from a luxury to a survival skill for most organizations, the Camper's penchant for preserving the box may prove costly, if not fatal.

What happens physically and intellectually to a person if he or she camps in one place too long? Atrophy. The longer one camps, the greater the atrophy. Over time, Campers lose the ability to climb. And as they atrophy, they feel increasingly threatened by those Ascending. Campers may also lose their edge, getting slower and weaker, showing a gradual decrease in performance and results. As time goes by, they come to the cold realization that by attempting to stay in one place, *they ultimately lose ground.*

Unlike Campers and Quitters, Climbers embrace challenges, and they live with a sense of urgency. They are self-motivated, highly driven, and strive to get the utmost out of life. Climbers are catalysts for action; *they tend to make things happen.*

Because Climbers are dedicated to growth and lifelong learning, they feel a strong kinship with the Japanese principle of *Kaizan,* or continuous improvement, being instilled in many organizations. Climbers do not settle for title or position alone. They constantly seek new ways to grow and contribute.

Former President Jimmy Carter's mission is to use his skills and talents to help those less fortunate than himself. While most Presidents retire into relative obscurity, he has chosen a different path. Since losing miserably to Ronald Reagan in 1980, he and Rosalynn continued with their mission of helping others through the Carter Center, by fighting illnesses in Africa, overseeing contentious elections in Third World countries, building houses for the homeless, and negotiating peace around the globe. Many argue that Jimmy Carter is having a greater impact now than when he was the leader of the most powerful nation in the world. He has created this impact by continuing in his Ascent, by continuing to learn, grow, and apply himself to the Climb. He could have quit or camped. He had reached a place higher than most ever dream, but his Ascent will continue until he dies. Regardless of his political setbacks, Jimmy Carter remains a Climber.

Climbers work with vision. They are often inspirational and, as a result, make good leaders. Mohandas Gandhi, the spiritual leader of India, had no formal authority when he overthrew British rule. It was his undying dedication to fairness and freedom that made him the reluctant leader of an entire nation. His devotion to the Ascent continues to inspire the world. Climbers find ways to make things happen.

Quitter, Camper, and Climber Relationships

Relationships are at the heart of all that we do. Perhaps the greatest opportunity for fulfilling one's potential lies in creating a lifelong, synergistic partnership with another person. Such an accomplishment requires intense faith, dedication, commitment, vulnerability, and emotional fluency.

Quitters are not necessarily lonely people, for they have little difficulty finding others who are more than happy to share wasted time or to commiserate about the climb that could have been. Together they nurture their helplessness or build deep cynicism about "the system" and the world that is passing them by.

Quitters also tend to shy away from the deep challenges of true commitments. Their lives may be filled with acquaintances, with few if any genuine friendships, except those built upon a shared resentment of the mountain and all it represents. Quitters lose out in the richest areas of growth and fulfillment—deep, meaningful relationships.

In an effort to be satisfied, Campers sacrifice their individual potential, even in relationships. They tend to seek and successfully interact with other Camping buddies. They may have ventured into commitments that resulted in unbearable pain. Because of their scars and accumulated wisdom, Campers learn to pick satisfaction at the price of fulfillment. Their marriages are likely to reflect the years of playing it safe, offering little room for the discomfort and risk of growing the relationship into increasingly new and more enriching dimensions. They will only go so far, and in so doing, lose much.

Climbers, on the other hand, are not afraid to explore the boundless frontier of potential that exists between two people. They welcome meaningful commitments with potential climbing partners. They recognize the power and rewards of a true marriage of souls. Climbers understand and embrace the raw risk that ultimate vulnerability represents. As a result, Climbers may experience the lowest of lows that comes with the ending of a relationship in which both parties have deeply invested. However, they also may enjoy the highest of highs, or the unbridled ecstasy and rich fulfillment that accompany the highest forms of love.

Like conditions on the mountain, Climbers' relationships will not be easy—sunny, and pain-free all of the time. However, the commitment to advance, to move forward and higher transcends the challenges and fears that will inevitably arise. Climbers accept these challenges and continue to strive for the highest connections with another human being.

How Quitters, Campers, and Climbers Respond to Change

When consulting with executives about change, the same statistic always seems to rear its ugly head. At a recent meeting with a senior executive for a worldwide semiconductor manufacturer, my client complained, "Whenever we introduce a change, we can generally predict that around 20 percent of the people will jump on board, no matter what it is. Another 60 percent kind of hang back, playing the game of 'wait and see.' The remaining 20 percent reject the change out of hand, regardless of what it can offer." Generally, these are the Quitters. They react to change with the classic fight/flight response. Quitters tend to either resist the change and sabotage any chance of its success, or they will avoid it and actively steer clear.

The 60 percent that hangs back describes the Campers. Because they are motivated by fear and comfort, Campers have a limited capacity for change—especially big change. They may support some modifications (upgrading the computers at work, for example) to their campground, but, over time, they may passively or actively resist bigger transitions (such as restructuring the organization). Campers who want to preserve their hard-fought comforts and the predictability of their world, dig in. This is much easier than resuming their Ascent. The collective caution exhibited by Campers can be enough to bring a vital change effort to its knees.

At best, Campers will be uninspired participants in significant change. They may welcome, even forward, acceptable variations to the ways things are done, as long as they do not rock the foundation

of their controlled existences. At worst, Campers will actively undermine the organization's success, recognizing the genuine threat
to their hard-earned status quo.

Change sometimes forces Campers to rediscover the lost joy of
climbing. Despite the obstacles, however, dedicated and focused
Campers can—once again—make the Ascent.

Climbers are most likely to embrace, if not drive, positive
change. They thrive on the challenge change represents and welcome the opportunity to move forward and up in any endeavor. In
fact, Climbers are typically the people you can count on to help
make change happen. Climbers know that change is an inevitable
reality on the mountain. A favorite saying about weather in the high
country is, "If you don't like the weather, blink and it will change."
An inability to adapt to and capitalize on change will destroy one's
ability to Ascend. Climbers *thrive* on change.

Quitter, Camper, and Climber Language

Predictably, Quitters are adroit at using the language of limitations. They are quick to find ways things cannot work. They
use words like "can't," "won't," "impossible," and phrases like,
"We've always done it this way," "Who cares," "It's not worth it,"
"Well I tried," "It's not fair," "This is stupid," "Here we go again,"
"I'm too old (fat, skinny, tall, short, stupid, dark, light, weak,
male, female, etc.)," and "I could if I wanted to." I'll never forget
a retired sales manager whose favorite response to the question
"How are you doing?" was "Every day above ground is a good
one." What linguistic creativity Quitters show comes through in
the excuses and responses they manufacture.

You can find the roots of compromise in Campers' language.
They use expression such as, "This is good enough," "What's the
minimum needed to do the job?" "This is as far as we need to go,"
"Things could be worse," "Remember when . . . ?" "It's not worth
it," "In my younger days . . ." Campers can be heard rationalizing
why the Climb isn't all it's cracked up to be—why it should be
avoided.

Climber language, on the other hand, is filled with possibilities. Climbers speak about what can be done and how to do it. They

speak of action, growing impatient with words that are not backed with deeds.

Lou Holtz, Notre Dame football coaching legend, has no tolerance for excuses or inaction. Holtz had a miserably poor childhood. He was a social misfit with a terrible lisp. He feared public speaking so violently that he would skip class on days of oral presentations.

One day he learned the power of setting goals. He set 107 goals, including dining with the President of the United States, rafting the Snake River, meeting the Pope, skydiving, coaching Notre Dame, winning Coach of the Year, and winning a national championship. Today, as of last count, he has accomplished 98 of his 107 goals. Holtz has earned fame as a man who creates the capacity to win and talks about what can be, not why it can't be.

You can hear Climbers like Lou Holtz say, "Do right," "Do your best," "Don't flinch," "What can we do to make this happen?" "There's always a way," "The question isn't if, but how," "Just because it hasn't been done doesn't mean it *can't*," "Lead, follow, or get out of my way," "Let's do it!" "The time to act is now." Climbers drive toward results, and their language reflects their direction.

Quitters', Campers', and Climbers' Contributions

Quitters lack vision and faith in the future. As a result, they see little reason to invest the time, money, and heartache required to improve themselves. Quitters, therefore, deliver little; they make minimal contributions. As a Quitter's life goes by, his or her contribution capacity actually shrinks. Whatever potential was originally sacrificed, will dry and wither on the vine like unharvested fruit. As a result, Quitters may experience the anguish of a life unlived or they may be entirely numb to the possibilities that once existed. Either represents a tragic end.

Take note: Quitters are not always found in the bowels of society, buying cheap bottles of booze in the wee hours of the morning from the corner convenience store. They can be found in most walks of life—in our schools, organizations, families, and in our streets.

Certainly many who benefit from our government programs are in genuine need and may be physically and/or mentally incapable of achieving financial self-sufficiency. However, there is a growing wave of resentment toward those who are capable of becoming self-sufficient, but simply choose not to.

Yet, not all Quitters deserve to be harshly judged. Many really want to reenergize their climbs and deserve our heartfelt sympathy, if not empathy. You probably have had moments when you wanted to high tail it back down the mountain. I am a firm believer that the first step to transforming Quitters is to hold them accountable for decisions, and help them recognize they have the power to *choose not to quit.*

Campers do not breathe the rarefied air of ultimate achievement and contribution. While they probably have racked up some significant accomplishments and recognition—plaques, awards, and maybe even the gold watch—Campers, by definition, do not reach their full potential. The same can be said for their contributions. Campers stop short in learning, growing, and achieving!

According to the Torah (the Old Testament), "Deeds of giving are the very foundation of the world." Today, more than ever, our lives need to be about contribution. Douglas Lawson, in his book *Giving to Live,* offers compelling evidence that contributing to others enhances the length of our lives, our immune functions, our spiritual well being, and our mental health.

Of the three kinds of people I have identified, *Climbers contribute the most.* Climbers come the closest to fulfilling their potential, which continues to grow throughout their lives. Climbers enlarge their capacity to contribute through a lifetime of learning and improvement.

The fact is, in today's highly competitive world, a team of Climbers can virtually blow away a whole organization of Campers. We have watched giants like IBM and General Motors stagger while smaller, more agile, focused, and determined companies eat their market share for lunch. Fortunately for IBM and General Motors, they were able to reignite the Climber instinct and continue their Ascent.

Likewise the historically agile Microsoft was caught standing still. The more scrappy Netscape headed by Jim Clark, former chairman of Silicon Graphics, Inc., and Marc Andreessen, the technical genius and visionary behind NCSA Mosaic, developed the revolutionary, award-winning software browser. Netscape exploded into a multibillion dollar company literally overnight. The larger-than-expected response turned the heat up on Microsoft, testing its ability to continue the Ascent or settle into camp. With the aggressive, multimillion dollar launch of *Explorer,* its version of a web-browser, Microsoft is behind, but it is back on the path. Today Microsoft is poised to become the largest company in existence, early in the twenty-first century.

Climbers will take the risks, withstand the challenges, overcome the fear, maintain their vision, take the lead, and tough it out until the job is finished.

Quitters', Campers', and Climbers' Capacity for Adversity

Let's face it, no one can promise that life is fair, although many assume it should be. Quitters have little or no capacity. That's why they quit. The good news is that Quitters are not predestined to always see the mountain from afar. With help, they can be brought back, and their core drive to Ascend re-ignited.

Campers may have weathered considerable adversity to earn their spot on the mountain. Unfortunately, it is adversity that eventually leads the Camper to weigh the risks and the rewards and abandon the Climb. Campers, like Quitters, have a limited adversity threshold, finding powerful reasons to give up the Ascent. Campers operate on the belief that after a certain number of years or amount of effort, life should be relatively free of adversity. The price of the Climb is significant, but so are the rewards. Permanent Campers pay the immeasurable price of never knowing or accomplishing what they could.

Climbers are not strangers to adversity. Indeed, their lives have been about facing and overcoming an endless stream of adversity. Climbers do not, therefore, continue the Ascent because they experience any *less* adversity than Campers and Quitters. Quite the contrary. Climbing is akin to swimming upstream. It demands unending energy, sacrifice, and dedication. In fact, many Climbers come from disadvantaged backgrounds, or worlds submerged in adversity. As we read about the common traits of entrepreneurs, we learn that they usually have faced significant adversity at some time in their lives. Climbers understand adversity is part of life—by avoiding adversity, one avoids life.

Every year *Success* magazine publishes stories of the year's greatest comebacks and entrepreneurs. Common to their tales is the powerful obstacles and setbacks these individuals faced along the way. Steve Jobs, one of the founders of Apple Computer and more recently of Pixar Studios, is a classic example. Jobs started Apple with a powerful vision of putting computing power in the hands of the common citizen. When he was forced out of Apple, Jobs was wealthy and a legendary folk hero. He had every reason to quit trying. Instead he started Next, a rival computer company which lost to the cut-throat competition of the hardware industry. Next is now providing a new operating system for Apple computers while moving into software and internet applications which are expected to help the company rebound.

Jobs' next big hit came with his formation of Pixar Studios, the makers of *Toy Story,* a landmark animated movie. On the day Pixar went public, Jobs was worth over $1.2 billion. Along the way, all he had to do was round up funding, hire the best people, convince the world that this was a world-class animation studio, land major contracts, and take his company public. In creating Pixar as a state-of-the-art computer graphics producer, Jobs envisioned something before it existed and then he was relentless in making it happen. Jobs' success is directly tied to his ability to face and overcome adversity long after others would have given up. These are the indicators of a high AQ. Jobs' latest efforts are meant to help Apple reclaim its position in the computer industry. It should be interesting to watch.

THE ADVERSITY DILEMMA

Perhaps the most significant effect of facing greater adversity is what I call the *Adversity Dilemma.* This is similar to a dilemma faced by the pioneers who explored and homesteaded the American frontier. As winter approached, the weather grew colder. As the temperature dropped, the more calories were required for survival—yet, the less food there was to survive the cold. There was an inverse relationship between cold and food.

This same relationship exists between adversity and Climbers. The worse the weather, the fewer Climbers remain to attack the challenge. In practical terms, the more difficult the situation, the fewer people there are who are capable or willing to resolve it (Figure 1–4). As a leader, parent, or concerned citizen, you no doubt find this phenomenon alarming. Consider the decline in registered voters over the last two decades.

There may be no greater threat to our future livelihood and survival as a species than the epidemic of quitting and the commensurate loss of hope that is provoked by a mounting wall of adversity. Giving up and losing hope results in greater adversity for all, since whatever challenge existed has now become worse, and even fewer people are willing to attack the vertical wall now confronting them.

This relationship between hope (belief it will work out), helplessness (the belief that what one does will not matter), and adversity is depicted in Figure 1–5. Notice that *AQ* is the determining variable in whether one remains hopeful and in control through

FIGURE 1–4   The Adversity Dilemma

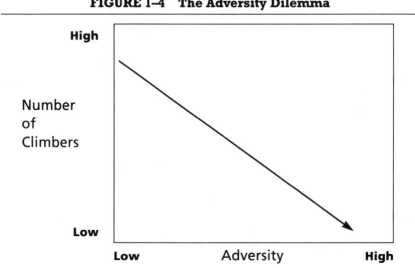

FIGURE 1–5 AQ as the Determining Variable in Hope and Control

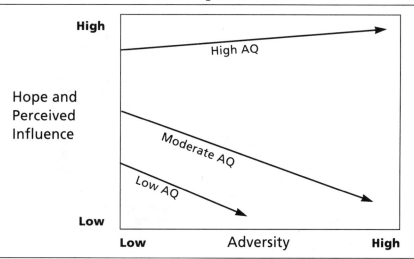

difficult times. The ability to climb through adversity is determined by your AQ. Consider the role AQ plays in your overall success.

THE TREE OF SUCCESS

Once when scaling a rock, I came across a lone pine tree proudly jutting from the granite. I was so taken by the power of that tree and its ability to withstand the bitter cold, relentless winds, and scorching sun to flourish in a place on the mountain where no other tree could grow. What gave that lone pine the power to thrive amidst adversity?

Most of us know what it takes to succeed. Like the tree, we are given varying amounts of the essential ingredients for success. The truth is, however, if individuals have a relatively low AQ and therefore lack the ability to withstand adversity, they will remain stunted in their potential. On the other hand, given a sufficiently high AQ, people can, like the tree, flourish on the mountain. A new, integrated model, the Tree of Success (Figure 1–6) clarifies

FIGURE 1-6   The Tree of Success

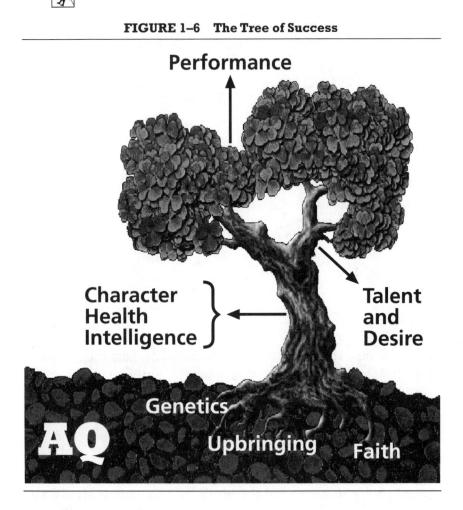

the foundational role AQ plays in unleashing all aspects of our life-long potential, no matter how hard the wind may blow.

The Leaves: Performance

The leaves of the tree are labeled performance, referring to that part of us that is most visible to others. You can readily see a person's output. Because it is most visible, this is what is most frequently evaluated or assessed. Be it for a promotion, friendship, a date, a marriage offer, or a job, we are constantly assessing and evaluating other people's performance and results. Yet, your performance does not grow out of thin air. Leaves must grow on branches.

The Branches: Talent and Desire

The first branch refers to what I call *the resume factor*. A resume describes your skills, competencies, experience, knowledge—what you know and are capable of doing. I refer to this synthesis of knowledge and ability as talent. The majority of training dollars are spent building talent. Yet, if you were interviewing job candidates, and you ran across one with a stellar resume, would you automatically hire that person? Probably not.

That candidate must also display what I call *the interview factor* or desire. Desire describes the motivation, enthusiasm, passion, drive, ambition, fire in the belly, spark in the eye that we seek when hiring someone. You could have all the talent in the world, but without desire, it would all go to waste. You cannot be great at anything difficult without the desire to be so. Would you hire a person who lacked desire? Of course not!

You need *both* talent and desire to succeed. Yet, these, like the branches on a tree, do not grow out of thin air. For this reason, we must focus on the trunk issues.

The Trunk: Intelligence, Health, and Character

What is *intelligence?* For many people, it is equated with traditional measurements such as IQ, GPA, or SAT. Howard Gardner, a professor of psychology at Harvard University, is one of many researchers who has expanded our entire notion of intelligence by showing us that intelligence has seven forms: linguistic, kinesthetic, spatial, logical-mathematical, musical, interpersonal, and intrapersonal.

You possess all forms of intelligence to varying degrees. Some are predominant. If you are like most people, your predominant intelligence affects which career you may pursue, which classes you may have chosen, and which hobbies you enjoy. Regardless of which form is strongest or weakest, it is clear that your intelligence will impact your success. It is a trunk issue.

Your *emotional* and *physical health* will also affect your ability to succeed. If you are seriously ill, the disease can detract substantially from your focus on the mountain. Your ascent can be merely a battle for survival or a daily struggle to maintain. On the other hand, emotional and physical vigor can greatly enhance your ascent. For these reasons, health is a trunk issue.

Character has gained great attention thanks, in part, to the writings of Stephen Covey *(Seven Habits of Highly Effective People), Poor Richard's Almanac,* William Bennett *(Book of Virtues, The Moral Compass),* Laura Schlesinger *(I Can't Believe You Did That: The Abdication of Courage, Character, and Compassion),* and many others. These authors remind us of some fundamental laws of human civilization, as described by Aristotle nearly 2400 years ago and in the Old and New Testaments. Fairness, justice, honesty, prudence, kindness, courage, generosity—all are essential to our successful and peaceful coexistence. One might argue that a society without virtue is no society at all. Character is a trunk issue.

The Roots: Genetics, Upbringing, and Faith

All of the factors just discussed are important to your success. However, none of these can grow without the root factors. Consider genetics. While your genetic heritage need not *determine* your destiny, it certainly influences it. In fact, there is a recent burst of research indicating that genetics may underlie far more of our behavior than we may be willing to admit.

The most famous study of the genetic influence on behavior was the Twins' studies at the University of Minnesota. The studies tracked hundreds of sets of identical twins separated at birth . Even though these twins were bought up in dramatically different environments, the similarities were astounding.

In one example, a set of twins reared separately discovered each other for the first time after forty years. Their similarities included:

- Both were named Jim.
- Both had named their dogs Toy.

- Both took law enforcement classes.
- Both had similar hobbies.
- Both had first wives named Linda and second wives named Betty.
- Both had named their sons James Alan.

Similarities found in studies of other twins included favoring the same foods, using the same gestures, demonstrating the same mannerisms, choosing similar careers, marrying similar spouses, some spouses with the same names, liking the same music, dressing the same, gravitating toward identical hobbies, using the same colognes, looking identical. These studies showed that much of what we consider to be choice is influenced by our genetics. More recent research indicates a genetic link to mood and level of anxiety.

The second root factor keeps many a therapist in business. Without a doubt one of the most popular subjects of discussion while enjoying a hot cup of java with friends is one's upbringing. I was sitting with a group of safety and facilities managers recently. The conversation was classic.

"My parents never gave me the female subservience script that my friends received," explained one manager over lunch. "So I just did what all my male friends did."

"My father was into the 'Daddy's little princess' thing," said another. "He never let me get dirty or tough. Now I'm paying for that every day of my life."

Like genetics, your upbringing can influence intelligence, the formation of healthful habits, character development, and the resulting skill, desire, and performance.

The third root factor is *faith*. A common trait among business and political leaders currently and throughout history is a deep and abiding faith in something or someone greater than oneself. M. Scott Peck, in *The Call to Community*, considers this faith to be pivotal to the survival of our society. No matter what "brand" one's faith may be, a substantial portion of highly successful people share this root factor.

Herbert Benson of Harvard University, a pioneering researcher into the role of faith in health, argues that "Our genetic blueprint has made believing in an Infinite Absolute part of our nature." According to Benson, praying affects epinephrine and other corticosteroid messengers or stress hormones in the body leading to lower blood pressure, more relaxed heart rate and respiration as well as other benefits.

World leaders like Vaclav Havel and Nelson Mandela cite faith as an essential element of the survival of our societies. Business leaders more openly discuss the spiritual health of their organizations and cultures. Whereas few books on spirituality could be found in the business section of the bookstore a few years ago, today there are many. Books like *Jesus as CEO, Handbook for the Soul, The Soul of Leadership, The Path,* and *Seven Spiritual Laws for Success* are on many bestselling business book lists. Faith is a compelling and essential factor in hope, action, morality, contribution, and how we treat our fellow humans.

ADVERSITY QUOTIENT

Good timber does not grow with ease; the stronger the wind, the stronger the trees.

J. Willard Marriott

As you read these paragraphs and consider the diagram in Figure 1–6, you may be thinking, "Well, this is my life's work! All I need to do is strengthen my faith, overcome my genetics, decode my upbringing, fortify my health, develop seven forms of intelligence, hone my character, and I'll constantly improve my talent and desire, resulting in a thick canopy of performance." Right? *Perhaps.*

Even given all of these factors, there is no guarantee that a person, or tree, will stand strong when faced with the winds of adversity. If that tree is planted in sand, it will topple. If it is anchored in rock and nourished with the essential resilience, it will bend, but never fall.

Your AQ determines whether you, regardless of all other factors I've mentioned, will stand strong and true, continuing to grow when faced with adversity, or if you will be crippled or destroyed. AQ is the nutrient rich soil, the key, foundational factor of success that can determine how, if, and to what degree your attitudes, abilities, and performance are manifested in the world. Like the composition of the soil in your garden, AQ can be enriched and strengthened. It is here that we can begin to truly grasp the practical implications of AQ.

Fortunately, unlike genetic traits, your AQ is *learned.* Carol Dweck, a professor in the Department of Psychology at the University of Illinois and one of the foremost researchers on emotional development, has conducted studies that indicate that your response to adversity is formed through the influences of parents, teachers, peers, and other key people during childhood.

In studies that examined how children respond to the adversity of failure, Dweck discovered that, early on, teachers influence girls to attribute failures to their lack of ability whereas boys are taught to attribute failure to a lack of motivation—a far more temporary and adjustable cause. Fortunately, these patterns can be interrupted and permanently changed; you can rewire your brain for success.

By discovering, measuring, and applying AQ to our world, we can understand how and why some people consistently exceed the predictions and expectations of those around them. It makes sense that those who cannot prevail over adversity will suffer on all fronts, while those with sufficiently high AQs are likely to persist until they succeed. They will reap benefits in all areas of their lives. This is why some people are able to stay motivated even in the most adverse conditions. *AQ is what separates Climbers from Campers and Quitters.* When the going gets tough, Quitters give up and Campers entrench, while Climbers dig in and ascend.

All the talent and the desire in the world will go unrealized when undermined by a low AQ. Rather than focusing your attention on and committing any further resources to gathering more intellectual gear, it is time to fortify yourself for the climb ahead. The remainder of this book will guide you through the knowledge and skills you need to substantially and permanently boost your AQ.

The Age of Adversity

All adversity is really an opportunity for our souls to grow.
John Gray

Try this experiment—ask older Americans "Do you think life is easier now than when you were young?" You will be as surprised by the answer as I was when I asked my energetic, optimistic 88-year-old grandmother, my 92-year-old-grandfather, and a larger sample of more than 200 people between 75- and 95-years-old. I expected to be reminded of how they had to fight tooth and nail just to put bread on the table to feed a large family during the Great Depression. I waited to hear the heart-rending sagas of surviving two World Wars and the incredible sacrifices made by all. I anticipated the tales of trudging uphill through four feet of snow to and from school. Surely they would make me appreciate the conveniences of modern life by reminding me of the days of only the most basic foods, rudimentary medicine, no air conditioning, poor roads, undependable communication systems, and a far more limited menu of recreational options.

"Oh, it's much harder now!" my grandparents exclaimed in unison, without pause. "I wouldn't want to be a parent today," my grandmother explained gravely. "With both parents working—I think children have it much tougher than we did!"

37

"I wouldn't want to be working today," my grandfather, the man who had sold men's clothing on the road, store-to-store for 45 years added, shaking his head. "Competition, information, . . . the pace just gets faster and faster. I always had time for my family and friends. People just don't have any time anymore."

My grandparents, the more than 200 older Americans I have interviewed over the past 30 months, corporate leaders, and the thousands of people who have attended the AQ Programs agree. Life is hard, and it is getting harder.

Today we are facing a crisis of hope. Look around you. Despair is sucking vitality from our corporations, institutions, families, children, schools—from our very hearts and souls. We are living in the *Age of Adversity,* and it is eating us alive.

The world has changed in some powerful and significant ways. I am a firm believer that your ability to succeed will be affected, at least to some degree, by the conditions on the trail. It's time to take a good hard look at what has changed, to prepare for some sizable roadblocks, so that you can ultimately break through, continue your ascent, and persevere.

THREE LEVELS OF ADVERSITY

Your AQ becomes more and more important as your daily dose of adversity rises. Business leaders, children, entrepreneurs, teachers, professionals, parents, and teenagers alike describe ever-greater challenges—a relentless barrage of adversity in their lives. Regardless of how effectively one handles these challenges, their magnitude and frequency continues to mount. Adversity is on the rise, and it strikes earlier and more unremittingly than ever.

To help frame the challenges we face in life, consider the "Three Levels of Adversity" (Figure 2–1). Unlike most pyramid-shaped models which begin at the bottom and work up, this model begins at the top and works down to you, the individual. In this way the model describes two effects. First, it describes the accumulated burden of societal, workplace, and individual adversity that each of us confronts along our perilous journey. This model depicts the growing reality that adversity is a pervasive, real, and inevitable part of life. However, it need not crush your spirit.

FIGURE 2-1   Three Levels of Adversity

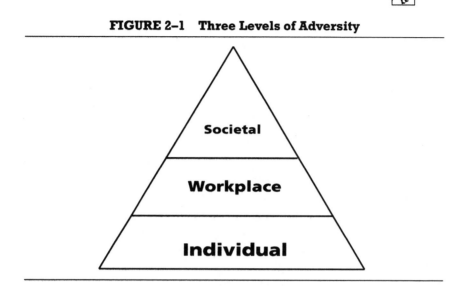

The Three Levels of Adversity also shows that positive change at all three levels starts with you, the individual, and works up, affecting the workplace, and ultimately society-at-large. In order to create change, you must have the relentless fortitude to climb through adversity. *You must develop a sufficiently high AQ.*

Ultimately, adversity can serve as the vital fuel for rejecting the Camper's complacency and strengthening your Climber's resolve to succeed. To successfully convert adversity into climbing fuel and progress in your ascent, you must first consider the conditions on the mountain.

Societal Adversity

We are experiencing a profound shift in wealth, a pervasive sense of uncertainty about the future, a dramatic rise in crime, a heightened sense of anxiety about our economic security, unprecedented environmental destruction, a radical redefinition of the home, a nationwide moral crisis, and a loss of faith in our institutions, including our educational system. Together, these changes are what I call *societal adversity.*

Our greatest fear is of violence from a nameless, faceless stranger. Law enforcement agencies have always reassured citizens by stating that the great majority of murders are committed by a relative or an acquaintance of the victim's. Now that falsehood has been unmasked.

Atlantic Monthly

Crime is the number one concern among Americans and with good cause. According to the *Atlantic Monthly,* eight out of ten American adults will be victims of violent crime. One in four will be victims of three or more violent crimes. In response, President Bill Clinton passed a crime bill in 1994 that would add 100,000 officers to our streets. In order to return to the ratio of police officers to crimes we enjoyed in 1960, 5,000,000 new officers would have to be hired.

Our streets are particularly dangerous for minorities. According to the Department of Justice, one in every twenty-one black men can expect to be murdered. This is more than double the death rate of American servicemen in the Second World War.

Most alarming is the trend toward younger criminals and more deadly weapons. Schools are no longer a safe haven for our children. Twenty percent of high school students carry a weapon on any given day, including 100,000 handguns. According to *USA Today,* 42 percent of high school students report an increase in violence over the past year, with 25 percent being regularly in fear for their safety. The problem is especially acute for teenage women, 30 percent of whom are sexually assaulted. Juvenile murders alone are up 93 percent since 1982.

Dean Fox of Northeastern University, the nation's foremost criminologist, warns that despite the recent dip in urban crime, "we haven't seen anything yet." As a new generation of undersupervised children reach their teens, crime levels are expected to reach unprecedented highs.

Drugs are sure to exacerbate an already disturbing trend as drug use among 12- to 17-year-olds has risen by 78 percent since 1992. Of the growing menu of mind-altering substances, heroin is the drug with the fastest growing number of users. The strength of the drug used is up from 10 percent to 40 to 90 percent in some major cities. And the price of heroin has dropped 75 to 90 percent on the streets.

The home has become both a cause and symptom of the rising level of societal adversity. Today we are told 60 percent of new marriages will end in divorce or separation. Traditional family homes (two biological parents with children) made up only 8 percent of all homes in 1984. There has been a 200 percent increase in single-parent homes since 1970. Children from these homes are 164 percent more likely to give birth out of wedlock and 93 percent more likely to get divorced should they get married.

More and more children are having children. In 1996, there were 500,000 babies born to teenage mothers. Since 1960, illegitimate births are up 400 percent. It may be no surprise, therefore, that children make up 48 percent of our poor.

Children suffer the most from their fragmented upbringing. Many lose hope. Teen suicide has tripled since 1960—59 percent of our teenagers know someone who has attempted suicide, 26 percent know someone who has succeeded. The numbers are more alarming among Native American children with 30 percent having attempted suicide. Divorce contributes to as many as 3 out of 4 teen suicides and 4 out of 5 teen psychiatric admissions. The experts tell us that these and other means are ways teenagers are expressing a loss of control over their lives. Psychologists report a disturbing trend of self-mutilation, including burning, cutting, and disfiguring among teenage women.

The impact on our children's moral development is severe. Two thirds of America's youth do not believe in the Ten Commandments or any rules of right and wrong, and 76 percent of Americans believe we are in a state of moral decline.

Many turn to our educational system for answers. Yet, we must ask, *who is raising our children?* Preschoolers watch an average of four hours of television per day. A teenager spends, on average, 1.8 hours per week reading, 5.6 hours working on homework, and 21 hours watching television. On a given day, teenagers spend, on average, five minutes with their fathers and twenty minutes with their mothers. Due to the unfiltered viewing of television, children see 100,000 acts of violence by the end of grade school.

For many, education fails to provide the much-needed hope. 35 percent of college graduates take jobs that don't require a college degree, up from 15 percent five years ago.

Comparing the results of two nationwide surveys of teachers—one in 1940 and one in 1990—says much about the changes that have taken place.

Top Problems Reported by Teachers in 1940	**Top Problems Reported by Teachers in 1990**
■ Talking out of turn.	■ Drug abuse.
■ Making noise.	■ Alcohol abuse.
■ Running in the halls.	■ Pregnancy.
■ Cutting in line.	■ Suicide.
■ Dress code violations.	■ Rape.
■ Lingering.	■ Robbery.
■ Chewing gum.	■ Assault.

Workplace Adversity

Okay, job security is dead. Where do we go from here?

BusinessWeek

The cover of *Newsweek* magazine declares, "Work Is Hell." The article describes the incessant pummeling of demands and uncertainty today's workers must face. "Constant change is here to stay" has become the mantra of the workplace as we move toward a new millenium. The security blanket of a regular paycheck, long-term employment, social security, and a pension has been weakened for all, and ripped to shreds for millions. *USA Today* reports that worker anxiety is at an all time high. People go to work each day with all the optimism of a Bosnian minesweeper. "What will happen today?" is the question on everyone's mind. Reengineering, restructuring, rightsizing, downsizing, revitalizing, and decentralizing have all taken their toll on millions of workers over recent years.

As long as there is tangible fear out there—and there is—people are going to work harder. Workers will learn to be more selfish, not expect very much from management, and it has to mean a decline in productivity.

Jeffrey M. Humphreys, University of Georgia Economist

As a result, workers must constantly scramble to upgrade their knowledge and skills—scared into action by the realization that everyone is self-employed. So what's the pay off for doing more with less? In the last 20 years, American workers have added one month per year to their work schedules. They work more and earn less, and as a result frustrations mount.

Adversity in the workplace is on the rise. We see it in an escalation of violence and a loss of real income. Median net worth for 35- to 44-year-olds has dropped 33 percent since 1980. Loss of income and job security has spawned pervasive fear and, for many, a sense of desperation. In some cases, the response is extreme. Nationwide, more than 2 million people were attacked in the workplace in 1995.

These trends are simply the manifested fears of millions of people. Many worry about their place in this new global information-age economy.

Most people who lose their jobs midlife do wind up making less money in new ones.
James L. Medoff Professor, Harvard University

Individual Adversity

As you move down the model from societal through workplace adversity, the third and final level is individual adversity. Individual adversity is at the bottom because, as one AQ program participant put it, "Stuff flows downhill." You are the one who carries around the accumulated burden of all three levels.

One of the most revealing facts I have uncovered is: The average 6-year-old laughs 300 times per day. The average adult laughs just 17. This is the accumulated effect of adversity over time. For most people, life is nothing to laugh at.

Conversely, the individual is on the bottom, because that is where change begins and control is instigated. It is the level at which you can make a difference.

As you consider your own challenges along with those listed above, you may be thinking, "I knew it was bad, but," or you may be asking yourself, "How did all of this ever happen?"

HOW DID IT GET SO BAD?

Few events can trigger greater introspection, sweet recollections, or even depression, than a high school reunion. It is a time of fond reminiscence, painful memories, and traditions relived. A friend of mine shared this story of his reunion.

Flagstaff, Arizona, is nestled in the foothills of the San Francisco Peaks, which soar from their base at 7,000 feet to a pinnacle of 12,643 feet. In 1980, the year Eric graduated from high school, Flagstaff was a rural western-style town of 28,000 people. The night of their graduation, Eric and his high school buddies decided to create a tradition. That night, after the ceremony, like many graduates, they went out drinking. They bought their stash and hit the road. They drove off the paved roads and past the outskirts of town, parking in a deserted dirt clearing.

As if to celebrate their immortality, every guy was required to down a six-pack of beer. Then, they hiked up the 9,300 feet of Mt. Eldon in the moonlight, while bellowing the school fight song at the top of their lungs. At the top, they lay on their backs, looking at the stars, and shared their deepest dreams about life into the cool, crisp, hours of dawn. Bucky, Eric's closest friend at the time, vividly described how he would play college ball, and travel the world, meeting beautiful women and creating an international import-export business. He spoke with great passion and bravado.

That night, the world was perfect, and theirs for the taking. It seemed such a fitting conclusion to their high school careers, that Eric and his friends decided to relive the moment.

At their fifteen-year high school reunion, Eric and his buddies got together. Eric was stunned by how much some of them had aged. Yet, they frantically attempted to rekindle the old fire. Finally, after a couple of cocktails, "Bucky" (now "Bernard," a manufacturing manager), grabbed Eric by the elbow. "Hey guys! Remember grad night?" (He looked around the circle.) They nodded their understanding. "Let's do it! What do you guys say?" In a courageous burst of forced enthusiasm, all agreed. Except that night was different.

It is said that you can never go back. Likewise, their ritual could not be relived. That night they drove the same roads they had fifteen years before—roads now populated with malls and fast-food franchises. Flagstaff was now a mountain-chic city of 56,000. The dirt clearing was now a fully-lit parking area patrolled by the National Forest Service. They were greeted by a huge trail sign, welcoming them and enumerating a long list of hikers do's

*and don'ts. Yes, they brought beer. But, more sensible now, no one dared
drink an entire six-pack. Instead, three guys drank a couple of light beers,
and another guy, a recovering alcoholic, responsibly chose an alcohol-free
brand. After making a fairly weak display of downing their beverages, they
started their hike. They started out singing, but this time the trail seemed
steeper, the song gave way to the panting of these thirty-something-year-old
hikers—the hike had become a climb. Eric, still in reasonably good shape,
was dismayed by how soft his friends had become. Even Bucky, the ex-
running back, was struggling. It seemed like yesterday that they had bounded
up this hill, half-drunk, singing at the tops of their lungs. Now they gasped
and panted, and the hill had become as formidable as Mount Everest.*

*Half way up, three guys reluctantly called it quits, probably sparing
themselves a coronary. The rest persevered. At the top, they laid on their
backs, more exhausted than exhilarated, looking at the stars. Except this
time, there was pain in their voices as most of them reflected on their dreams
for the first time in over a decade, and each rationalized the compromises he
had made along the way. The entire group was strangely quiet on the way
down. How had all of the others aged so much? Eric wondered. What had
happened to their spirits and strength? It struck Eric as odd, if not chilling,
that, had he told his friend Bucky fifteen years ago that he would some day
be bald, overweight, divorced, and never travel beyond the West Coast, Bucky
would have punched him in the face. Tonight, Bucky was matter-of-fact, if
not resigned. Eric was stunned by the power of gradual change. Fifteen years
ago, had he and his buddies awoke to the malls, concrete, government reg-
ulations, receding hairlines, and pot-bellies-in-the-making, they would have
been immobilized with shock. Yet, when these changes occur over time, they
are accepted if not completely unnoticed.*

*Upon returning home, Eric walked by the bathroom mirror and paused.
This time, for the first time, he saw the face his friends must have seen. Although healthy and strong, he too had aged. In a moment, he saw the pas-
sage of fifteen years.*

Eric experienced the powerful realization of gradual change accumulated over time. As you consider the preceding lists of societal,
workplace, and your own individual adversity, you may have been
struck with a similar realization.

Confronting the accumulated effects of the gradual accretion
of adversity can be brutal. Whether it is the slow disintegration of
a relationship, the loss of enthusiasm for a job, the amassing of
unwanted pounds, the daily march of a receding hair line, the

year-by-year weathering of a house, the rusting of a car, the dilapidation of a neighborhood, the degradation of our environment, or the aging of our parents, none of these happen overnight. These are examples of *gradual* change. Yet when confronted with the total effect over time, we may be shocked.

The same could be said for confronting the gradual, yet dramatic rise in adversity. Imagine opening a newspaper in 1950 and reading that 20 percent of high school students were going to carry weapons to school that day! How would you respond? Most likely you would be shocked and scared. You might jump to your feet, turn to the person next to you and yell, "Call out the National Guard!" Or imagine the response a teacher would get if he stood up in a school board meeting today and announced, "I have an extremely serious problem which we must address immediately. I have children chewing gum in my classroom!" People would die with laughter! The changes I have described are the most insidious kind: They are *gradual.*

While inspiring some to action, the accumulated effects of large-scale adversity can weigh heavily on one's soul. For many people, the danger is a loss of hope.

Hope is the lifeblood of possibilities. You need not lose hope. You need not resign yourself to this "fate." Quite the contrary, unlike the inevitability of aging, you need not accept a world gone awry. You have the remainder of your life to make a difference, but only if you *refuse* to abandon the ascent.

I have discovered that improving how you *respond* to adversity improves your ability to overcome it and persevere. This is done by understanding, measuring, and raising your AQ. When adversity is on the rise, you need greater creativity, courage, fortitude, persistence, and resilience.

But, beware: Without a sufficiently high AQ, you may choose a dangerous fork in the road.

FOUR DANGEROUS FORKS IN THE TRAIL TO THE TOP

As adversity increases, the trail to the top becomes more rigorous. Saddled with the weight of your mounting burden, you confront the challenge every day. Your trail is strewn by the boulders resulting from an avalanche of change, washed out by the flood-waters of fear, scorched by the searing heat of global competition, eroded by failed attempts, and blasted by the incessant winds of time. Yet, *ascend you must.* Giving up on the climb is nothing short of giving up on your potential,on your contribution—on your *life.*

Any deviation is an irretrievable loss of time, life, and opportunity. Yet, as the trail becomes increasingly difficult, more and more people may abandon the ascent. As a result, they may opt for one of four dangerous forks in the trail. These are potentially damaging responses to the adversity in our lives—responses you can avoid.

Fork 1: The Climber-Turned-Camper Option

The mountain appears insurmountable. The increasing adversity of the ascent makes it more daring and riskier to climb than ever before. As a result, more and more people stop striving to move forward and up in their lives and take the trail-less-challenging (see Figure 1–2 in Chapter 1). Be it in their own growth, careers, relationships, contribution, or self-awareness, they come to a halt part way up their mountain, setting up camp and living under the false assumption that their little campsite on the mountain will remain forever stable.

In camping, these individuals risk spiritual, physical, mental, and emotional atrophy. Campers can lose their ability to ascend. They sacrifice dreams, fulfillment, and self-actualization in order to preserve the facade of comfort and stability they worked so hard to build.

Yet, campers are not to be judged harshly. They make up the bulk of our society and our workplaces. They are fortified by the growing multitude of other campers who make similar choices. Campers are making what seems to be a sound decision, protecting themselves from the winds of change that pound incessantly at their tents. However, in reality, the storm is never-ending. By waiting out the storm, they wait out life. Constant change *is here to stay!*

The campground has its own gravitational force. The temptation to camp in hope of waiting out the storm of change or simply to avoid the incessant challenge of the climb is powerful. Yet, the consequences of camping are severe and the joys of fighting the pull and not getting sucked into the easy path are great.

I remember my summer working in the Grand Teton National Park. I waited tables at the local grill. One day, a heavyset man from New York arrived with his family in tow. He waved me over. "What's there to do around here?" he asked impatiently. I pointed toward the mountains and smiled. "Oh, we're in no shape to do that!" he exclaimed. I told him that if he left early and took it slow, he and his family could experience the magic of the mountains, maybe viewing some wildlife. He looked at me as if I were crazy.

The next morning, as I set out for a 22-mile hike up the Grand Teton, I saw this man and his family standing in the trail, frozen in their tracks. Not 20 yards away stood a bull moose proudly displaying a full rack. The moose slowly shambled away, vanishing into the morning mist. I walked by the man, and he turned, smiling and said, "Now I understand. This is what it's all about." And he and his family continued their gradual but courageous hike into the unknown.

For this moment at least, he had begun to shift from a Camper to a Climber.

Fork 2: The Technology-as-God Option

A second, alarming trend has been the shift away from faith in human solutions toward technological ones. As the ascent becomes increasingly challenging, it is easy to turn from the higher power of purpose and one's own abilities toward technology. But with this shift comes a dangerous loss of perceived control over our lives. An analysis of the thirty years of literature regarding the environmental movement from the first Earth Day through today illustrates my point. In 1971, people believed that the environment would be saved by politicians, leaders, community involvement, and grassroots campaigns. In short, people would, through persistence and determination, rise up, join together, and save the planet.

Today, almost without exception, we believe the rare positive developments in the environment are the result of technological advances. We read about gains in wind power, solar energy, nuclear waste removal, electric cars, and desalinization plants. We have not increased collaboration or improved sensitivity to implement win-win solutions. These are *technological* gains.

These observations are in stride with today's business environment. A sales manager I met with M&M Mars in New Jersey articulated this shift. "Nothing can match the power of technological innovation," he said. "Within fifty years, a handful of geniuses will have quietly tackled the really big problems while we are still shouting at each other in our city council meetings." Technology, we are told, not teams of people working together will tackle major issues. One might say we believe more in our machines than in ourselves.

The danger lies in the shift of faith away from a "together we (I) can (or must) do what's necessary to solve the problem," to a "I can't (won't) do anything, but someone else will invent something someday" mentality. This perilous transition represents an abdication of essential accountability and responsibility for our role in contributing to either the problems or the solutions. Once a person abdicates responsibility, he or she also lets go of control, power, and accountability. Today, there are more than 350 billion silicon chips and 15 billion microprocessors. According to *Newsweek* magazine, "That's more than two silicon brains for every person on earth." Federico Faggin, CEO of Synaptics, Inc. believes there will soon be machines with autonomous intelligence, "You just tell them what to do, and they'll figure out how to do it." The thought of computers running our cars, phones, climate control systems, databases, communication lines, airplane travel, and national security is the stuff of many a sci-fi thriller. We have already given over control of many facets of our lives to faceless machines comprised of "smart" chips. To many, the power is not in ourselves, but in technology. The result is a heightened sense of helplessness and a reduced commitment to act.

Fork 3: The Pump-Up Option

Ultimate Power with Freddy Savage* *boasted the marquis in front of the Phoenix Convention Center. This was the big event. I was guided to my seat by a member of Freddy's perfectly groomed entourage. At that moment, the rock music pounding through a Superdome-sized sound system softened noticeably. A Master of Ceremonies took over the microphone on stage.*

As he went through his introduction, I scanned the room. I saw the full range—individuals who later introduced themselves as students,

---

* Freddy Savage is a fictitious character pieced together from a number of motivational speakers I have seen.

professionals, entrepreneurs, and the temporarily unemployed—good, earnest people—executives, salespeople, children, retirees, laborers, home-makers, investing their hard-earned money for one reason—to find some-thing they had lost along the way: their motivation. They sought an escape from the pervasive sense of helplessness that surrounded them. They wanted to feel good again. They wanted to feel in control.

"Finally it's here," the man with the microphone announced. "The big moment you've all been waiting for. The Sultan of Success, The Professor of Personal Power, The Monster of Motivation, . . . Freddeeeeee Saaavage!" The crowd roared.

There he was, larger than life, Freddy Savage. He bounded across the stage and grabbed the microphone. "Yes!" his voice boomed forth.

"Yes!" The crowd roared back.

"Everybody up!" he demanded. All 2,000 people jumped to their feet. "Form groups of three now!" We formed groups of three. "Put one person in the middle. Go!" One person jumped in the middle. "Give that person a full body massage. Go!"

I found myself and some guy in a suit rubbing from head to toe a com-munity college secretary we'd never met. "Does it feel good?" Freddy asked.

"It feels good." Three-hundred people responded.

"No, does it feeeeel goooood?" Freddy challenged.

"Oooooh! It feeeeels gooood!" 666 people bellowed.

"Take a seat," Freddy directed. Everyone sat.

"You are in charge of your own destiny. You are in control." He paused as he flashed his million-dollar smile at his adoring fans. "You can fly with the buffalo, you can swim with the eagles, you can roam with the sharks" (or something like that). And so it went for eleven hours straight. I watched as 2,000 people from all walks of life soaked up every word. The energy was palpable. I had never seen so many hard-working individuals so completely energized at the end of an eleven-hour day. They were pumped! But were they changed?

In response to the growing weight of everyday adversity, people want to feel good. Yet, as you persist through your daily challenges, how long does the "pumped" feeling last, and why is it necessary? For that matter, why does the self-help section in the bookstore seem to grow larger by the day? The trend is clear. Life is hard, and we are looking for something to get us through the day.

A growing number of people are deviating from the trail to the top, seeking an escape from the rigor of their ascents. Motivational programs and products seem the perfect elixir. The search for quick-fix, pump-up solutions has formed a particularly dangerous fork in the trail to the top. Many perceive it to be a short cut, but it is, in truth, a dead end.

As skilled as some of the great motivators are at giving you valuable nourishment, you must consider, and may have experienced the potential downside of programs that offer more pump than sustainable content. Unfortunately, for many, the motivational injection provided by a certain kind of book, programed affirmation, or guru may be more like a cup of coffee in the morning providing a temporary lift. You get a dose of something you desperately need, which makes you feel better for a limited period of time. Once it wears off, however, you desperately need another dose.

For my doctoral dissertation, I explored the effectivenss of leadership and self-development programs, such as Outward Bound. After forging swamps, climbing cliffs, and surviving solos with minimal supplies, these programs end on a real high. This high is called *Post-Group Euphoria*. While programs such as Outward Bound serve a valuable function challenging people and their limitations, I discovered that the pump, and with it much of the motivation to make changes in one's life, quickly died.

I have witnessed this motivational phenomenon first hand on countless occasions. Motivation by injection and the hope it can create will wear off. Yet, people are buying season tickets to motivational seminars and satellite dishes that beam down daily motivational programs in order to receive their monthly or nightly pump. The Pump-Up Option has been the engine driving the growth of the $24 billion motivational industry, and it's addictive!

Fork 4: Helpless-Hopeless Option

People at all levels of corporate America feel increasingly helpless about their work. They struggle with an endless avalanche of change and the pressures of doing more and more with less and less. An alarming number feel nothing they do will make a difference. Helplessness left untreated metastasizes into hopelessness. This is the Spiral of Despair (Figure 2–2). Drawing from the landmark research of Dr. Martin Seligman at the University of

FIGURE 2–2 The Spiral of Despair

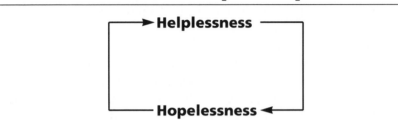

Pennsylvania, Joel Barker, prominent futurist and author of *Para-digms,* describes the relationship between helplessness and hope-lessness as a feedback loop. Helplessness validates the loss of hope. Hopelessness becomes a self-fulfilling prophecy, proving how help-less one truly is. One confirms and feeds the other.

Hopelessness is the cancer of the soul. It sucks the life and en-ergy from its host. People throughout our society have grown hopeless about ever surpassing, let alone matching, the lifestyles they had when they were kids. They question the value of at-tempting greatness while floating in a sea of apparent mediocrity. They feel increasingly despairing about their lives, their futures, and their children's futures.

This fork appears at that point in the trail of greatest challenge and greatest potential reward. Rather than surmount life's obsta-cles, a startling number of people are motivationally dismantled. *They simply give up.*

A SAFER PATH

Rather than opting for any of these choices, you can find a safer path toward a higher AQ, which I have clearly marked. The re-maining chapters will provide you with the knowledge, skills, and tools you need to remain true to your purpose and stay on your path, no matter what challenges you might face along the way. You need not be tempted by a fork in the trail. You *can* stay on track.

The Science of AQ

The event is not important, but the response to the event is everything.

I Ching

This chapter builds on the work of many prominent scholars, to whom I am deeply indebted, and a substantial body of 35 years of research. From this knowledge, I have combined and assembled several major findings for the first time, resulting in a new practical theory of human performance, and effectiveness.

THE THREE BUILDING BLOCKS OF YOUR AQ

AQ, the underlying factor that determines your ability to Ascend, is based on breakthroughs in three different scientific fields. Each of these represents a building block, which, when taken together, forms your AQ—the foundation of your success.

Building Block 1: Cognitive Psychology

This building block is comprised of the extensive and growing body of research related to the human need for control or mastery over one's life. It includes some essential concepts for understanding human motivation, effectiveness, and performance. In all, these theories are based on more than 600 studies at hundreds of universities and institutions around the world.

Learned Helplessness: The Landmark Theory of the Century

Learned helplessness is considered by the American Psychological Association to be the Landmark Theory of the Century, and with good cause. It explains *why* many people give up or stop short when faced with life's challenges. For this reason, this theory is the most significant ingredient in the formation of AQ.

Nearly thirty years ago, Martin Seligman, then a graduate student at the University of Pennsylvania, conducted an experiment that resulted in one of the major breakthroughs in the field of human psychology.

After observing a number of experiments in which dogs received an electric shock, Dr. Seligman noticed that some of them simply didn't respond. They just laid down and endured the pain. At the time, there was no theory in the field of psychology that could explain this behavior.

Seligman created an ingenious two-stage experiment to determine why some dogs simply gave up. In Stage One, dogs in Group A were put in a harness and administered a mild shock. They could stop the shock by pressing a bar with their nose, and they soon learned to do this. Group B dogs were placed in the same harness and administered the same shock but had no method of stopping it. These dogs just took the pain. Group C was called the control group. They were put in a harness and given no shock.

The next day, Seligman conducted Stage Two of his experiment. One at a time, he put all of the same dogs in a device called a shuttle box—a box with a low barrier down the middle. Each dog was placed on one side where it received a mild shock. All that the dog had to do to stop the shock was to jump the low barrier to get to the other side.

The Group A dogs (those that could control the shock) and the Group C dogs (those given no shock) quickly figured out how to jump the barrier and get away from the discomfort. But the dogs who could not control the shock in Stage One had a different response. *They lay down and whimpered.* They didn't try to escape.

What Seligman and others discovered is that these dogs had learned to be helpless, a behavior that virtually destroyed their motivation to act. Scientists have since discovered that cats, fish, dogs, rats, cockroaches, mice, and people are all capable of acquiring this trait. *Learned helplessness is simply internalizing the belief that what you do does not matter,* sapping one's sense of control.

Inspired by Seligman's breakthrough, scientists, however, were not satisfied to know only how other animals experienced learned helplessness. Hundreds of studies were to follow. The primary scholars in this area are Martin Seligman, now president of the American Psychological Association, Chris Peterson, professor of psychology at the University of Michigan, and Steven Maier, professor of pyschology at the Univeristy of Colorado. Together, they authored the most complete overview of the research in this growing theory, *Learned Helplessness* (1993).

In one of the many human experiments in learned helplessness, Donald Hiroto, a graduate student at the University of Oregon, placed a group of people in a room and turned on a loud noise. He then gave them the task of learning how to stop the noise. They attempted every combination of buttons on the panel at their fingertips, but the noise could not be stopped. No pattern would turn it off. Another group could stop the noise by hitting the right combination of buttons. Still another was subjected to no noise at all.

As with the dogs, Hiroto then took his subjects to a room where he placed their hands, one-by-one in a shuttle box. If they put their hand on one side, the annoying noise continued. If they moved their hand to the other side, the noise stopped.

Even though the time, place, and situation had been changed, the majority of those who had been earlier presented with an unstoppable noise just sat there. Like the dogs, they didn't even try to end their pain. Those who had earlier controlled the noise learned to shut it off by moving their hands in the shuttle box.

Similar results have been achieved in related experiments by a host of scientists. Howard Tennan and Sandra Eller of the State

University of New York at Albany, for example, conducted a study with 49 students. They demonstrated that people were taught to be helpless by being given unsolvable puzzles. Those who became helpless later performed poorly when compared with a control group who were given solvable puzzles.

Learned helplessness is about the loss of perceived control over adverse events. Perhaps one of the most dramatic examples can be derived from the experiences of Vicktor Frankl, Nazi concentration camp survivor and one of the prominent psychologists of this century. In his book, *Man's Search for Meaning*, Frankl described the moment at which many prisoners learned to be helpless. At one camp, the guard turned to the prisoners as they entered and told them they would never leave. According to Frankl, those who bought into this belief died soon after. Among the inmates who were not killed, those who rejected the guard's ominous prediction and retained a faith that "This too shall pass" survived. However, the moment the prisoner lost hope was the day he or she couldn't get out of bed. And that was the day of his or her death.

There are countless stories of those who, even in desperate situations, somehow fended off helplessness and overcame seemingly insurmountable odds.

Born with a rare degenerative eye disease, Erik Weihenmayer became completely blind at age thirteen. He was told he would never be able to do the things other people did. He had a disability. Yet, Weihenmayer refused to accept a life with such limitations. After fighting his blindness for years, Erik learned to embrace his adversity, making it part of him.

First, he joined his high school wrestling team, became co-captain, and state champion runner-up in his class. Next, Weihenmayer took on the challenge of rock climbing—a difficult hobby for those with perfect eyesight. "Blindness won't keep me from having fun," Weihenmayer insist. He took his adversity—his blindness—and turned it into his strength, using his heightened senses to take on challenges few will conquer.

In 1995 he scaled 20,320 foot Mt. McKinley, North America's highest peak. In 1996, he became the first blind person to ever scale the 3000-foot granite monolith—El Capitan in Yosemite. Says Weihenmayer, a teacher at the private Phoenix Country Day School, "Blindness is just a nuisance." As for climbing, he says, "You just have to find a different way of doing it."

You will discover that Erik's response to his adversity demonstrates a high AQ. Learned helplessness describes the power of believing that what one does does not make a difference. Conversely, if Erik Weihenmayer by possessing a high AQ—the ingredient that immunized him against helplessness in the face of adversity—could climb a sheer 3000-foot granite wall without the benefit of sight, imagine what obstacles you and others are capable of surmounting with a sufficiently high AQ.

The Definitive Barrier to Empowerment. Without a doubt, you know the importance of being empowered. Children are supposed to be empowered to say "No" to drugs, sex, and abusive situations. Parents need to be empowered to act on behalf of their children; keep a healthy, loving household; and guide their children's development. Business leaders must be empowered to overcome the adversity they face from all sides every day. You must be empowered to continue your ascent.

Learned helplessness and empowerment are mutually exclusive terms (see Figure 3–1). They cannot, by definition, coexist. A person who suffers from learned helplessness cannot be empowered,

FIGURE 3–1   Learned Helplessness and Empowerment

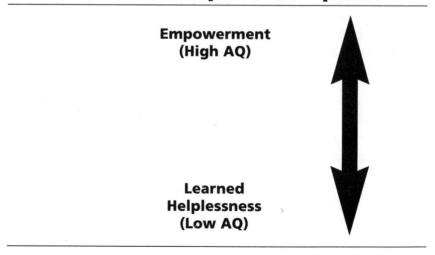

**Empowerment
(High AQ)**

**Learned
Helplessness
(Low AQ)**

and a person who feels empowered does not suffer from being help-less. *Learned helplessness is a definitive barrier to empowerment,* and therefore to your ascent. It is a definable pattern of thought that can undermine all facets of success.

Many of our major corporations are being brought to their knees by a workforce debilitated by learned helplessness. One executive describes his effort to introduce change to a workforce ravaged by learned helplessness. "It's like calling a caged dog," he said. "The dog won't move, because he knows it won't matter."

Individuals who respond poorly to adversity suffer in all aspects of their lives. In my research work with a wide range of organizations, I have discovered that learned helplessness saps performance, productivity, motivation, energy, learning, improvement, risk taking, creativity, health, vitality, resilience, and persistence. It creates Campers and Quitters.

Nurturing Helplessness in Others.   Grace Ferrari, a faculty member in mass communication at Quinnipiac College conducted a study of the content of local news broadcasts and their effect on people. Her study revealed that 71 percent of the content was helplessness-invoking. An example might be the plight of a victim who is helpless to escape her fate at the hands of a rapist, or a couple who turns their back for a second and loses a child. A mere 12 percent of the messages demonstrated control over the situation! These were situations where effort paid off.

A number of studies conducted by Seligman, Dweck, and others indicate that helplessness is taught to children early in life. A father who does everything for his daughter, inadvertently teaches helplessness by never letting her face her own challenges. A teacher who explains bad grades on stable characteristics such as smarts or personality creates a more helpless response than the educator who uses more temporary explanations such as effort or task-specific motivation.

Helplessness can also be taught or reinforced later in life. The spouse who constantly finds a reason not to be alone with her husband, teaches him to stop trying. The boss who punishes new ideas soon finds that fewer and fewer ideas emerge. The man who makes

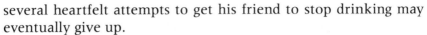

several heartfelt attempts to get his friend to stop drinking may eventually give up.

Everyday, intimacy, innovation, and improvement are crushed. The opportunities for helplessness are everywhere. But not all individuals are affected. Some are taught to *be immune.*

Immunization from Hopelessness. In his research, Dr. Seligman discovered that while most dogs learned to be helpless, some could not be taught this disabling lesson. They had somehow been *immunized.* Seligman explored what made them different and discovered that early in life they had been taught that their actions did make a difference. As a result, they kept trying long after others had quit. In fact, they never stopped trying! Later research developed skills for people to immunize themselves against helplessness. In Chapter 6, you will learn a rapid-response system to enhance your AQ, prevent helplessness, and become a Climber.

Attributional Theory, Explanatory Style, and Optimism

Strongly related to and evolving from learned helplessness theory is the idea that a person's success may be largely determined by the way he or she explains or responds to life's events. Seligman and others discovered that those who respond to adversity as *stable, internal,* and *generalizable* to other areas of their life tend to suffer in all areas of life, while those who explain adverse events as external, temporary, and limited tend to enjoy benefits ranging from performance to health.

Carol Dweck, from the University of Illinois, is one of the world's leading researchers on emotional development. She demonstrated that among children, those who perceived the cause of adversity as stable ("I'm dumb") *learned* less than those who perceived the causes as temporary ("I didn't try very hard"). Helpless children focused on the cause of the failure (generally themselves), and mastery-oriented students focused on remedies for failure. Helpless children attributed failure to lack of ability—a stable trait.

In a separate study, Dweck showed that girls responded much differently than boys to the criticism they received from their teachers and peers. Girls were more likely to receive criticism that was both permanent and pervasive, such as "You're not very good at math." Boys' criticism was more temporary, such as "You weren't paying attention." Girls, therefore, learned to attribute their failures to permanent traits, whereas boys learned to attribute failures to more temporary sources, such as lack of motivation. These are meaningful lessons for any concerned parent or dedicated teacher.

Dweck revealed an important difference between how men and women respond to adversity. Females are more likely to explain the adversity as their fault and due to an enduring characteristic, such as stupidity. Males, on the other hand, are more likely to attribute failure to something temporary, such as "I didn't try hard enough." I have also consistently found this difference in the AQ Programs.

Martin Seligman at the University of Pennsylvania describes these differences as *pessimism* versus *optimism*. Those who explain adversity as permanent ("It will never change"), pervasive ("It will ruin everything"), and personal ("It's all my fault") have pessimistic explanatory styles. Those who respond to adversity as temporary, external, and limited have optimistic explanatory styles (Figure 3–2).

Seligman and others have shown that explanatory or attributional style—how you respond to adversity—is a strong predictor of success in many arenas. In a five-year study involving thousands of insurance agents, Seligman and his colleagues showed that those with more optimistic explanatory styles sold substantially more policies and hung in there longer than the pessimists. Optimistic

FIGURE 3–2   Optimists versus Pessimists

	Response to Adversity		
Pessimists	Permanent	Pervasive	Personal
Optimists	Temporary	Limited	External

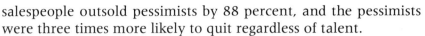

salespeople outsold pessimists by 88 percent, and the pessimists were three times more likely to quit regardless of talent.

A special force of agents was hired based purely on how they responded to adversity. The astounding feature of this group was that they would normally have been rejected in the hiring process because they did not match the traditional profile of a successful agent. They were hired as the ultimate test of the role of how one's response to adversity impacts one's performance. Over time, this group of rejects became the top sellers.

The natural link between how people respond to adversity and their ability to sell was strengthened by a two-year study, in which Seligman discovered that optimistic real estate agents sell 250 to 320 percent more than pessimistic agents.

Further studies by Seligman and his colleagues have revealed dramatic differences between those who respond to adversity as optimists versus pessimists. Optimistic managers outperform pessimistic managers. Optimistic students outperform pessimistic students. Optimistic cadets at West Point outlast the pessimists. People elect optimistic leaders. Optimistic teams outperform pessimistic teams. The list goes on and on. In all of these cases, it comes down to how one responds to adversity.

In the largest longitudinal study of its kind, Seligman and George Vaillant demonstrated that those who responded optimistically to adversity *outlived* those who responded pessimistically.

Melanie O. Burns and Martin Seligman, both from the University of Pennsylvania, demonstrated that the way people explain or respond to adverse events remains stable over their *entire life.* (However, through the tools provided in this book, this habit can be unlearned and permanently improved.)

Through an innovative analysis of diaries of elderly people, their study measured how people responded to adversity over a lifetime. The results showed a consistency in these responses over a span of 52 years.

After working with people in dozens of companies, I discovered that individuals who respond to adversity destructively (low AQ) suffer, while those with more constructive response patterns (high AQ) excel. These findings are substantiated by several related theories.

From Martin Seligman, Christopher Peterson, Steven Maier, Carol Dweck and the dozens of researchers inspired by their work, we learn:

- Learned helplessness explains why many people give up.
- Learned helplessness is the definitive barrier to empowerment.
- Once learned, it is easy to justify one's helplessness.
- People can be *immunized* against helplessness.
- Those immunized against learned helplessness never give up.
- The upsurge in depression is caused by an epidemic of learned helpessness.
- Optimists respond differently to adversity than do pessimists.
- Optimists sell more, perform better, persist longer, and live longer than pessimists.
- Males and females are taught differently and, as a result, tend to respond differently to adversity.
- People can be taught to improve how they respond to adversity.

Hardiness and the Ability to Withstand Adversity

Why is it some people seem better able to cope with life's hardships than others? Suzanne Oullette, professor of psychology at the City University of New York, has spent over 20 years researching a human trait she calls *hardiness*. People who are hardy suffer less of the negative fallout from adversity.

Horticulturists use hardiness to describe a plant's ability to thicken its cell walls before going dormant so it can outlast the coldest weather over the course of a Midwestern winter. Hardiness in humans refers to your ability to withstand the harsh conditions of life.

In a major study of executives at Illinois Bell Telephone around the time of the break up of AT&T, Oullette found out that those executives whose response to the adversity of massive reorganization, uncertainty, and stress demonstrated hardiness—a measurable sense of challenge, commitment, and control—suffered half as much illness as those whose responses were less hardy. *Hardiness is a predictor of health and overall quality of life.*

Oullette also discovered, in a study of hundreds of women, that those who scored higher on her hardiness questionnaire developed fewer mental and physical illnesses.

In a separate study, Oullette and her colleagues at the City University of New York, discovered that, in women with high-risk pregnancies, those with greater hardiness showed fewer residual symptoms, such as anxiety and depression, one to three months after the crisis had passed. *Hardy people tend to suffer less and for a shorter time.*

Morris Okun, a psychologist at Arizona State University strengthened the link between hardiness and performance in a 1988 study evaluating the hardiness of 33 women with rheumatoid arthritis. Okun discovered that women with greater hardiness had a significantly higher percentages of T-cells—meaning their *immune systems were stronger.* Those who scored lower on hardiness had more B cells, which have been found when the disease flares up.

Jon Kabat-Zinn, head of the Stress Reduction Clinic at the University of Massachusetts Medical Center, discovered that mind-body techniques that teach awareness and ways of coping with pain, *increased hardiness measurably* over an eight-week period.

Victim or Master? *Hardiness, like optimism, is a strong predictor of physical and mental health* in the face of adversity. Those who respond to adversity as an opportunity, with a sense of purpose and a sense of control—or what I call *"Advertunity"*—remain strong, while those who are victimized by the adversity, responding to it helplessly, become weak.

In Chapter 1, you learned about the Adversity Paradox—how as adversity rises fewer people persist to solve the problems which caused it (Figure 1–2). Adversity also spurs a victim mentality in many who adopt the belief that "the system" is the source of all ills. We can see victimhood in epidemic proportions in our courts and the lines in the offices of our government entitlement programs. If one is a "victim," one cannot be held responsible for one's outcomes or actions.

We see both the role of AQ and the victimhood mentality take hold whenever a corporate downsizing is announced. Those with high AQs recover quickly, responding with a sense of Advertunity (adversity as an opportunity), whereas low AQ employees become instant victims of the system. It is bigger than they are, out of their control, far reaching, but the job of someone else to resolve. Some take charge, others give up. Although the adversity is real, the victimhood is negotiable.

While a popular escape from accountability, victimhood reeks of helplessness and induces one to quit rather than Ascend. The consequences extend from one's vitality to one's performance, attitude, motivation, and longevity.

Mastery and Health.   In its essence, hardiness, like learned helplessness and attributional theory, is about *control,* or mastery over one's life. Social psychologists Ellen Langer and Judith Rodin (now president of the University of Pennsylvania) conducted a study which demonstrated that among nursing home residents, those who had the opportunity to interact with something they could control actually lived longer! Over the course of a year and a half, those who were given a plant which the staff would tend died at twice the rate of those who were given a plant for which they were solely responsible. Perception of control, or mastery, is an essential element in avoiding learned helplessness, developing hardiness, and raising your AQ.

Resilience: Building Invincible Kids

The cover of *US News & World Report* boasts new research and hope for immunizing children against adversity. Child psychologist Emmy Werner began her research 40 years ago in Hawaii where she studied young people with traumatic childhoods. Expecting to see trauma passed from one generation to the next, Werner discovered that one-third of the kids had beaten the odds, heading for success rather than disaster. They had become *resilient.*

When Hurricane Iniki battered Kauai in 1992, the 160-mile per hour winds left one in six residents homeless, but somehow seemed to spare the homes of the resilient kids, now in their 30s.

They created their own luck as Werner discovered. Resilient kids were better planners and preparers than less resilient kids. While they couldn't avoid the adversity of the storm, they could control several factors such as boarding up their houses, arranging insurance, and having the necessary financial security to weather the loss. According to Werner, **resilient kids** are "planners, problem solvers, and picker-uppers." The less resilient kids simply gave up.

Werner's research is especially timely as kids face mounting adversity. With one in five living in poverty and surges in child abuse, drug abuse, teen violence, and teen pregnancy, the need to develop resilience is greater than ever.

Unlike genetics, *resilience can be molded*. Research in this field helps us reshape our notion of adversity. Those who face and overcome adversity as children appear to fare better later in life than those with less adverse childhoods. *US News* reports that these individuals enjoy stronger marriages and better health than those with less stressful upbringings. Once in mid-life, these resilient individuals were more likely to report being happy, and were one-third less likely to report emotional health problems.

> *We're all inbred with a certain amount of resiliency. It's not until it's tested . . . that we recognize inner strength.*
> Kweisi Mfume, Head of the NAACP

Resilience programs for chldren are sprouting up across the nation, and it appears *AQ may play a pivotal role*. The ability to permanently improve how one deals with adversity is fundamental to any child's future. Each child must develop the ability to turn obstacles into opportunities.

> *I've never believed adversity is a harbinger of failure. On the contrary, [it] can provide a wellspring of strength.*
> Diane Feinstein, U.S. Senator

Like optimists, resilient individuals possess the ability to spring back from adversity. They are the Climbers. This ability stems not from the adversity itself, but from how they *respond* to it.

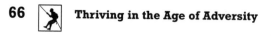

From Oullette, Werner, and other researchers, we learn:
- Hardiness and resilience are predictors of performance and health.
- Hardiness is based on a sense of commitment, challenge, and control.
- People who demonstrate hardiness and/or resilience handle adversity better than those who do not.

Self-Efficacy, Locus of Control

The belief in your mastery over your life and your ability to meet challenges as they arise is what psychologists call *self-efficacy*—it's yourself being effective. Albert Bandura, a Stanford psychologist and the leading researcher on self-efficacy puts it clearly, "People who have a sense of self-efficacy bounce back from failures, they approach things in terms of how to handle them rather than worrying about what can go wrong."

In 1966, Julian Rotter proposed that people who believe that they control their rewards and punishments (internal locus of control) are less likely to be depressed and more likely to take action to improve a bad situation than those who perceive that rewards and punishments are due to outside factors (external locus of control), such as bad luck, weather, or chance. Those with *external loci of control* tend to passively accept both rewards and punishments, while those with *internal loci of control* actively pursue or avoid them. Those with external loci of control are more likely to be depressed. Rotter's work has since been substantiated and further developed by researchers around the world.

Like the preceding theories, locus of control is about the relationship between control over life's events and motivation and success.

A Master Theory of Control

We can draw some powerful conclusions or truths from this extensive research on learned helplessness, attributional theory, explanatory style, optimism, hardiness, resilience, and locus of control.

From the combination of these theories we learn:

- Success is significantly influenced by your sense of control or mastery over your life.
- Success is greatly influenced and can be predicted by how you respond to and explain adversity.
- Individuals respond to adversity in specific patterns.
- These patterns, *if unchecked,* remain consistent over your entire life.
- These patterns are subconscious, and therefore, operate outside your awareness.

We can further hypothesize that:

- If you can measure and strengthen how you respond to adversity, you should be able to enjoy greater productivity, performance, vitality, resilience, health, learning, improvement, motivation, and success.

The Role of Your AQ in Life

These scientifically grounded and implied factors of success are influenced, if not determined, by our perceived sense of control and how we respond to adversity. They cover everything it takes to Ascend.

Competitiveness. Jason Satterfield and Martin Seligman conducted a study comparing the rhetoric of Saddam Hussein and George Bush during the Gulf War. They discovered that those who responded to the adversity more optimistically would predictably be more aggressive and take more risks, where the more pessimistic reaction to adversity resulted in more passivity and caution.

People who respond constructively to adversity are more apt to maintain the energy, focus, and vigor required to successfully compete. Those who respond destructively tend to lose steam, or simply stop trying. Competition is largely about hope, agility, and resilience which are highly determined by how one deals with life's setbacks and challenges.

Productivity. In a number of studies conducted in organizations, people who responded destructively to adversity were measurably less productive than people who did not. In 1996, I compared individuals' AQs with their performance as perceived by their supervisors for a Big Six client services firm. Preliminary findings reflect a strong correlation between performance and how the employees responds to adversity. Based on conducting the AQ Programs around the world, it is clearly the perception of organizational leaders that high AQ people dramatically outproduce low AQ people. In his work with the Metropolitan Life Insurance Company, Seligman showed that people who do not respond well to adversity sell less, produce less, and perform worse than people who do.

Creativity. Innovation is, in essence, an act of hope. It requires the belief that something that did not previously exist could be possible. According to futurist Joel Barker, creativity also comes out of desperation. It, therefore, requires the essential ability to *overcome* the adversity of uncertainty. If you believe that what you do does not make a difference, how can you possibly be creative? I have watched learned helplessness crush the creativity of bright, capable people. Those who are not able to withstand adversity become incapable of being creative.

Motivation. I recently asked a director at a pharmaceutical company to rank his team in terms of their apparent motivation. We then measured the team members' AQs. Without exception, those with the highest AQs were perceived as the most motivated both on a daily basis and over time.

Risk Taking. With a lack of perceived control, there is no reason to take risks. In fact, risks make no sense. Believing that what you do does not matter saps the burst of energy required to leap into unknown territory. As Satterfield and Seligman showed, those who respond to adversity more constructively are willing to take more risks. Risks are an essential aspect of the Ascent.

Improvement. We are in an era of continuous improvement in order to survive. Whether in a business or in personal life, you must improve to avoid becoming obsolete in your career and relationships. In measuring the performance and AQs of swimmers, I found that those with higher AQs improved, while those with lower AQs did worse.

Persistence.   Persistence is the essence of the Ascent and your AQ. It is the ability to keep on trying, even when faced with setbacks or failure. Few traits gain more results over time than sheer persistence, especially when combined with a little creativity. Seligman showed that salespeople, military cadets, students, and sports teams who responded well to adversity recovered from defeat and persisted. Those who responded poorly when faced with adversity gave up. AQ determines the resilience it takes to persevere.

Learning.   At the heart of the information age is the need to constantly accumulate and process a never-ending stream of knowledge. You may recall that Seligman and others showed that pessimists respond to adversity as permanent, personal, and pervasive (Figure 3–2). Carol Dweck showed that children with pessimistic responses to adversity, learned and achieved less than those with more optimistic patterns.

Embracing Change.   As we experience a constant avalanche of change, our ability to deal with uncertainty and shifting ground becomes ever more critical. Rock slides, fickle weather, unexpected floods, and eruptions all challenge even the most skilled Climber. In order to succeed, you must effectively deal with and embrace change. However, if you believe that what you do makes little difference, then you may feel overwhelmed and incapacitated by change. In fact, it may be the very force that induces you to quit.

Executives and managers at Mott's are using AQ to help speed the change process by helping people embrace change more readily. Collective change begins with the individual. If you can alter the AQs of a critical mass of people, you can make change take place more smoothly and efficiently. Change becomes a welcome part of life, rather than an overwhelming burden.

For many of the individuals I have encountered in my work, change *is* overwhelming. They perceive it as an enduring, far-reaching threat that is beyond their control. There is a clear pattern that has emerged from AQ programs. Those who embrace change tend to respond most constructively to adversity—using it to strengthen their resolve. They respond with advertunity. Those who are crushed by change are crushed by adversity.

In responding to a major restructuring resulting in layoffs at U.S. West's Denver office, employees who perceived control over their situation were more likely to stay on the job and perform well. Those who felt helpless were reported to suffer in their health, motivation, and performance. They were more likely to camp or quit.

Resilience, Stress, Pressure, Setbacks.   Most likely you have no lack of stress in your life. Be it from the daily pressures of keeping up or making headway in your work, or the larger setbacks of losing a loved one, surviving the break-up of a relationship, losing your job, suffering financial difficulties, becoming ill or injured, or feeling isolated and alone, you are probably no stranger to pain. People who respond poorly to adversity are often devastated by setbacks. Some recover slowly, others never do.

In more extreme cases, a lack of perceived control robs you of your resilience—your ability to spring back. Climbers must be resilient. They are constantly facing the adversity and unpredictibility of the climb. Sometimes you will work hard to move forward and up along a particular route only to discover an insurmountable obstacle. Sometimes Climbers fall. Resilience enables you to get back up. Climbers must be emotionally and physically pliable enough to recover from the disappointment and fatigue to pick a new route, sometimes moving backward to move forward, and continue the ascent.

Suzanne Oullette, the prominent researcher on hardiness, demonstrated that those responding to adversity with hardiness—control, challenge, and commitment—remain resilient in the face of difficulties. Those who do not respond with control, challenge, and commitment tend to be weakened by adverse situations. I found this to be true in my own research. Emmy Werner, child psychologist, found those who responded positively to adversity became resilient, springing back from major setbacks.

Creating Resilient Swimmers

In 1996, I set out to examine the relationship between AQ and performance at the High Altitude Training Complex at Northern Arizona University. The Complex draws Olympic athletes, especially swimmers from around the world anxious to gain the advantage that comes with conditioning at 7,000 feet above sea level.

My research team and I measured the AQs of the members of successful NCAA Division I collegiate men's and women's swim teams. Next, we threw the swimmers into the water and told them to swim their best time for 50 meters. We then gave them their results—but they were doctored. Building on earlier research by Martin Seligman, we added 1.2 seconds to swimmers' actual times, without their knowledge. Many were horribly upset. We then instructed the swimmers to try again. With the exception of one competitor, all of those in the top half of AQs swam better after the setback, and everyone who scored in the lower half of AQs swam slower the second time.

AQ proved to be an accurate predictor of an athlete's ability to respond to adversity. While this finding is important, the critical question is *can AQ be enhanced?*

Next, we put these elite student-athletes through an abbreviated version of the standard one-day program that teaches them the scientifically grounded skills for raising their AQs. Without revealing our intentions, they were told only that this was a sports psychology program. Following this tightly condensed training, all swimmers significantly enhanced their AQs. The following day we repeated the swim test. Eighty-six percent improved both their ability to bounce back from a setback and *their overall performance.* AQ predicts who will improve and who will prevail, and *AQ can be enhanced,* significantly impacting performance levels. Additional studies using AQ to enhance recruiting accuracy and sports performance are now under way.

This critical ability to overcome adversity has long been the fuel for many inspirational stories, yet it seemed to be a quality one either possessed or lacked from birth. Now we know better. The ability to overcome adversity can help every person, no matter how successful or destitute, and it can be *learned.*

Predicting AQ

People are not intuitively able to predict how an individual will respond when faced with adversity. One of the significant and somewhat surprising findings of our study was that a skilled, experienced, and highly successful coach was unable to predict, with any degree of accuracy, how an athlete would respond to receiving a slower time. We asked the coach to predict who would improve and who would do worse. Despite knowing these athletes for as long as four years, the coach was accurate only 25 percent of the time, where random guessing would result in 50 percent accuracy!

People are not instinctively good judges of AQ. It must be *measured*.

Mental Health.   There is a powerful connection between your AQ and your mental health. One of the largest bodies of research related to learned helplessness establishes the powerful link between this syndrome and depression. Dr. Gerald Klerman, former director of the government's Alcohol, Drug Abuse, and Mental Health Agency coined the term *Age of Melancholy* for our current era. Klerman sponsored two major studies, which revealed that depression strikes earlier in life and in unprecedented numbers of people. As Seligman and others demonstrated, this epidemic of depression coincides with an epidemic of learned helplessness and the Age of Adversity. Those who suffer as a result of adversity tend to feel helpless, and, in turn, get depressed.

Physical Health.   In the largest longitudinal study of its kind, Chris Peterson (University of Pennsylvania), George Vaillant (Stanford), and Martin Seligman (University of Pennsylvania) showed that pessimism (what I closely equate with a low AQ) proved to be a significant health risk for later life. Pessimists who were healthy at 25, suffered worse health between 45 and 60 years of age than optimists (which correlates with higher AQ). Resiliency research further indicates that those who spring back from adversity enjoy better health.

According to a report in the *Minneapolis Tribune* a study conducted by Dr. Daniel Mark, a heart specialist at Duke University, demonstrated the importance of AQ (my term) in recovery from major surgery. In the study 1,719 men and women who had undergone heart catheterization were interviewed to assess their response to the adversity of heart disease. The death rate among those who perceived the adversity as severe and long lasting (low AQ), was more than double that among those who responded to the adversity as more limited and fleeting (high AQ).

In a follow-up study, Dr. Nancy Frasure-Smith of the Montreal Heart Institute discovered that among 222 heart patients, those who responded to the adversity with depression and anxiety had double to triple the death rate of those who remained upbeat.

Clearly, AQ, or how one responds to adversity, is an emerging and fundamental factor in emotional and physical health.

Vitality, Happiness, Joy. While the most subjective elements of success on this list, vitality, happiness, and joy are perhaps the most important. It only makes sense that in a world rife with adversity, those who are able to overcome and climb through adversity will experience the greatest joy. Those who perceive adversity as far-reaching, out of their control, and enduring are most likely to suffer. The resilience research cited earlier has shown that those who develop resilience as kids reported greater happiness as adults.

Nothing can sap your vitality, happiness, and joy more readily than walking around with the belief that you have no control over far-reaching, long-lasting adversity. When you consider the volatile combination of reduced productivity, creativity, motivation, energy, resilience, and health, you can begin to understand the way in which such a destructive response to adversity can suck the life out of an otherwise happy, upbeat person. This tragic loss results in people who are going through the motions of life with none of the zeal, passion, or enthusiasm that makes the journey enjoyable.

The award-winning research in learned helplessness combined with the research in hardiness, resilience, self-efficacy, and locus of control, explains why some people become Quitters or Campers, why they give up, underperform, underproduce, fail to create, run from change, are unmotivated, lack energy, are unassertive, suffer depression, are incapable of being empowered, are prone to illness, lack persistence, are easily devastated, and shrink from competition.

This first building block connects tightly with the second which answers the question: "What is the relationship between how you respond to adversity and your emotional and physical health?"

Building Block 2: The New Science of Health

There is a radical shift afoot in the way we think about health and human performance. For centuries, thanks to leading seventeenth-century thinkers, in particular the French doctor and philosopher René Descartes, scientists considered and treated the mind and body as separate entities. This continues to this day. You may know people who treat their bodies as mere vehicles to get their brains from one place to another. Such dualistic thinking has led to a major criticism of Western medicine—treating an individual's symptoms rather than the person, disease, or cause. Another criticism has been that Western medicine has traditionally focused on illness rather than on *health*.

As scientists began to explore health and became more sophisticated in their efforts to discover the potential causes for a variety of medical conditions, many found themselves entering new territory and questioning old ways of thinking. They wanted to know:

- Why some people seem to weather major surgery better than others.
- Why some people remain robust into old age while others, of similar genetic heritage, become ill and frail when much younger.
- How does brain activity affect the likelihood that one will contract cancer, diabetes, or other major diseases?
- What effects specific patterns of thought or emotion have upon your health.

Recent research in the field of psychoneuroimmunology has answered some of these questions. It has proven, for example, that *there is a direct, measurable link between what you think and feel and what goes on in your body.*

According to Henry Dreher, author of *The Immune Power Personality*, "To the astonishment of many immunologists, it turns out that our thoughts and feelings are mediated by brain chemicals that also regulate our body's defenses. In other words, the chemical carriers of our human emotions directly influence our physical health."

How you respond to life's events can have profound implications for your health and your ability to ascend. Many exciting new developments provide evidence for this hypothesis.

As early as the 1950s, Lawrence LeShan observed that cancer patients often suffered a significant loss accompanied by a loss of control shortly before being diagnosed. What he discovered was that their reaction to that loss (adversity!) was more important than the adversity itself!

The perception of control over your life plays a central role in the vigor of your emotional and physical health. You may recall the earlier Yale study where Ellen Langer and Judy Rodin found that residents of nursing homes who, over the course of eighteen months, were given basic control over activities as simple as when to water their plants, were more active, happier, and *lived longer* than those who were given no control. Control is a pivotal factor in living a disease-free, healthy life.

A pioneering British study followed 69 women with breast cancer for five years. Women who did not suffer a recurrence tended to be those who had a "fighting spirit." Those who suffered a recurrence or died tended to respond to their initial diagnosis with acceptance and helplessness.

In a later study, Seligman assessed the optimism of 34 women with breast cancer. Those who responded to life's events most constructively lived the longest.

Madelon Visintainer, now chairperson of the Department of Pediatric Nursing at Yale School of Medicine, conducted a brilliant experiment at the University of Pennsylvania where she injected mice with a precise number of cancer cells. She split the rats into three groups. One group was taught mastery, controlling shock by pressing a bar. Another group was taught helplessness, and a control group remained psychologically unchanged. The rate of cancer in the helpless rats was more than two and a half times that of the mastery rats, and nearly double that of the unchanged rats. This was the first experiment that demonstrated that learned helplessness, or loss of perceived control, can influence the spread of and perhaps even *cause* cancer.

The University of Minnesota has since reported that patients with a strong sense of hope seem to recover from major cardiac surgery more readily than those with little hope or sense of control over their futures.

Emotions and thought patterns play a powerful role in mental and physical health. Dr. Steven Locke examined a group of Harvard undergraduates for levels of stress, how they responded to adversity, and immunity. He discovered that "poor copers"—those who reported high levels of depression and anxiety in response to stress (one form of adversity) had significantly weaker natural killer cells. How an individual responds to adversity influences the chemical composition and rigor of his or her immune functions.

In December 1992, *Sports Illustrated* wrote the following about Arthur Ashe, the accomplished tennis champion, months before he died from AIDS (caused by an infected blood transfusion):

> *If sportsmanship is also the ability to transform loss into fresh, competitive, creative fire, then Ashe's has been unparalleled . . .*

The article chronicles how Ashe turned his own adversity into an opportunity to change society's view of AIDS and to raise hundreds of thousands of dollars for AIDS research. Arthur Ashe's adversity response was extremely positive. Not coincidentally, Ashe had been the longest known survivor of toxoplasmosis, an infection of the brain, and one of the longest known survivors of AIDS. His AQ (my term) or ability to turn adversity into opportunity was considered instrumental in keeping his immune system strong and functioning for such a long time.

George Solomon, professor of psychiatry and biobehavioral sciences at UCLA Medical Center, has shown that a destructive adversity response creates a quicker decline in infection-fighting helper T-cells in HIV-positive persons. Clearly, some disease just happens. However, a growing body of research suggests that your AQ (my term) has a direct bearing on your health.

A low AQ comes with a price. For example, Christopher Peterson from Virginia Polytechnic Institute and State University, evaluated 122 men who had their first heart attack on how they respond to life's events. Eight years later, of the 25 with the most destructive patterns (more internal and stable), 21 had died. Of the 25 with the most constructive patterns (more temporary and external), only 6 had perished. Their responses to adversity proved a better predictor of survival than any other medical factor, including the blockage in their arteries, the damage created by the first heart attack, cholesterol level, or blood pressure. Those with more constructive responses recovered much faster and with fewer complications than their counterparts with weaker responses to adversity.

The health-related implications extend to our ability to express our feelings and deal with others. David McClelland, a distinguished professor of psychology at Boston University, showed, through a variety of studies, that certain emotions were strong predictors of health. Those who exhibited mistrust proved twice as likely to contract a major illness than people who showed trust.

James Pennebaker, a psychology professor at Southern Methodist University, showed through a series of related studies that writing down your feelings has a positive and enduring effect on your immune system. Those who journaled were tested and shown to have significantly bolstered their immune functions compared with those who did not keep a journal. These benefits resulted in enduring improvements and fewer doctor visits compared to control groups. Expressing feelings in writing creates chemical changes in your body, resulting in better health. Perhaps because it enhances one's sense of control.

One of the most powerful and most substantiated findings stemming from the dozens of studies conducted by Seligman and his colleagues around the world was the causal link between learned helplessness and depression. It makes perfect sense that, if you walk around with the belief that what you do does not matter, you are prone to depression. With depression hitting people of all ages, in particular our young in epidemic proportions, instilling the ability to prevail through adversity and retain a sense of mastery over one's life becomes ever more critical.

In the largest longitudinal study of its kind, Christopher Peterson (University of Pennsylvania), George Vaillant (Stanford), and Martin Seligman (University of Pennsylvania) showed that what I call a destructive AQ (pessimism) proved to be a significant health risk for later life. Even those with poor adversity responses who were healthy at 25, suffered worse health between 45 and 60 years of age than the constructive responders.

In fact, Peterson, Vaillant, and Seligman's work indicates that people who suffer from learned helplessness—a severe response to adversity—die sooner!

From the various researchers in psychoneuroimmunology, we learn:

- There is direct link between how you respond to adversity and your mental and physical health.
- Control is essential to health and longevity.
- How one responds to adversity (AQ) influences immune functions, recovery from surgery, and vulnerability to life-threatening disease.
- A weak pattern of response to adversity can cause depression.

Building Block 3: The Science of the Brain

Due to recent breakthroughs in neurophysiology—the science of the brain—we now have a much clearer picture of how AQ is formed and what must happen in order for you to change it and to develop the mental habits of a Climber. How does learning take place, and how do you form habits of thought or behavior? With new findings in computer-imaging technology, scientists can now see what goes on in your brain.

Over the years, I have attended hundreds of seminars where I have heard a dozen different "experts" stand up in front of a group and declare, "It takes twenty-one days to form a habit." "After twenty-one days, you've got it down cold." So I approached these "experts" and told them I was interested in that fact and would like to learn more. I asked for the source for the twenty-one day miracle, at which point they often said, "Give me your card, and I'll give you a call with that information." Needless to say, I never received a call. In fact, even when I called them, no one had a viable source for that myth.

This wild-goose chase only fueled my curiosity about how we form habits and how long it takes to form new, more constructive ones. I decided to find out for myself. I began by contacting Dr. Mark Nuwer, head of neurophysiology at UCLA Medical Center.

I asked the million dollar question: "How long does it take to form a habit?" I expected to hear about the scientific complexity involved in forming a habit, which surely must take weeks, if not months.

"How long does it take for you to learn not to touch a hot stove?" Nuwer replied.

"About a second." I said, playing along.

"Actually, it's a hundred milliseconds."

I paused, stunned. "What are you saying, Dr. Nuwer?" I asked, wanting to hear it from his mouth.

"When you touch a hot stove, a loud alarm goes off in your brain, immediately making you keenly aware of where you placed your hand." That loud alarm, as Nuwer explained, is instrumental in interrupting the subconscious thought pattern in the basal ganglia—a subconscious, automatic region of the brain—and bringing it to the conscious region of the brain (cerebral cortex).

I explained to Dr. Nuwer what was at stake in one's response to adversity. I recited the potential consequences of a low AQ and the likely benefits of a high AQ. "Sounds like a loud alarm to me!" was Nuwer's response.

The idea that one's AQ could be instantly changed, thus altering that person's entire life was a powerful revelation.

The Anatomy of a Habit

Dr. Nuwer explained to me that learning takes place in the outer conscious region, or gray matter of the brain. This region is called the cerebral cortex. Initial learning is a blood and oxygen-rich activity. You are aware of what you are doing. If you have ever watched young children tackle brushing their teeth or tying their shoes for the first time, you have witnessed their intense concentration as they learn these new skills.

But, over time, as you repeat a new thought pattern or behavior, that activity migrates to the subconscious, automatic region of the brain. This region is called the basal ganglia (Figure 3–3). The more you do something, the more automatic and subconscious it becomes. The habit changes immediately and becomes strengthened over time.

What would happen if I sent you on a hike that had no blazed trail? How would that affect the speed and efficiency of your hike? Obviously, it would slow you down substantially. The same thing

FIGURE 3–3   The Anatomy of a Habit

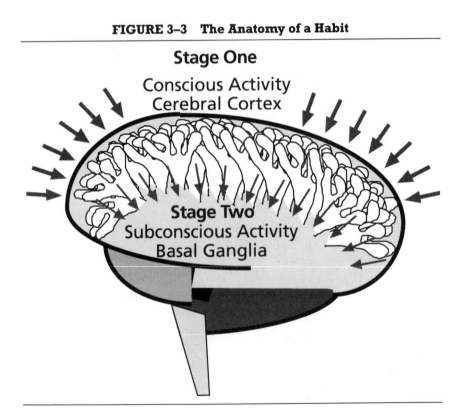

occurs in the brain. When you first start out, the neurological "trail" is undeveloped. The resulting connections are relatively inefficient. But the more you do or think something, the more efficient those connections become. In fact, the dendrites or connectors in your brain become thicker and process the impulse with greater speed.

As you do or think something repeatedly, your brain adapts by creating denser and more efficient neuropathways in your brain (Figure 3–4). The "trail" eventually becomes a neurological super-highway. This becomes part of the physiological structure of a habit.

FIGURE 3–4   The Brain Adapts by Creating Neuropathways

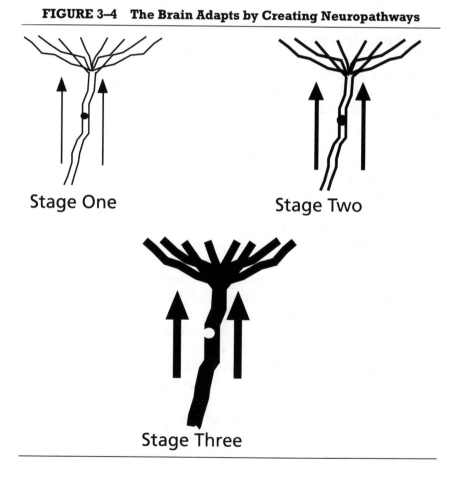

Stage One

Stage Two

Stage Three

This explanation was strengthened by my interview with Dr. Larry Squire of the University of California, San Diego Medical Center and president of the Society of Neuroscience. According to Dr. Squire, as you repeat a thought or behavior the strength of the synapses in your brain increases, and you literally form more transmitters and receptors for that pathway. Dr. Squire described the growth in the cortical map, or brain development which occurs as you generate and repeat a pattern of thought or behavior.

If you could peer into Andre Agassi's brain and locate the portion related to the forehand in tennis, you would find a thick and efficient set of neuro-pathways related to that behavior. We have this ability with the new Positron Emission Technology (PET) scans. With it, you could see denser development in that portion of his brain. However, if you looked for dense forehand dendrites in my brain, you wouldn't find much there!

Since speaking with Dr. Nuwer and Dr. Squire, I have interviewed other neurophysiologists. They concur. The gist of their findings is that the brain has an amazing ability to take repeated thoughts or behaviors and hardwire them into subconscious, automatic patterns or habits. This process begins with your first conscious choice, and with repetition the habit begins to migrate to the quiet background of your subconscious mind.

It is the neurological equivalent of having a "habits only" lane on the freeway. This lane or neuro-pathway allows your habits to travel more directly, predictably, and efficiently than the more random thoughts or neurological impulses.

That's great when you want to learn a new skill. However, the bad news is that the more you repeat a *destructive* thought or action, the deeper, faster, and more automatic it becomes, too. If you are in the habit of violating the speed limit when driving, chances are you do so automatically. You may slow down at times; but when your mind wanders, you find yourself whizzing down the freeway, traffic permitting, at 80 miles per hour. Like the cruise control in your car, your brain is very effective at following the pattern of behaviors required to speed. You may not consider this to be a destructive pattern until you see the red lights in your rear view mirror, or until your sixteen-year-old asks, "Why is it okay for you to speed when you yell at me whenever I go over the limit?" As with AQ,

FIGURE 3–5   The Three Building Blocks of AQ

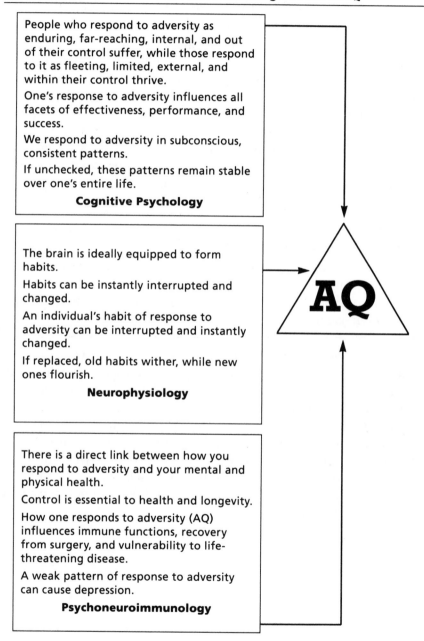

People who respond to adversity as enduring, far-reaching, internal, and out of their control suffer, while those respond to it as fleeting, limited, external, and within their control thrive.

One's response to adversity influences all facets of effectiveness, performance, and success.

We respond to adversity in subconscious, consistent patterns.

If unchecked, these patterns remain stable over one's entire life.

Cognitive Psychology

The brain is ideally equipped to form habits.

Habits can be instantly interrupted and changed.

An individual's habit of response to adversity can be interrupted and instantly changed.

If replaced, old habits wither, while new ones flourish.

Neurophysiology

There is a direct link between how you respond to adversity and your mental and physical health.

Control is essential to health and longevity.

How one responds to adversity (AQ) influences immune functions, recovery from surgery, and vulnerability to life-threatening disease.

A weak pattern of response to adversity can cause depression.

Psychoneuroimmunology

these "alarms" awaken you, immediately triggering the change to a more constructive habit (driving closer to the speed limit).

The good news is that the more you repeat a constructive thought or action, the deeper, faster, and more automatic it becomes. You probably are quite proficient at combing your hair, buttoning your shirt or blouse, and tying your shoes. You do these things without thinking, yet they help you avoid a lot of embarrassing stares!

To unlearn a bad or destructive habit, such as a low AQ, you must start at the conscious region of your brain and initiate new neuro-pathways. As Dr. Nuwer points out, *this can occur in an instant.* Change *can* be immediate, and the old, destructive patterns will atrophy and dwindle from lack of use.

Based on the research of leading neurophysiologists, we learn:

- The brain is ideally equipped to form habits.
- Habits become hardwired in the subconscious region of the brain.
- Subconscious habits, such as AQ, can be immediately altered, readily forming new habits that are strengthened over time.

These three building blocks—cognitive psychology, psychoneuroimmunology, and neurophysiology—come together to form AQ (Figure 3–5). the result is a new understanding, measure, and set of tools to enhance human effectiveness.

These new breakthroughs in these three sciences explain much of why people, teams, organizations, and societies quit or camp where others persevere. These findings also reveal what you must do in order to immediately reroute your AQ, and begin to hardwire your brain for success. In Chapter 6, I'll explain exactly how to achieve just that.

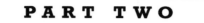

PART TWO

MEASURING AND UNDERSTANDING YOUR AQ

The Adversity Response Profile™

Measuring Your AQ and Your Ability to Climb

Know thyself.
Socrates

Beck Weathers used his ability to climb through adversity to overcome certain death on Mt. Everest. You will now have the opportunity to measure this ability in yourself. Unlike other measures, tests, or instruments you may have completed in the past, the Adversity Response Profile provides an entirely new, essential glimpse at what propels you and what might stand in the way of unleashing your full potential.

In Chapter 5, you will interpret your results from the Adversity Response Profile. You will learn about and graph your AQ—the habitual patterns that underlie how you perceive and respond to life's events. Like thousands of others, you'll find the results compelling and the implications pivotal to your further success and development as a climber.

VALIDITY AND RELIABILITY

The Adversity Response Profile (ARP) has been completed by more than 7,500 people from around the world representing a broad range of careers, ages, races, and cultures. Formal analysis of the results reveals that the instrument is a valid measure of how people respond to adversity and a powerful predictor of success. Studies in organizations, schools, and with athletes have shown that the ARP is an effective predictor of performance as well as a host of other facets of success. According to my clients, it also has great face validity—in other words, it makes sense, no matter what one's background. They see it as a source of major insight into their lives and the lives of those around them.

Through repeat and follow-up tests, the Adversity Response Profile has also proven to be highly reliable. Professionals, students, executives, and athletes who complete the tool more than once over a number of months, without participating in the AQ training program, demonstrate strong consistency in their results. And those who attend the program show marked improvement in their responses to adversity.

THE ADVERSITY RESPONSE PROFILE (ARP) QUICK TAKE™

You will be completing a special version of the Adversity Response Profile designed for your use in this book to provide you with quick results. The full version used in the AQ Programs has greater length and depth, providing more extensive graphing, insights, interpretation, and customization of the results. The ARP Quick Take™ will provide you with ample information to measure and interpret your AQ for the purposes of the activities within this book, without overwhelming you with additional detail.

If you are like most people, you will want to share this tool with a friend. Use the one in this chapter for yourself. Provide your friend with the opportunity to measure his or her AQ by using the blank Adversity Response Profile Quick Take™ located in the Appendix. In case you know more than one person who might benefit from completing this instrument, information on where to obtain additional tools as well as the full version of the Adversity Response Profile is provided at the end of the Appendix.

To get full value from this chapter and book, invest a few minutes in carefully following the instructions and filling out the questions that follow.

Tips:

- This is not a test. This tool is simply meant to give you new insights into an important aspect of how you think and function.
- Your first response is your best. Don't waste time trying to second guess this tool or your response.

Instructions

There are 30 events listed. Complete the questions for each event as follows:

1. Vividly imagine each event as if it is happening now, even if it seems unrealistic.
2. For both of the questions following each event, circle a number 1 through 5 that represents your response.

1. Your coworkers are not receptive to your ideas.

The reason my coworkers are not receptive to my ideas is something over which I have:

No control   1   2   3   4   5   *Complete Control*

C−

The reason my coworkers are not receptive to my ideas is something that completely has to do with:

Me   1   2   3   4   5   *Other people or factors*

O_r-

2. People are unresponsive to your presentation at a meeting.

The reason people are unresponsive to my presentation is something that:

Relates to all aspects of my life   1   2   3   4   5   *Just relates to this situation*

R−

The reason people are unresponsive to my presentation will:

Always exist   1   2   3   4   5   *Never exist again*

E−

3. You make a lot of money from a major investment.

The reason I am making a lot of money is something that:

Relates to all aspects of my life   1   2   3   4   5   *Just relates to this situation*

R+

The reason I am making a lot of money will:

Always exist   1   2   3   4   5   *Never exist again*

E+

4. You and your loved ones seem to be drifting further and further apart.

The reason we seem to be drifting further apart is something that:

Relates to all
aspects of my life   1   2   3   4   5   Just relates to
this situation

$R-$

The reason we seem to be drifting further apart will:

Always exist   1   2   3   4   5   Never exist again

$E-$

5. Someone you respect calls you for advice.

The reason this person called me for advice is something that:

Relates to all
aspects of my life   1   2   3   4   5   Just relates to
this situation

$R+$

The reason this person called me for advice will:

Always exist   1   2   3   4   5   Never exist again

$E+$

6. You have a heated argument with your spouse (significant other).

The reason we have a heated argument is something over which I have:

No control   1   2   3   4   5   Complete control

$C-$

The outcome of this event is something for which I feel:

Not at all
responsible   1   2   3   4   5   Completely
responsible

O_w-

(Continued)

7. You are required to relocate in order to keep your job.

The reason I am required to relocate is something that:

Relates to all aspects of my life	1	2	3	4	5	Just relates to this situation

$R-$

The reason I am required to relocate will:

Always exist	1	2	3	4	5	Never exist again

$E-$

8. A valued friend doesn't call on your birthday.

The reason my friend didn't call me is something over which I have:

No control	1	2	3	4	5	Complete control

$C-$

The reason my friend didn't call me is something that completely has to do with:

Me	1	2	3	4	5	Other people or factors

O_r-

9. A close friend becomes seriously ill.

The reason my friend is seriously ill is something over which I have:

No control	1	2	3	4	5	Complete control

$C-$

The outcome of this event is something for which I feel:

Not at all responsible	1	2	3	4	5	Completely responsible

O_w-

10. You are invited to an important event.

The reason I am being invited is something over which I have:

No control   1   2   3   4   5   Complete control

$$C+$$

The reason I am being invited is something that completely has to do with:

Me   1   2   3   4   5   Other people or factors

$$O_r+$$

11. You are turned down for an important assignment.

The reason I am being turned down for this assignment is something that:

Relates to all aspects of my life   1   2   3   4   5   Just relates to this situation

$$R-$$

The reason I am being turned down for this assignment will:

Always exist   1   2   3   4   5   Never exist again

$$E-$$

12. You receive some negative feedback from a valued coworker.

The reason I am receiving negative feedback is something that:

Relates to all aspects of my life   1   2   3   4   5   Just relates to this situation

$$R-$$

The reason I am receiving negative feedback will:

Always exist   1   2   3   4   5   Never exist again

$$E-$$

(Continued)

13. You receive a pay increase.

The reason I am receiving a pay increase is something over which I have:

No control   1   2   3   4   5   *Complete control*

$C+$

The reason I am receiving a pay increase is something that completely has do do with:

Me   1   2   3   4   5   *Other people or factors*

O_r+

14. Someone close to you is diagnosed with cancer.

The reason he or she has cancer is something that:

Relates to all aspects of my life   1   2   3   4   5   *Just relates to this situation*

$R-$

The reason he or she has cancer will:

Always exist   1   2   3   4   5   *Never exist again*

$E-$

15. Your latest investment strategy backfires.

The reason my strategy is backfiring is something that:

Relates to all aspects of my life   1   2   3   4   5   *Just relates to this situation*

$R-$

The reason my strategy is backfiring will:

Always exist   1   2   3   4   5   *Never exist again*

$E-$

16. You miss your airplane flight.

The reason I missed my flight is something over which I have:

No control   1   2   3   4   5   *Complete control*

$C-$

The reason I missed my flight is something that completely has to do with:

Me   1   2   3   4   5   *Other people or factors*

O_r-

17. You are selected for an important project.

The reason I am being selected for this project is something over which I have:

No control   1   2   3   4   5   Complete control

$C+$

The outcome of this event is something for which I feel:

Not at all responsible   1   2   3   4   5   Completely responsible

O_w+

18. The project you are in charge of fails.

The reason the project is failing is something over which I have:

No control   1   2   3   4   5   Complete control

$C-$

The outcome of this event is something for which I feel:

Not at all responsible   1   2   3   4   5   Completely responsible

O_w-

19. Your employer offers you a 30 percent pay cut to keep your job.

The reason I am asked to take the pay cut is something over which I have:

No control   1   2   3   4   5   Complete control

$C-$

The reason I am asked to take the pay cut is something that completely has to do with:

Me   1   2   3   4   5   Other people or factors

O_r-

20. You receive an unexpected gift on your birthday.

The reason I received this gift is something that:

Relates to all aspects of my life   1   2   3   4   5   Just relates to this situation

$R+$

The reason I received this gift will:

Always exist   1   2   3   4   5   Never exist again

$E+$

(Continued)

21. Your car breaks down on the way to an appointment.

The reason my car broke down is something that:

Relates to all aspects of my life	1	2	3	4	5	*Just relates to this situation*

R—

The reason my car broke down will:

Always exist	1	2	3	4	5	*Never exist again*

E—

22. Your doctor calls to tell you that your cholesterol level is too high.

The reason my cholesterol is too high is something that:

Relates to all aspects of my life	1	2	3	4	5	*Just relates to this situation*

R—

The reason my cholesterol is too high will:

Always exist	1	2	3	4	5	*Never exist again*

E—

23. You are chosen to lead a major project.

The reason I am being chosen is something over which I have:

No control	1	2	3	4	5	*Complete control*

C+

The reason I am being chosen is something that completely has to do with:

Me	1	2	3	4	5	*Other people or factors*

O_r+

24. You place several phone calls to a friend, and not one of them is returned.

The reason my friend did not return my call is something that:

Relates to all aspects of my life   1   2   3   4   5   Just relates to this situation

R−

The reason my friend did not return my call will:

Always exist   1   2   3   4   5   Never exist again

E−

25. You are publicly praised for your work.

The reason I am being praised is something that:

Relates to all aspects of my life   1   2   3   4   5   Just relates to this situation

R+

The reason I am being praised will:

Always exist   1   2   3   4   5   Never exist again

E+

26. At your physical exam, your doctor cautions you on your health.

The reason my doctor is cautioning me is something over which I have:

No control   1   2   3   4   5   Complete control

C−

The outcome of this event is something for which I feel:

Not at all responsible   1   2   3   4   5   Completely responsible

O_w-

(Continued)

27. Someone you respect pays you a compliment.

The reason I was paid a compliment is something over which I have:

No control	1	2	3	4	5	Complete control

$C+$

The outcome of this event is something for which I feel:

Not at all responsible	1	2	3	4	5	Completely responsible

O_w+

28. You receive an unfavorable performance appraisal.

The reason I am receiving this appraisal is something over which I have:

No control	1	2	3	4	5	Complete control

$C-$

The outcome of this event is something for which I feel:

Not at all responsible	1	2	3	4	5	Completely responsible

O_w-

29. You do not receive a much-anticipated promotion.

The reason I did not receive a promotion is something over which I have:

No control	1	2	3	4	5	Complete control

$C-$

The reason I did not receive a promotion is something that completely has to do with:

Me	1	2	3	4	5	Other people or factors

O_r-

30. You are elected by your peers to head an important committee.

The reason I am being elected is something that:

Relates to all aspects of my life	1	2	3	4	5	Just relates to this situation

$R+$

The reason I am being elected will:

Always exist	1	2	3	4	5	Never exist again

$E+$

Scoring

You will notice a small C, O_r, O_w, R, or E next to each question where you circled a response. Some have pluses, others have minuses. Since we are most concerned with your responses to *adversity*, you will only be scoring those answers with minus signs next to them. These are the adverse events, and only these are listed in order on the worksheet provided on the next page.

1. In the worksheet provided, insert your responses in the blanks next to the number for each event.
2. Follow the sequential instructions on the worksheet to calculate your CO_2RE dimensions and your overall AQ.

Congratulations! Now that you've just completed the Adversity Response Profile (ARP), you may be wondering, what's it all for? How will you use it?

In analyzing the thousands of individuals' responses to the ARP, I have discovered that people exhibit a wide range of AQs or discernible patterns of responses to adversity. Understanding these patterns can be as valuable as mapping your genetic code, although a tad easier. Knowing what underlies your behavior can shed a powerful light on who you are and how to improve. This understanding can help you climb.

In many ways, the tool you just completed is like any diagnostic test you might have taken at the doctor's office. The hardest part of having a blood test or an MRI may be the test itself. But, once you've had your vein tapped or your brain scanned, you still need some information. You want to know how to interpret your scores.

Chapter 5 will provide you with the answers. But, mark the previous page. You will want to return to your totals and grand total as you unravel the mystery of how you respond to life's events.

Event	C−	O_r-	O_w-	R−	E−
1					
2					
4					
6					
7					
8					
9					
11					
12					
14					
15					
16					
18					
19					
21					
22					
24					
26					
28					
29					

1. Vertically total your O_r and O_w scores.

   Insert them in the boxes.

2. Add your O_r and O_w totals to get your O_2 total.

   Insert it in the O_2 box.

3. Separately calculate your C, R, and E totals be adding the numbers in each column.

   Insert them in the appropriate boxes.

4. Going left to right, add your C, O_2, R, and E totals together to get your overall AQ.

   Insert it in the triangle below.

$$\boxed{O_r} + \boxed{O_w}$$

$$\boxed{C} + \boxed{O_2} + \boxed{R} + \boxed{E} = \triangle\!AQ$$

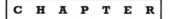

Interpreting Your Adversity Quotient and Your Power to Ascend

Difficulty, my brethren, is the nurse of greatness—a harsh nurse, who roughly rocks her foster-children into strength and athletic proportion.

William Cullen Bryant

"So, in order to remain competitive," the new CEO announced, "we will have to make significant adjustments in the allocation of human resources."

"Another downsizing," Marguerite thought to herself. "Let's see, that makes three in the past two years." Except they weren't calling it downsizing anymore, Marguerite mused. Nowadays it was called positioning for growth, realignment, or reallocating human resources. Fancy terms aside, it was all the same. More instability, more fear, more tears, more damaged morale, and certainly more work.

The day after the meeting Marguerite made a beeline for the coffee urn as she entered the conference center where she was to attend the AQ Program. It was 8:20 A.M. and she already felt sapped. She had awakened at six after a fitful night, which gave her just enough time to get herself and her two boys ready for school, feed everyone, clean the kitchen, and head out the door. On the way to the program, while waiting in traffic, Marguerite grabbed her cellular phone to pick up nine messages from her voice mail and returned two of the more urgent ones. By the time she arrived, there were several crises brewing at work, and the program hadn't yet begun!

"Everything seems lackluster lately," Marguerite thought as she reflected on some questions in her notebook. Her work, her life, and her marriage all seemed flat and lifeless, especially her marriage! Her husband, Randy, had been working late hours with lots of travel. Logically, she understood. He needed to work extra hard to keep his job. So did she. He had several opportunities for advancement that he had worked toward for a long time. Now was his time to dig in and prove himself.

Nonetheless, Marguerite felt needy. Needy and tired.

She remembered a time when she was fired up about her job and excited about the challenge of raising kids, managing a household, and having a committed marriage. Now it all seemed like too much. At times, Marguerite felt overwhelmed. She couldn't remember the last time she had smiled and felt it inside, not just on her face. Yet, everyone always told her how successful she was. "Why don't I *feel* more successful?" Marguerite wondered.

Ever since her company had reengineered for the second time, Marguerite had lost her zest for her career. Yesterday's announcement took what little wind she had left out of her sails. "Why work so hard if all they're going to do is lay off people anyway?" she reasoned. "What's the payoff in playing supermom? It only means more headaches down the road." Nothing Marguerite did brought her joy, just varying levels of stress. Some things were simply less stressful than others, but none were fun.

During the program, Marguerite learned about the three building blocks of her AQ and how it is the foundation of her success. She measured her AQ. "How can it be this low?" Marguerite fretted. "I'm a successful person!" she silently proclaimed, defending her accomplishments, if only to herself.

Over time, however, Marguerite came to realize that her AQ was not a tattoo or a judgment. It was more of a *snapshot*, an invaluable insight into an essential part of herself that had remained hidden, influencing her behavior and emotions from its secret room in the subconscious shadows of her mind.

Gradually, it dawned on her that how she was experiencing her life could be traced to her AQ. "It's no wonder I'm feeling so dead inside," she thought. As the program leader explained the three levels that comprise the Age of Adversity, Marguerite turned to the participant seated next to her and said, "Gee! I face more adversity than I realized!" Her reaction to the CEO's announcement could be traced directly to her AQ. She couldn't help noticing that others in the room seemed to be affected much less adversely as a result of the news.

As she interpreted her AQ, Marguerite realized that she tended to respond to adversity as something enduring and far-reaching and, like most women, she tended to blame herself, even when she wasn't responsible for whatever went wrong. Marguerite soon understood the critical role her AQ played in her energy, happiness, motivation, performance, and success. She thought about Randy and how he seemed tougher, almost happier when things got hard. "I bet he's got a high AQ!" she thought. "No wonder we've been growing apart. I'm probably dragging him and our marriage down."

Over the course of the day, Marguerite learned the important role her awareness played in changing her AQ. She thought back to the information about the brain and how, by being aware of her response, she can immediately begin to hardwire a new response pattern.

Marguerite practiced her new skills with the partner she joined from across the room. Together they honed their ability to reroute their response and create a stronger, more effective response to adversity.

By the end of the day, Marguerite had a long list of actions she wanted to take, including teaching the new material to Randy. She also felt a sense of lightness, as if the sun had emerged after a prolonged period of rain. Marguerite knew that, if she took advantage of some of the tools and devices which she had learned during the program, she could strengthen herself from the inside out and re-ignite her ascent and passion for life. She felt centered, with a deep inner resolve to improve her life and get back on her path. Marguerite left equipped to improve her AQ, and with it, her life.

The purpose of this chapter is to provide you with the information you need to understand the four CO_2RE dimensions of your AQ or Adversity Quotient and to create your own AQ Profile. The chapter is divided into two parts: The CO_2RE Dimensions of Your AQ, and Graphing Your CO_2RE. The first part will provide you with a detailed understanding of the high, moderate, and low CO_2RE dimension. The second section will give you the opportunity to graph your CO_2RE and learn about your own positive and negative tendencies. Ultimately, this information will provide you with essential insights to strengthen your ascent, contribution, and sense of purpose.

THE AQ CONTINUUM

As you analyze your AQ, you will discover that AQs are not simply categorized as "high" or "low"; rather, they fall on a continuum. The higher you score, the more likely you are to enjoy the benefits of a high AQ. But, even if your AQ is very high, you will find ways to better understand and fine tune your success, while helping others continue their ascents.

AQs tend to fall more frequently in the middle than at either extreme of the continuum in a normal distribution or bell-shaped curve (Figure 5–1).

AQ is not a matter of black and white, yes or no, successful or unsuccessful. It is a matter of *degree*.

INTERPRETING YOUR OVERALL AQ

Next you will find some general descriptions of people whose AQs fall within different ranges. Remember, these are general statements meant to help you learn more about yourself. Because AQs fall on a continuum, these cut offs are somewhat arbitrary. There

FIGURE 5–1 Normal Distribution of Adversity Quotient Scores Based on a Norm Base of Over 7,500 Respondents

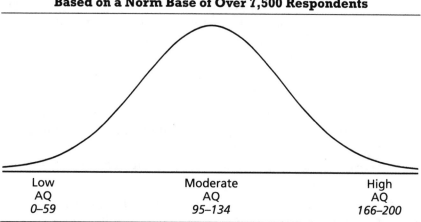

| Low AQ 0–59 | Moderate AQ 95–134 | High AQ 166–200 |

is not a discernible difference between someone with an AQ of 134 and someone with an AQ of 135. There is, however, a difference between people with low, moderate, and high AQs. Use these descriptions to *learn*, not to categorize yourself or seal your fate.

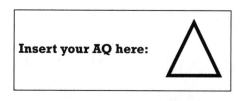

Insert your AQ here:

- *166–200* If your overall AQ is in this range, you probably have the ability to withstand significant adversity and continue to move forward and upward in your life. You can use the tools found in this book to continually hone your climbing skills and to teach others in your life how to prevail.

- *135–165* If your AQ falls within this range, you probably do a fairly good job of persisting through challenges and tapping a good portion of your growing potential on a daily basis. You can increase your effectiveness by fine tuning certain aspects of your AQ.

- *95–134* You usually do a decent job of navigating life as long as everything is going relatively smoothly. However, you may suffer unnecessarily from larger setbacks, or may be disheartened by the accumulated burden of life's frustrations and challenges. By using the tools presented in the remaining chapters, you can raise your AQ and substantially strengthen your effectiveness in life.

- *60–94* You are likely to be underutilizing your potential. Adversity can take a significant and unnecessary toll, making it difficult to continue your Ascent. You may battle a sense of helplessness and despair. You *can* escape this conundrum by raising your AQ.

- *59 and below* If your AQ falls within this range, you have probably suffered unnecessarily in an number of ways. Your motivation, energy, health, vitality, performance, persistence, and hope can be greatly revitalized by learning and practicing the tools you'll find in this book. My experience in working with those whose AQ scores fall within this point range has proven that you can experience a transformation in your personal and professional life by approaching adversity in a new way. So, take heart, you can make great progress quickly.

THE CO_2RE DIMENSIONS OF YOUR AQ

Your AQ is comprised of four CO_2RE dimensions. CO_2RE is an acronym for the four dimensions of your AQ. They are derived from the research described in Chapter 3 (Figure 5–2). Much the way your strength, speed, coordination, and intelligence may determine your score on the tennis court, these CO_2RE dimensions will determine your overall AQ. However, your tennis score provides little information as to why you received that score or what you may need to work on to improve your game. Likewise, your overall AQ, while significant, reveals little about *why* your AQ is in the upper, middle, or lower ranges. Nor does it tell you what you need to work on to raise it. You must look more closely at your CO_2RE to fully understand your AQ.

FIGURE 5–2   Forming the CO_2RE

Hybrid Control Theory*	Optimism	AQ
Control		C = Control
Ownership	Personal	O_2 = Origin and Ownership
	Pervasive	R = Reach
	Permanent	E = Endurance

*Derived from a combination of hardiness, locus of control, resilience, self-efficacy, attributional theory.

C = Control

C stands for "control." It asks the question: How much control do you perceive that you have over an adverse event? Notice, the key word here is *perceive*. Actual control in a given situation is nearly impossible to measure. Perceived control is far more important.

This AQ dimension is one of the most important departures from and additions to Seligman's theory of optimism. While related research strongly supports the inclusion of this dimension, Seligman's theory stopped short of fully accounting for the impact perceived control has over how one responds to and handles adversity. Control strikes directly at empowerment and influence, and impacts all other CO_2RE dimensions.

Life is filled with situations in which one might solidly predict, "there's nothing you can do about it" yet, someone changes the face of history. When Mohandas Gandhi decided to take on the British Empire through passive resistance, he had no formal authority. He was just "a little brown man" with an impenetrable sense of purpose and a relentless determination to seek justice for his people. Centuries of domination had led to a pervasive feeling of helplessness. Much like Seligman's dogs, people in Gandhi's time accepted their situation as their desperate fate.

Gandhi's entire campaign against the British depended on one thing—*his ability to alter the Indian's perceived control over their oppressors*. While no one would have bet on Gandhi in the early years of his effort, he proved that independence could be gained and justice would prevail. He turned around perceptions, then he turned perceptions into reality.

It is difficult to overestimate the power of perceived control. Without it, hope and action are crushed. With it, lives can be transformed and destinies fulfilled. Had Gandhi not perceived control where none seemed to exist, India and its nearly one billion citizens might be under British rule today.

Control begins with the perception that something, anything, can be done. The same could be said for:

- Every executive who turns around a faltering company.
- Every student who takes on an impossible subject.
- Every leader who goes against the common wisdom of the day.
- Every teacher who innovates in spite of a deeply entrenched bureaucracy.
- Every neighborhood volunteer who fights back the tide of drugs and gangs.
- Every salesperson who finds a "yes" in a sea of "no's."
- Every entrepreneur who takes on the corporate behemoths.
- Every child who continues to pick himself up and hop back on after having failed at yet another attempt to ride his or her bicycle.
- Every person attempting to create change or improve.

From day one, nothing happens without the perception of control.

The difference between lower and higher AQ responses on this dimension are, therefore, quite dramatic. Those with higher AQs simply perceive greater control over life's events than do those with lower AQs. As a result, they take action, which results in more control. Those with higher AQs are more likely to climb, whereas those with lower AQs are more likely to camp or quit. The self-fulfilling prophecy is real.

Those who score low on the C dimension might think:

- This is out of my reach!
- There's nothing I can do about it.
- Oh well, there's no use banging your head against a brick wall.
- You can't take on City Hall.

Whereas those with higher AQs, given the same situation, might think:

- Whew! This is tough! But, I've seen tougher.
- There must be something I can do. . . . . I refuse to believe I'm helpless in this situation.
- There's always a way.
- Nothing ventured, nothing gained.
- I've got to figure out a way . . .

Even in these sample responses you can sense the resilience and gritty determination that comes from having a high AQ. High AQ people are relatively immunized from feeling helpless. It is as if they are protected by an impenetrable force field that keeps them from bottomless despair. Perceiving even the smallest degree of control has a radical and powerful effect on the actions and thoughts that follow.

Find your score on the C dimension from Chapter 4, insert it in the box, and see how it fits with the descriptions that follow.

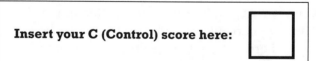

Insert your C (Control) score here:

At the High End (38–50 points)

The higher your AQ and your score on this dimension, the more likely you are to perceive that you have a strong degree of control over most adverse events. Greater perceived control leads to a more empowered, proactive approach. High control has far reaching, positive implications and bodes well for your long-term performance, productivity, and health. The higher your C score, the more likely you are to persist through difficulties, and remain both steadfast in your determination and agile in your approach to finding a solution.

> *Sheila felt some measure of control in her life. Twenty-two years after graduating from college, she overcame her fears and decided to take night classes in German at the local community college. Despite her hard work and strong language aptitude, she received a B- on her midterm exam. Sheila was perplexed by her grade. She instantly reviewed the test, double-checking her answers. After close scrutiny, Sheila realized that her professor had taken off points for several accurate answers. Sheila immediately arranged to meet with her professor after class. Despite Sheila's diplomatic approach, the professor was initially defensive. As Sheila persisted, the professor softened and realized that her instructions to Sheila were unclear. She awarded Sheila full-credit for her work, raising her grade from a B− to an A−.*

In the Mid-Range (24–37 points)

You may respond to adverse events as at least partially within your control, depending on the magnitude of the event. You probably are not easily disheartened. But, it may be more difficult to maintain a sense of control when faced with more serious setbacks or challenges.

At the Low End (10–23 points)

The lower your AQ and your score on this dimension, the more likely you are to perceive that adverse events are beyond your control and that there is little, if anything, you can do to prevent them or limit their damages. Low perceived control can have a highly detrimental affect on your sense of power to alter the situation. Those with significantly low perceived control often feel frozen in the face of adversity. This undermines their ability to ascend. In more severe cases, this may result in a resigned, fatalistic view of life. Scores on the lower end of the scale may indicate a dangerous vulnerability to adversity, increasing it's potential toll on one's performance, energy, and soul. The lower your score on this dimension, the more you may be worn down than necessary by life's daily vicissitudes.

> *Imagine how Sheila would respond if she had scored low on the C dimension. Probably, she would be instantly shocked and deflated when she saw her grade. The more she ruminated about it, the worse she would feel. She might think she was in over her head. It would never even cross her mind to question the grade! Deep within, she would assume her professor is right, the grade is set in stone, and there is nothing she can do.*

Control is generally internal and often highly individual. There are even instances where, to an outside observer, a person seems to have no control whatsoever. The extreme occurred in the Nazi concentration camps. Vicktor Frankl's now famous realization was that even in such unfathomable conditions, he, as a prisoner, had greater control than the guard who was torturing him, because Frankl could control how he *responded!*

We need not turn to the concentration camps to find examples of where apparent lack of control exists. Many of our organizations and families are populated with individuals who are told they have control but are severely punished when they exercise it. They are put into double binds with no apparent way out. Is the child who is told to speak his mind and then punished for doing so really any different than the "empowered" employee who is reprimanded for exercising control? I remember a cartoon in which the son tells his dad what he thinks about living with rules, and the dad turns to his son and says, "That's a very interesting and thought-provoking comment. Now go to your room."

Even in the most dire of circumstances, there is always a modicum of control. You *always* control how you respond. This is the seed from which hope and action sprout.

O_2 = Origin and Ownership

O_2 stands for "origin" and "ownership." It asks two questions: Who or what was the origin of the adversity? and To what degree do I own the outcomes of the adversity? On the surface, these two questions of origin and ownership may appear identical. Upon closer examination, however, you will discover that there is a powerful difference between *origin* and *ownership*. Let's begin with origin, which has to do with blame.

People with lower AQs tend to place undue blame upon themselves for bad events. In many cases, they see themselves as the sole cause or *origin* of the adversity.

Blame serves two valuable functions. First it helps you to learn. By blaming yourself you are more likely to consider, learn from, and adjust your behavior. This is what improvement is all about. Second, blaming leads to remorse. Remorse can compel you to search your soul and weigh the ways in which you might have hurt someone else. Remorse is a powerful motivator. Used properly it can help heal real, perceived, or potential damage to an important relationship.

We all have moments where we wish we could take back what we said and do it over. When you do something awful to someone, it is important to them that you experience some remorse and learn from your mistakes.

A fair and accurate degree of self-blame is required to create the critical learning or feedback loop needed to continuously improve. The ability to assess what you did right or wrong and how you might improve is fundamental to developing yourself as a person. Lower origin responses may squash this feedback loop under the burden of relentless self-blame, undermining your ability to learn from your mistakes.

Like criticism, blame, and its cousin remorse, are only beneficial in measured doses. Too much of either can be severely demoralizing and *destructive*. Once blame becomes destructive, it can devastate your energy, hope, self-worth, and immune system. Blame in the right measure spurs one to action. Blame overdone creates inaction.

The accumulated effect of low perceived control, overwhelming remorse, and exaggerated self-blame can be debilitating. If things go continually bad in your family or work team and you believe there's little that can be done and that the bad things are mostly your fault, you may become worn down, disheartened, and depressed. You may, in fact, decide to *quit*.

People with lower origin scores tend to think:

- It's all my fault.
- I'm such an idiot.
- I should have known better.
- What was I thinking?
- I was in way over my head.
- I've ruined everything!
- I'm such a failure.

The lower your origin score, the more likely you are to heap blame upon yourself, beyond the point of it being constructive.

Insert your O$_2$ (Origin) score here:

On the other hand, the higher your origin score, the greater your tendency to consider other, external sources of the adversity and put your own role into perspective. Ideally, you will assess your role and learn from your behavior so you can be smarter, quicker, better, or more effective next time you encounter a similar situation.

People with higher origin response might think:

- It was lousy timing.
- The whole industry is suffering.
- Everyone is having a hard time right now.
- She is just in a bad mood.
- Several team members didn't contribute.
- My son is ill, and I had to stay up all night taking care of him.
- No one could have seen this one coming!
- There were several factors at play.
- The whole team fell short of our expectations.

- All things considered, I can see ways in which I could have done my job better, and I will next time I am in this situation.

Owning versus Blaming

You may be reading this section and thinking, "Yeah, but isn't blaming yourself a good thing?" Remember, self-blame is important and effective, *to a point*. Excessive self-blame, however, that goes beyond one's role in causing the adversity is *destructive*. Of far greater importance is to what degree you are willing to *own the outcome* of the adversity. Blame is not the same as *accountability*. Owning the outcomes reflects accountability, and that's the second half of the O_2 dimension.

This is one of the significant additions to the current theory. The major sticking point in teaching people about optimism versus pessimism is the implied message that it is preferable to deflect accountability. But many executives, managers, administrators, and parents find this message unacceptable in a time when accountability is foremost. I have spoken to countless leaders whose greatest frustration comes from people unwilling to own results of bad events, whether or not they are the cause.

A common misconception generated from earlier theory is that those with higher AQs simply deflect bad events, blaming everyone else and learning nothing. It would be irritating if they went around blowing off responsibility every time things went awry. The result might be utter chaos! People place a premium on taking responsibility. Accountability is one of the most revered yet rarest character traits in our society.

AQ teaches people to *enhance* their accountability as a way to enlarge their control, empowerment, and motivation to take action (Figure 5–3). This message is a welcome framework for change.

Recently, Tom, the neighborhood landscaping "expert" stopped by. A couple of months earlier he had called, asking to include me in his special, ecologically friendly lawn fertilization program. I consented, deciding to give the guy a break. He sounded like he knew what he was doing.

A few weeks later he sent out a member of his crew to do the job. Within a month, the lawn was dead. To make matters worse, Tom had the nerve to bill me for it!

FIGURE 5–3   AQ, Learning, and Accountability

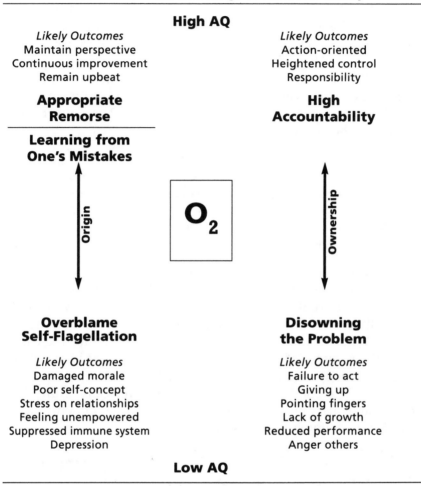

High AQ

Likely Outcomes
Maintain perspective
Continuous improvement
Remain upbeat

**Appropriate
Remorse**

**Learning from
One's Mistakes**

Origin

O₂

Likely Outcomes
Action-oriented
Heightened control
Responsibility

**High
Accountability**

Ownership

**Overblame
Self-Flagellation**

Likely Outcomes
Damaged morale
Poor self-concept
Stress on relationships
Feeling unempowered
Suppressed immune system
Depression

**Disowning
the Problem**

Likely Outcomes
Failure to act
Giving up
Pointing fingers
Lack of growth
Reduced performance
Anger others

Low AQ

So, I called him, and that's when he stopped by. As he entered my back-yard and surveyed the damage he said, "Darn it! I hired that new kid, and he told me he knew how to do the job. I even trained him, but he has killed several of my best customers' lawns! Well, Paul, I just want you to know, I am 100 percent accountable for what's happened here. And, I will do what-ever it takes to make things right, even if it means putting in a new lawn, at my expense!"

Notice that Tom was not blaming himself as the origin or cause of the adversity, any more than was realistic. He acknowledge that he had hired and trained the kid, but it was the kid who did the poor job. I had no problem with Tom's response, because, what I cared about was *him learning from his mistake and his owning* the outcome, or holding himself accountable for the ruined lawn.

Imagine if Tom had blamed himself entirely as the only origin of the adversity, but failed to own the outcome. The conversation would have been severely aggravating for me.

> *Oh, Geez! I can't believe I did this Dr. Stoltz. I mean it's all my fault. I hired the kid who killed your lawn, and I should have known better. I guess I'm not a very good judge of people. I trained him, but I must have done a terrible job, because look what happened! I'm so stupid! Your beautiful lawn is ruined, and I did it! Well, there's nothing I can do about it. You'll just have to call someone more competent and put in new sod. I am so, so sorry."*

Can you imagine how you would respond? First you'd feel so bad for the guy flogging himself with merciless self-blame that you would want to comfort him or send him to therapy. But, you would just as likely become angry as you would think, "Hey, wait a minute! What do you mean I'll have to pay for resodding the whole lawn? *You're* responsible for the damage, not me!" He blames himself (low O_r) but *owns* nothing (low O_w). *No one wins.*

So O_2, the second CO_2RE dimension of your AQ, measures *both* origin and ownership. Find your O_w score on the O_2 dimension and consider the following discussion.

Insert your O_w (Ownership) score here:

The higher your ownership score, the more you own the outcomes, regardless of their cause. The lower your ownership score, the more you *disown* the outcomes, regardless of their cause.

Obviously this tendency to blow off bad events or deflect accountability is highly undesirable. As a result, strategies that increase employee ownership abound in corporate America. There are many large, highly successful companies that are over 70 percent employee owned, including Weirsten Steel, ranking 288 in the Fortune 500, and Avis Corporation, now privately owned, but, (as everyone knows) America's Number 2 car rental company. Employees own a majority of the stock in three of the country's ten largest steel manufacturers, two of the ten largest private hospital management companies, two of the three largest shipbuilders, United Airlines, two of the ten largest construction firms, and so on.

The growth in such plans is a direct result of the need to enhance perceived ownership through real ownership. People act with great responsibility and accountability if they believe they own a piece of the result. It is the leader's imperative to communicate and specify each person's ownership, closing the gap between behavior and outcomes.

Therefore, it is not that people with high AQs simply blame others while dodging the bullet. In fact, high AQ people are superior to those with lower AQs in their ability to learn from their mistakes (Figure 5–3). They also tend to own the outcomes of the adversity, often regardless of its cause. Such accountability compels them to take action, making them far more empowered than their low AQ counterparts.

Like Tom the landscaper, people with high AQs simply do a better job of putting their own role into perspective. They recognize what portion of the responsibility is genuinely theirs. Think about it. When was the last time something bad happened? How much of it was truly your fault? You are *rarely* 100 percent at fault.

You may recall from Chapter 3 that there is a gender difference on this dimension. Women tend to blame themselves more than men do as the cause of bad events. Carol Dweck of the University of Illinois has conducted several studies which reveal that this pattern of behavior forms early in life. Women's self-blame could be traced, at least in part, to the kind of feedback teachers gave them when they were children.

I have found Dweck's discovery to hold true in my AQ programs and my consulting work with individuals in organizations. In fact, there is an immediate response from women participating in my program when I describe this phenomenon. They often laugh in recognition saying, "Well, *that* explains it!"

Women do tend to take on more destructive self-blame, while men tend to focus more on the outcomes than their role in causing the adversity. Through the program, I teach women to put their blame in check, and I teach men to accept the appropriate amount of blame for them to learn from their mistakes and heal any wounds they may have caused in their relationships. Both men and women seem to find this a refreshing perspective and a useful skill.

Find your O_2 score and consider the following discussion.

Insert your O_2 (Origin + Ownership) score here:

At the High End (38–50 points)

The higher your AQ and your score on this dimension, the more likely you are to view success as your doing and adversity as originating primarily from some external source. Higher scores on this dimension typically reflect an ability to avoid unnecessary self-blame while putting one's own responsibility into perspective. They indicate the empowering combination of blaming yourself only for what you did while owning the outcomes of the adversity, which propelled you toward action. Ideally this reflects an ability to feel appropriate remorse (Figure 5–3) and learn from your mistakes.

Upon arriving at work, Frank was instantly accosted by an anxious team member. After a few minutes of listening to this person's panicked explanation, Frank discovered that the computer hard drive containing the 145-page report they had been preparing for the Executive Committee had crashed during a power surge the night before. Everything was lost, and the last back-up was at least a week old.

Frank, recognizing the severity of the situation, reflected back on the heavy thunderstorm that had hit in the middle of the night, knocking out electricity to the entire area. Frank shrugged. "It was an act of nature. We're lucky we didn't blow out the whole network."

As team leader, however, Frank felt responsible for exploring every creative alternative to recover the lost data. He acknowledged that the team had to take immediate action to reconstruct the report, as best it could, and strengthen its enforcement of company policy to regularly back up all hard drives. Frank contacted the data recovery experts to see what, if anything could be recovered. Next he called a team meeting to make the necessary adjustments in schedules so members could reconstruct the lost data as quickly as possible. Frank reported the loss to his supervisor, holding himself accountable for doing whatever it took to come up with the final report.

In the Mid-Range (24–37 points)

You may respond to adverse events as sometimes originating from without and sometimes from yourself. You may, on occasion, blame yourself unnecessarily for bad outcomes. You probably hold yourself somewhat accountable for the outcomes of the adversity, but may limit your accountability to only those things for which you were the direct cause, being unwilling to contribute in a larger way.

At the Low End (10–23 points)

The lower your AQ and your score on this dimension, the more you may view adversity as primarily your fault (whether or not it is) and good events as strokes of luck due to external forces. Perceiving yourself as the origin of bad events can be hard on your stress level, ego, and motivation. You may also deflect ownership, avoiding holding yourself accountable for working to solve the situation. Over time, such a response may lead to self-doubt and withdrawal from major challenges.

If Frank had a low O score, he would be crushed by the news. As team leader, he would mercilessly blame himself for the lost data. He might be inconsolable. "In hindsight it's all so clear. I should have reinforced the back-up policy more rigidly," he might have thought. "I can't believe I didn't have a hard copy and updated back-up in safe storage. What kind of leader would let this kind of disaster occur? I should have seen this coming." Frank would begin to question his leadership and ability to handle major responsibilities.

At no point would he recognize that this was a shared responsibility of the entire team, especially those who worked on the document since its last back up. Nor would he acknowledge that they might all have had to start from scratch had he not suggested regular back-ups months ago.

At the same time, Frank, dispirited by his burden of blame, would lack the energizing sense of ownership necessary for recovering the lost data. He would have sat around, licking his wounds, while time slipped by and little was being done to correct the error. He would have assumed it was someone else's responsibility to deal with the problem. Frank's response would have demoralized the other team members who were concerned with recovering the data.

R = Reach

The R dimension asks the question: How far will the adversity reach into other areas of my life? Lower AQ responses allow the adversity to bleed over into other facets of one's life. A bad meeting becomes a ruined day; a conflict becomes a failed relationship; a negative performance appraisal becomes a career failure, which becomes financial panic, sleeplessness, bitterness, distancing one's self from others, and poor decision making.

Indeed, the lower your R score, the more likely you are to catastrophize bad events, allowing them to spread, consuming your happiness and peace of mind in the process. Catastrophizing, like wildfire, can be dangerous, causing significant damage if allowed to go unchecked.

On the other hand, the higher your R score, the more you may limit the reach of the problem to the event at hand. A cold-call rejection is just one rejection—nothing more and nothing less. A tough performance appraisal is a tough performance appraisal, if not a learning experience. A conflict is a conflict, an event that may warrant additional commitment and action. A misunderstanding with a loved one, although painful, is a misunderstanding, not a sign that your life is falling apart.

Find your score on the R dimension and consider the following descriptions.

Insert your R (Reach) score here:

At the High End (38–50 points)

The higher your AQ and your score on this dimension, the more you may respond to adversity as specific and limited. The more effectively you contain or compartmentalize the reach of the adversity, the more empowered and less overwhelmed you are likely to feel. Keeping adversity in its place makes life's difficulties, frustrations, and challenges more manageable. To people with high R scores, a bad day is simply a bad day, not a major setback; a tough meeting is a tough meeting, not a failure; a conflict with a loved one is a misunderstanding, not the disintegration of the relationship.

> *Three days before her wedding Lilly discovered that the band she had hired for her reception had never received her confirmation and deposit check. As a result, they had booked another gig for the same evening. Lilly immediately limited the reach of the adversity by recognizing that this was but one facet of the wedding. She went through a mental checklist of all the things that were well-planned and in place. The loss of the band was a setback, not a disaster. She immediately phoned her fiancé to share the news and brainstorm alternatives. Within five minutes they were laughing uproariously. They recognized that, at worst, they could hire a disc jockey with a professional sound system. The wedding was on track, and they had overcome the adversity.*

In the Mid-Range (24–37 points)

You may respond to adverse events as somewhat specific. However, you may occasionally let them reach unnecessarily into other areas of your life. When you're feeling down, you might catastrophize, making bad events much more far-reaching and severe than they might otherwise be. In your weaker moments, you may succumb to the temptation to turn setbacks into disasters, relying on others to pull you out of this emotional pit.

At the Low End (10–23 points)

The lower your AQ and your score on this dimension, the more you may view adversity as bleeding into other areas of your life. You may perceive criticism from your boss as a ruined career. A financial loss may look like an impending bankruptcy. An unreturned phone call may mean the end of a valued friendship. Conversely, you may perceive good events as specific and limited in reach.

Allowing adversity to reach other areas of your life can greatly enhance the weight of the perceived burden and the energy required to make things right. As a result, this distorted view of adversity may, at times, render you helpless to take necessary action.

> *If she had a low R score, Lilly might hang up the phone, stunned when news of the band disaster hit. "No band. No band means no music, no music means no dancing, no dancing means no bride's and groom's dances. . . ." Within moments, Lilly might have convinced herself that the entire reception, indeed the entire wedding was ruined. She might vividly imagine people criticizing her blunder as they left the reception as soon as they finished eating. "What kind of reception doesn't have a band? Who planned this wedding anyway? This is pathetic!" Lilly might be in tears, debilitated with dread, incapacitated by the nightmare she would play over and over in her mind.*

Limiting the reach of the adversity is highly desirable. The further you allow the adversity to reach into other areas of your life, the more helpless and overwhelmed you may feel. Small annoyances can become disasters if allowed to fester and grow in the fertile darkness of your subconscious. Limiting the reach of the adversity enables you to think clearly and take action. Allowing even a moderate reach of the adversity into one or more areas of your life can take the strength out of your climbing legs.

E = Endurance

E, or Endurance, is the final dimension of your AQ. It asks two related questions: *How long will the adversity last?* and *How long will the cause of the adversity last?*

The lower your E score, the more likely you are to perceive adversity and/or its causes lasting a long time, if not forever.

- This always happens.
- Things will never get better.
- I'm not good with computers.
- It's always been this way.

- My life is ruined.
- This company is doomed.
- My boss was right; I am not wired for success.
- The whole industry is going down the tubes.
- My family will never be close.
- I'll never be a good salesperson.
- No one will want to marry me.
- I've always been lazy.
- I've never been good with kids.
- I'm just a procrastinator.
- I have no will power.

All of these statements reek of permanence. Labels such as *loser, stupid failure,* and *procrastinator,* as well as words like *always* and *never* are insidious. They render you helpless to change. There is a world of difference between "I need to be careful not to postpone things to the last minute" and "I am a procrastinator." One is temporary the other is *permanent.* One implies action, the other is a label. One reflects self-knowledge, the other quickly becomes an excuse.

A friend struggles with his teenage stepson, who shrugs as he helplessly explains his bad grades with "I can't help it. I'm just lazy. My father told me that I inherited it from him." This teenager has taken his own difficulty in getting excited about geometry and, with the help of his father, turned it into a disease.

The same is true of the cause of the adversity. Building on Seligman's work, research on attributional theory, such as that conducted by Lorraine Johnson and Stuart Biddle from the University of Exeter in England, indicates that there is a dramatic difference between people who attribute adversity to something temporary versus something more permanent or enduring. In applying attributional theory to sports, they found that people who see their *ability* as the cause of their failure (stable cause) are less likely to persist than people who attribute failure to their *effort* (a temporary cause).

If you are turned down for a job, and you attribute the rejection to something temporary—such as a lack of effort, poor strategy, or a bad match—you are likely to believe that adjustments in these areas will improve your future chances of success. If, however, you attribute the rejection to something more enduring or stable—such as your intelligence, your ability to write a good cover letter, your appearance, or whether or not you are perceived as likable—you are more likely to give up. The relationship between the perceived stability of the cause of the adversity and empowerment to take action have been demonstrated in sports, education, and business.

Locate your score on the E dimension and consider the following descriptions of the high, mid, and low scores.

Insert your E (Endurance) score here: ☐

At the High End (38–50 points)

The higher your AQ and your score on this dimension, the more you may view success as enduring, if not permanent. Likewise, you may consider adversity and its causes to be temporary, fleeting, and unlikely to recur. This enhances your energy, optimism, and likelihood to take action. You have a healthy and natural tendency to see the light at the end of the tunnel, no matter how long the tunnel may be. The perception that adversity and its causes will eventually pass bolsters your ability to survive life's darker moments and greatest challenges.

> *Petra's assistant broke into a manufacturing group meeting to inform her that she had an urgent phone call from her son's principal. Slightly embarrassed, Petra left the meeting to handle the call. She couldn't believe her ears. In a solemn tone, Dr. Miller informed her that David, along with two of his ten-year-old friends, had been caught shoplifting. The idea of David stealing from Mr. Gruber, the local druggist, was inconceivable. Yet, the boys had been collared—their pockets filled with candy—walking out the door. After Petra hung up, she shut her office door and reflected on the gravity of her son's deed. Thinking back to her own childhood exploits, she took comfort in the belief that, if firmly and properly disciplined, David will likely learn from this experience and someday grow out of this vulnerable phase of his youth.*

In the Mid-Range (24–37 points)

You may respond to adverse events and their causes as somewhat enduring. This may, on occasion, delay you from taking constructive action. With life's small to moderate challenges, you probably do a reasonably good job of keeping faith and forging ahead. However, there may be moments when you are weakened and your hope dwindles, especially when experiencing a fairly severe setback.

At the Low End (10–23 points)

The lower your AQ and your score on this dimension, the more you may view adversity and its causes as enduring and positive events as temporary. This may indicate the kind of responses that evoke a feeling of helplessness or a loss of hope. Over time, you may feel cynical about certain aspects of your life. You may be less likely to take action against adversity which you perceive as permanent.

> *If Petra had a low E score, she might close her office door and put her head in her hands. She would imagine the unimaginable—her son David, a thief! Instantly Petra would imagine David's moral lapse years into the future. As she would ruminate on her son's impending immorality in future jobs and relationships, she might grow increasingly disheartened. With the belief that David's behavior was likely to endure and perhaps worsen, Petra would open herself to catastrophizing about his future, underestimating her control over his development, and allowing deep feelings of parental inadequacy to seep into her soul. She might in turn, treat him as a criminal, reinforce his destructive behavior, and make her worst nightmare a reality.*

GRAPHING YOUR CO_2RE

You are now ready to score, graph, and interpret your four CO_2RE dimensions. This portion of the chapter is highly interactive and introspective. The more you involve yourself in honestly reflecting upon your response habits, the more you will learn. The information you are about to receive is both exciting and invaluable. You will benefit from learning as much as possible about the dimensions and practical subtleties of your AQ.

This information will help you in two important ways. Not only will you gain unique insights into yourself, but you will also learn a great deal about other people in your life. In the following chapters, I'll show you how to lead and assist them more effectively. For maximum benefit, allow yourself a peaceful setting and enough time.

Turn back to page 100 where you totaled your responses on CO_2RE. For the remainder of this book, we will focus exclusively on these totals. They represent your cumulative responses to adversity, which, as you know, once strengthened, have powerful implications for your future success.

Step One: Insert your four totals for C, O_2, R, and E in the boxes at the top of the graph.

Step Two: Graph your four totals by placing a dot on each of the corresponding number lines, as shown in the example. Odd numbers should be placed in between the two closest even numbers.

Step Three: Connect your dots with a single line, as shown.

Step Four: Circle your highest point on the graph. If you have two scores that are equally high, circle them both.

Step Five: On the following pages, you will find many examples of different CO_2RE profiles, along with descriptions of each. Each provides an example with specific insights into what behavioral tendencies people with each profile might experience. Find the one that most closely resembles your own and carefully consider the description.

Decoding Your Profile

The upper and lower case letters in CO_2RE are adjusted to reflect your relative score range on each dimension. For example, Co_2Re would reflect a profile which is higher on the C and R dimensions and lower on O_2 and E.

As you go over the remaining pages of this chapter, you will want to refer back to your graph of your CO_2RE profile that you just completed. You will notice that the aggregate description of your CO_2RE profile provides more in-depth information than just

C	O_2	R	E
50	50	50	50
48	48	48	48
46	46	46	46
44	44	44	44
42	42	42	42
40	40	40	40
38	38	38	38
36	36	36	36
34	34	34	34
32	32	32	32
30	30	30	30
28	28	28	28
26	26	26	26
24	24	24	24
22	22	22	22
20	20	20	20
18	18	18	18
16	16	16	16
14	14	14	14
12	12	12	12
10	10	10	10

Example

25	41	46	18
50	50	50	50
48	48	48	48
46	46	46	46
44	44	44	44
42	42	42	42
40	40	40	40
38	38	38	38
36	36	36	36
34	34	34	34
32	32	32	32
30	30	30	30
28	28	28	28
26	26	26	26
24	24	24	24
22	22	22	22
20	20	20	20
18	18	18	18
16	16	16	16
14	14	14	14
12	12	12	12
10	10	10	10

your AQ. There is an interplay among the dimensions which influences your overall profile. Your CO_2RE profile provides a meaningful starting point for improving your AQ.

Step One: Notice the high point(s) on your graph. This indicates the CO_2RE dimension(s) on which you scored highest. This shows your relative strength in how you respond to adversity.

Step Two: Notice the low point(s) on your graph. This indicates the CO_2RE dimension(s) on which you scored lowest. This may be an area that you will want to strengthen to improve your AQ.

Step Three: Find the graph that looks most like yours.

Step Four: Read the description following the graph. Pick out those aspects that most accurately describe your adversity response. Carefully read and consider the description, and reflect upon where and how it might apply in your life.

Most of the examples are relatively extreme to assist in clarifying the different dimensions. Real life situations are often more subtle. Therefore, your graph may be more moderate.

---

co_2re

It's all my fault, and I couldn't help it. Everything's falling apart, it'll never change, and there's nothing I can do about it. Someone had better come in and pick up the pieces.

If this is your profile, you are likely to unnecessarily suffer great difficulties when faced with adversity. The accumulated effect of excessively blaming yourself unnecessarily for bad events which you perceive as far-reaching and long-lasting can be devastating to your productivity, motivation, persistence, learning, health, and spirit. As with any of the lower AQ profiles presented here, learning the skills offered in this book can have a dramatic effect, restoring hope and energy, while elevating all facets of your success.

Co_2re

I knew this would happen! Things never change. I'm just not meant for these kinds of challenges. I should have known better. But, hey, it's not my responsibility! Now everything's ruined. Well, at least I can do something about it.

The combination of higher C and lower O_2, R, and E scores may result in feeling some sense of control over adversity and its causes which you perceive as far-reaching, long-lasting, and largely your fault. This sense of control may help you avoid feeling completely

Example co$_2$re			
15	**13**	**11**	**18**
50	50	50	50
48	48	48	48
46	46	46	46
44	44	44	44
42	42	42	42
40	40	40	40
38	38	38	38
36	36	36	36
34	34	34	34
32	32	32	32
30	30	30	30
28	28	28	28
26	26	26	26
24	24	24	24
22	22	22	22
20	20	20	20
18	18	18	18
16	16	16	16
14	14	14	14
12	12	12	12
10	10	10	10

Example Co$_2$re			
49	**29**	**13**	**18**
50	50	50	50
48	48	48	48
46	46	46	46
44	44	44	44
42	42	42	42
40	40	40	40
38	38	38	38
36	36	36	36
34	34	34	34
32	32	32	32
30	30	30	30
28	28	28	28
26	26	26	26
24	24	24	24
22	22	22	22
20	20	20	20
18	18	18	18
16	16	16	16
14	14	14	14
12	12	12	12
10	10	10	10

Example cO$_2$re			
25	**45**	**19**	**25**
50	50	50	50
48	48	48	48
46	46	46	46
44	44	44	44
42	42	42	42
40	40	40	40
38	38	38	38
36	36	36	36
34	34	34	34
32	32	32	32
30	30	30	30
28	28	28	28
26	26	26	26
24	24	24	24
22	22	22	22
20	20	20	20
18	18	18	18
16	16	16	16
14	14	14	14
12	12	12	12
10	10	10	10

demoralized, serving as a foothold to pull yourself free of the adversity.

At times, however, the low O_2 score may result in your being unnecessarily, if not brutally hard on yourself. You may blame yourself for causing adverse events that you may believe will both have a negative impact on other areas of your life and will last a long time.

Ultimately, you can use your sense of control to take action to limit the reach and endurance of the adversity.

cO$_2$re

There were a number of factors which caused this to happen and I can see where I went wrong. Nonetheless, I am responsible for making it right, if I only could.

It seems like an impossible situation. It's bound to destroy everything I've worked for, and it will last forever.

When bad events happen, people with an O-dominant profile tend to recognize and consider all possible origins or causes for the adversity, rather than instantly blaming themselves. They learn from their behavior. They also tend to own the outcomes, holding themselves accountable for doing something about the results. This creates the psychic freedom to take action to improve the situation. Those who put their own role and responsibility for adversity into perspective with all possible origins or causes while owning the outcome tend to be the most empowered to take action. They are in the healthiest position to improve the situation.

The combination of a higher O and lower C, R, and E scores may result in your considering all possible origins for and owning the results of bad events which you believe will endure, reach other areas of your life, and over which you have little, if any perceived control. Depending on how low the C, R, and E scores are, this can be a relatively unempowering profile. The ability to feel accountable and avoid unnecessary and distorted self-blame is, however, positive.

co$_2$Re

I did it again. Someone better deal with this, it's out of my control. I'll always be bad at these things. But a least it's in only this one area.

This profile indicates a strong tendency to keep adversity in its place. You compartmentalize bad events, preventing them from leaking into other areas of your life. This strength is offset by the negative tendencies to respond to adversity and its causes as at least partially out of your control, your fault (whether or not it is), someone else's responsibility, and enduring. In extreme cases, depending on how low your C, O, and E scores may be, you may suffer from a propensity to give up and lose hope. It is particularly difficult to take action when you perceive adversity as out of your control, entirely your fault, and lasting a long time. However, the higher R score provides you with the perspective to limit your suffering to one area of your life while continuing to be fueled by victories in other areas. This may help you avoid becoming demoralized about life and the challenge of the climb.

Example co₂Re

25	16	46	18

Example co₂rE

33	30	21	42

Example CO₂re

49	47	19	21

---

co₂rE

This a disaster! It's going to ruin everything, it's all my fault, and there's nothing I can do about it. Someone else who's more competent had better take care of this. Oh well, at least this too shall pass.

The higher E score indicates the tendency, when faced with adversity, to see the light at the end of the tunnel. This can buoy you through difficult times. Yet, this strength can be partially or wholly offset by the tendencies to perceive adversity as at least somewhat out of your control, largely your fault (whether or not it is), someone else's to resolve, and affecting other, if not all areas of your life.

CO_2re

Even though everything's ruined and nothing is going to change, I recognize what I could have done better and know what I can do to fix it.

This profile indicates a moderately empowered person with a healthy sense of control over bad events. He or she considers all possible origins for the adversity, putting his or her responsibility for it into perspective. This person takes ownership for and learns from his or her behavior, holding oneself accountable for bettering the situation. These strengths may be partially offset by the tendency to perceive adverse events and their causes as far-reaching and long lasting. If you perceive enough control, you may act to reduce the reach and endurance of the adversity, making it more manageable and less burdensome.

cO_2**Re**

I know what I could have done better and recognize that there are many areas in my life where things are going well. It's my job to fix it, but ultimately, nothing is going to change. It is out of my control.

This response may result in an inner stalemate when faced with the opportunity to take action. In more severe cases, this profile can be high on hopelessness and low on empowerment. This can form a dangerous brew that may sap one's energy, motivation, productivity, and health. A person with a moderate cO_2Re profile may do an effective job of owning his or her portion of the responsibility and not letting adversity get out of control.

co_2**RE**

It's really my fault and there's little, if anything, I can or need to do about it. But at least it's only in this one area, and it will pass.

This profile indicates the tendency to limit the reach and the endurance of adverse events and their causes. While this has a positive impact on hope and motivation, these benefits can be countered by a low sense of control, little accountability, and high self-blame. The accumulated effect of low perceived control over events that you believe you caused can be demoralizing. However, limiting the reach and the endurance can make your lack of control seem less overwhelming.

Co_2rE

Everything is ruined, and it's my fault. But hey, it will pass. I'm not going to sweat it. Someone will take care of it.

This response profile indicates a sense of control over events and their causes which don't endure any longer than necessary. However, a person with this profile may catastrophize when bad events arise. There is danger of being hard on yourself while refusing to hold yourself accountable for improving the situation.

Example cO_2Re	Example co_2RE	Example Co_2rE
19 45 49 21	21 29 49 47	45 19 21 49

$$C \quad O_2 \quad R \quad E$$

Low accountability coupled with overblame and catastrophizing may hinder one accurately assessing and learning from where one went wrong. It may also slow the momentum toward action. This person's morale is likely buoyed by a sense of control, or "I could if I wanted to."

Co_2Re

I totally blew it, and now we're stuck with the result. It's not my responsibility, but at least I know I can do something to make sure things don't get out of hand, if I want to.

This action-oriented profile reflects a high degree of control over adverse events and their causes that are limited to the circumstances at hand. The downside is the accumulated effect of the perception that adverse events are one's fault (whether or not they are), not one's responsibility to deal with, and will last a long time—partially offsetting the motivating sense of control.

cO_2rE

There were many factors that caused this to happen, and I am sure it will pass. In any event, it's mine to deal with. In the meantime, I wish I could do something to prevent this from turning into a major disaster.

This profile may indicate the tendency to take appropriate responsibility for what is perceived to be short-lived, adverse events, without suffering from unnecessary self-blame. If misused, the tendencies indicated by this profile might induce a person to wrongly deflect responsibility when things go wrong. While this person may feel unburdened by guilt, he or she is likely to suffer from the affects of low control over what are believed to be far-reaching events and their causes. In more severe cases, this combination of low perceived control over events which may infect many areas of one's life may result in periods of helplessness and hopelessness.

CO_2Re

Given everybody's role in this setback, I can see where I went wrong. Although the fallout may last for a long time, there is no way I will let this get any worse than it already is. Besides, it's my job to make it better.

Example Co₂Re

48	13	44	20

50	50	50	50
48	48	48	48
46	46	46	46
44	44	44	44
42	42	42	42
40	40	40	40
38	38	38	38
36	36	36	36
34	34	34	34
32	32	32	32
30	30	30	30
28	28	28	28
26	26	26	26
24	24	24	24
22	22	22	22
20	20	20	20
18	18	18	18
16	16	16	16
14	14	14	14
12	12	12	12
10	10	10	10

Example cO₂rE

18	47	16	47

50	50	50	50
48	48	48	48
46	46	46	46
44	44	44	44
42	42	42	42
40	40	40	40
38	38	38	38
36	36	36	36
34	34	34	34
32	32	32	32
30	30	30	30
28	28	28	28
26	26	26	26
24	24	24	24
22	22	22	22
20	20	20	20
18	18	18	18
16	16	16	16
14	14	14	14
12	12	12	12
10	10	10	10

Example CO₂Re

45	48	40	14

50	50	50	50
48	48	48	48
46	46	46	46
44	44	44	44
42	42	42	42
40	40	40	40
38	38	38	38
36	36	36	36
34	34	34	34
32	32	32	32
30	30	30	30
28	28	28	28
26	26	26	26
24	24	24	24
22	22	22	22
20	20	20	20
18	18	18	18
16	16	16	16
14	14	14	14
12	12	12	12
10	10	10	10

This relatively high AQ profile indicates the healthy tendencies to put one's own role into perspective and limit the reach of and perceived control over adverse events. These tendencies combine to form a sense of fortitude that may, on rare occasions, be weakened by the belief that the adversity and its causes will last a long time. However, the perception of control, accountability, and limited reach will compel this person to take action, which may, as a result, limit how long the adversity actually endures.

cO₂RE

There were many reasons why this happened, and even though it's my responsibility, there is little I can do about this. Fortunately, it is just this one specific situation, and it will pass.

The significant factor lacking in this higher AQ profile is the perception of control. Even if most adverse events are not entirely one's fault, are limited in reach, and will not last any longer than necessary, the perceived inability to impact the outcome can still be disheartening and damaging. High accountability coupled with low control can make for a disillusioning combination. In more severe cases, this individual might feel unnecessarily buffeted by the winds of fate. The upside of this profile is that this person does not perceive adversity and its causes as any bigger, longer lasting, or more burdensome than necessary. This response can keep him or her from being overwhelmed through difficult times.

CO_2rE

There are many reasons why this happened, and it could ruin everything. I'm accountable for working this out. Fortunately, I can prevent it from lasting any longer than necessary.

As long as one is able to take full responsibility for one's role in the event, a person with this profile is likely to feel somewhat empowered. The combined response of taking responsibility, putting one's role into perspective, along with a high sense of control over events that are seen as transient, can have a positive affect on one's ability to continue along the trail to the top. However, the counterbalancing force of catastrophizing bad events may create temporary swings in motivation and hope.

CO_2RE

I can see what went wrong and how I could do a better job next time. I am accountable for dealing with this, so I look forward to taking immediate action to limit both the reach of the adversity and how long this difficult situation will endure, while learning from the challenge.

For most people in most situations, this is the ideal, high AQ profile. A person with this pattern is likely to demonstrate optimum resilience, persistence, creativity, risk-taking, fortitude, motivation, energy, productivity, and strength when faced with adversity. He or she thrives on challenges and takes the necessary risks to grow, improve, and restore control. High accountability coupled with high

Example cO$_2$RE				Example CO$_2$rE				Example CO$_2$RE			
13	**48**	**44**	**49**	**39**	**47**	**16**	**47**	**45**	**48**	**40**	**49**
50	50	50	50	50	50	50	50	50	50	50	50
48	48	48	48	48	48	48	48	48	48	48	48
46	46	46	46	46	46	46	46	46	46	46	46
44	44	44	44	44	44	44	44	44	44	44	44
42	42	42	42	42	42	42	42	42	42	42	42
40	40	40	40	40	40	40	40	40	40	40	40
38	38	38	38	38	38	38	38	38	38	38	38
36	36	36	36	36	36	36	36	36	36	36	36
34	34	34	34	34	34	34	34	34	34	34	34
32	32	32	32	32	32	32	32	32	32	32	32
30	30	30	30	30	30	30	30	30	30	30	30
28	28	28	28	28	28	28	28	28	28	28	28
26	26	26	26	26	26	26	26	26	26	26	26
24	24	24	24	24	24	24	24	24	24	24	24
22	22	22	22	22	22	22	22	22	22	22	22
20	20	20	20	20	20	20	20	20	20	20	20
18	18	18	18	18	18	18	18	18	18	18	18
16	16	16	16	16	16	16	16	16	16	16	16
14	14	14	14	14	14	14	14	14	14	14	14
12	12	12	12	12	12	12	12	12	12	12	12
10	10	10	10	10	10	10	10	10	10	10	10

control result in genuine empowerment. Adversity is as much a part of life as the changing weather on the mountain, and this person grows stronger with each encounter.

LIFE IN THE MIDDLE: A MODERATE CO$_2$RE PROFILE

People with a moderate profile have no "typical" response to adversity. However, they are often relatively successful. However, a moderate sense of control and ownership, combined with moderate blame, reach, and endurance can be dampened by extended adversity. I find that most successful people have an inherent drive and curiosity about how to take their overall success in life to the next level. My experience is that those with moderate profiles simultaneously enjoy some of the benefits of a moderate AQ while experiencing some of the dispiriting limitations of a less-than-ideal AQ.

I love to go backpacking in the mountains. One of my favorite moments is when, after hiking for several hours up some significant inclines, I dump my 50-pound backpack on the ground. There is this moment of relative weightlessness when I feel like an astronaut walking on the moon. This can continue, to a lesser degree the rest of the day. Relatively successful people with moderate profiles report an analogous experience when they raise their AQs. It is as if they have dumped a 50-pound backpack and can now

Example CO_2RE			
30	**24**	**28**	**26**
50	50	50	50
48	48	48	48
46	46	46	46
44	44	44	44
42	42	42	42
40	40	40	40
38	38	38	38
36	36	36	36
34	34	34	34
32	32	32	32
30	30	30	30
28	28	28	28
26	26	26	26
24	24	24	24
22	22	22	22
20	20	20	20
18	18	18	18
16	16	16	16
14	14	14	14
12	12	12	12
10	10	10	10

float up the trail. The effort to succeed by fulfilling one's purpose in life becomes more joyous and rewarding once you move from a moderate to a high AQ.

PERSONALIZING YOUR PROFILE

Now it is time to take your understanding a level deeper by personalizing it to your work and your life. The better you integrate these concepts the more powerful the impact AQ will have upon your success.

Invest a few minutes to think through the following questions. If you are going to look at yourself naked in the mirror, you might as well turn on the lights and exercise total self-honesty!

1. On which dimension did you score highest?
2. As you consider the description of this dimension, what is one of the advantages of scoring high on this dimension?
3. On which dimension did you score lowest?
4. As you consider the description of this dimension, what is one of the disadvantages of scoring low on this dimension?
5. As you consider the description of your overall CO_2RE profile, what is one *negative* tendency with which you might identify?
6. Where have you witnessed or demonstrated this tendency in your work?
7. Where have you witnessed or demonstrated this tendency in other areas of your life?
8. As you consider the description of your overall CO_2RE profile, what is one *positive* tendency with which you identify?
9. What is the one tendency that, if eliminated, would have the most significant positive impact on your work and/or life?
10. If you were able to eliminate this tendency, in what way(s) would it affect your work?

11. If you were able to eliminate this tendency, in what way(s) would it affect other areas of your life?

12. What tendency would you most like to keep?

13. If you were able to keep or strengthen this tendency, in what way(s) would it affect your work?

14. If you were able to keep or strengthen this tendency, in what way(s) would it affect your life outside of work?

15. Based on what you know so far, which of your co-workers would most benefit from the information in this book?

16. Based on what you know so far, which person outside of your work would most benefit from the information in this book?

YOUR AQ AND TAKING ACTION

The lower your AQ, the more fatalistic you may become. "Well, that's just the way things are. There's nothing we can do about it, so we might as well swallow it." People with higher AQs are possibility thinkers. Their subconscious response is, "There must be a way, and I'll do whatever it takes to find it!"

My good friend, Mike, has a high AQ. He is a salesperson by day and a handyman by night. He buys, renovates, and resells properties. He explained to me that he thrives on a specific kind of challenge.

"I love it when I find an impossible project!" he said. "Recently, I found an old farmhouse. I brought in three electricians, all of whom told me there was no way I could ever wire the place. The whole structure was in shambles. It should have been bulldozed. But I kept working on the problem until I wired the entire building myself. Then I invited all three back over to see what I had done. You should have seen the looks on their faces! Ha! I live for those kinds of challenges!"

Mike climbs through adversity.

You could readily view the difference between higher and lower AQ tendencies when every television news channel interviewed the victims of the 1994 earthquake in Los Angeles. "Everything is gone. Our home, our possessions, our dreams . . . everything we had. We'll never get it back. We're destroyed . . . just destroyed," one woman complained.

"This happens every time we get our lives together. I don't know why we even bother," answered another victim, shaking his head.

In contrast, there were others who responded in a dramatically different manner. "It's only our stuff. We have some insurance, and we can always rebuild. The important thing is we're okay," explained an older woman, motioning toward the pile of rubble behind her that had been her house of thirty years.

"Well, we always wanted to remodel! There was nothing we could have done about it. You can't live your life in fear. It was one of those rare flukes of nature, and a damned scary one! . . . But you pick up the pieces, salvage what you can, and move on. Things could be a lot worse," reasoned a recent immigrant who was supporting an extended family of eight.

Now, you may question which response is more realistic, accurate, or true. Several of my friends and business associates lost their homes in that earthquake. Those who believed that their lives were forever ruined were much slower in responding to the situation. A few were in therapy for many months and took an inordinately long time to move into, let alone rebuild their homes. Those with higher AQs made do. In fact, they did more than make do. They somehow benefited from the tragedy, each in his or her own way. Charlie, a colleague who had lost his entire business started the company he had always wanted. He was up and running within fourteen days and was profitable from day one. My friend Bob, who was forced to move his family in with his parents, seized the opportunity to help repair their home, a chore he had long felt guilty about avoiding. "We've never been closer, and Carol and I got a couple of built-in babysitters out of the deal," he told me.

Which is more accurate? I believe, that in most situations, we shape our own reality. In fact, one of the fundamental truths in the field of communication is that *language shapes reality*. Those with lower AQs *created* the gloomy, enduring, far-reaching fate that they predicted. Those with moderate AQs saw and created a reality of tremendous loss and, at the least, an arduous comeback. Those with higher AQs somehow used the setback of losing their businesses and/or homes as a way to progress and move forward and up in their lives. Acts of God may demolish your home, but they need not hobble your hope or sap your soul.

Remember, no matter what your AQ is today, it can be permanently improved, and with improvement, you will increase your effectiveness. AQ is not your fate, it is a snapshot of your habitual response to adversity, a measure of the consistent subconscious pattern which you have developed over the years. AQ explains and measures your tendency to climb, camp, or quit, and teaches you the skills for the ascent.

In the next section, you will learn the scientifically-grounded techniques for boosting your and other's AQs, as well as how to apply these breakthroughs in your organization.

PART THREE

IMPROVING AQ IN YOURSELF, OTHERS, AND YOUR ORGANIZATION

LEAD

Improving Your AQ and Your Ability to Ascend

Nothing in the world can take the place of persistence.
Talent will not; nothing is more common than unsuccessful men
*   with talent.*
Genius will not; unrewarded genius is almost a proverb.
Education will not; the world is full of educated derelicts.
*   Persistence and determination alone are omnipotent.*
The slogan "Press on" has solved and always will solve the
*   problems of the human race.*

Calvin Coolidge

Doug's jaw dropped in amazement. Never, in eleven years of working together, had his assistant, Janice, done anything like this before! "She was always the one to come up with a hundred and one reasons why things wouldn't work, why they couldn't be done," Doug explained. "She'd suck the wind right out of our sails. This is something completely new for her." What had Doug so stunned?

Three weeks earlier, Janice had attended one of my AQ programs within her company, a large multinational pharmaceutical concern. Early in the day, Janice had been openly skeptical, asking,

"How is this going to be any different from all the other programs we get sent to?" But, she really came around toward late afternoon. She had enthusiastically listed over a dozen applications of the new skills she had learned. As she left the room, she shook my hand and said, "I can't wait to use this with my husband! He'll be amazed."

Three weeks had passed, and I was back, running a program for a group of managers from Doug's organization. Materials were shipped, refreshments ordered, lists of participants confirmed— everything was set. Everything, that is, except for the power cord for the laptop computer that held the multimedia portion of the program. At the last minute, we discovered that it was missing. Normally this would have been no big deal. We would simply re-sort to the old standbys—flipcharts and color transparencies. But this day was special. After having his entire team, including Janice, attend the program the month before, Doug had bragged about its impact to several top executives who were there to see it in all its glory, animated multimedia included.

Upon noticing the lost equipment, I flagged Janice down as she walked by. "We've got a challenge," I confessed to her. "The laptop's power cord is missing, and the program begins in thirty minutes."

Normally, Janice would have rattled off ten reasons why we were simply out of luck. But, today, she paused, as if checking her-self. Then she looked at me with a sparkle in her eyes and said, "Let me see what I can do." At that, she uncharacteristically bolted from the room.

Five minutes before show time, Janice ran up to me, short of breath, face flushed. "I've called thirteen computer suppliers, and none of them have your cord. They all say it is a special order item, and that there is no way I'll find it anywhere in the area on such short notice." She paused, looking at me expectantly.

"Gee, thank you so much for trying . . . " I offered.

"*No, wait!* I'm not through yet!" she declared. She dashed from the room a second time.

I began the program, operating the multimedia on battery power. Forty-five minutes into the program, Janice burst into the meeting, beaming triumphantly, cord held high. "I tried nine more suppliers! They all said there was no way, but I wouldn't take no for an answer! It was *incredible!* It was just like we learned in the program. I really tried to keep the adversity in check, re-programming my response right away. I not only found a cord, I got the company to deliver it *immediately!*" Janice got a rousing ovation from the group.

As Doug later told me, Janice had never before so relentlessly sought a solution to a seemingly insoluble problem. She was the last one to take on the impossible. It was a complete transformation. When I asked her about her stellar display of persistence, Janice beamed. "I used to get so stressed out by each new problem," she said. "I was going to quit my job and find something less demanding. Now I love challenges. . . . It has been three weeks, and I really look forward to going to work."

Janice had always had the talent, brains, and motivation to excel. What she had lacked was a sufficiently high AQ. Janice learned the LEAD sequence presented in this chapter and the Stoppers! in the next, and, as she proudly reports, has never been the same since.

HANDS-ON PROOF

My real-world experience in using the skills that you'll be learning began several years ago as I incorporated them into the early versions of my AQ programs. Originally, I was highly skeptical of any skills that were designed to do anything as dramatic as helping people interrupt and alter a lifelong pattern. But during the first year, as I taught these skills to several hundred people, my skepticism slowly gave way in light of the results.

Since then, I have witnessed secretaries, executives, salespeople, professionals, parents, students, educators, senior citizens, and children whose lives dramatically improved because of their ability to permanently alter their adversity response, raise their AQ, and fortify the soil that holds them in place when the winds of adversity blow.

The results are highly individualized. Some people experience a significant increase in energy, motivation, and vitality. Others see the greatest results in their performance at work. These improvements come in the form of sales, creativity, quality of work, learning comprehension, persistence, and the ability to embrace change. Many report dramatic improvements in their personal and professional relationships as they become naturally inspiring leaders capable of overcoming and breaking through adversity. Frequently, participants report a marked improvement in their health and emotional stability.

In my own studies, both formal and informal, with athletes and businesspeople, these skills appear not only to endure, but to *strengthen* over time. One group of salespeople for an electronics company reported greater gains in sales during the second quarter than in the first quarter following the program.

A team within a multinational pharmaceutical company measured their progress by assessing their readiness for change. Those who went through the AQ program demonstrated a leap in their readiness and ability to embrace change when compared with those who did not attend the program. The result was a dramatic reduction in the costly and demoralizing transition trough that accompanies most change. In this trough, many people and companies abandon change prematurely. By reducing this trough, people maintained the momentum of the change without sagging productivity and motivation.

I have taught these skills to leaders at Mott's as they strive for greater agility and to be "best in class" as they face greater turmoil and an avalanche of change. Each leader takes and applies these skills to whatever challenges arise. Frequently, the LEAD sequence and Stoppers! transcend the boundaries between personal and professional as described by Mott's human resources manager, Duane Giannini:

> *I have used your content and skills to dramatically improve my own ability to spring back from daily setbacks and remain resilient no matter what occurs. Ever since attending your program, I never have viewed or responded to adversity quite the same. My daughter used your practical, simple skills to handle and come back from a major basketball injury. Thanks to your techniques, she is playing better than ever, setting records and being recruited by Division One colleges. I've coached basketball, and I've never seen anything really take hold or have such a positive impact.*

It is often not until many months after the program that a participant will call and excitedly describe how the skills helped that person in his or her ascent that day.

Like climbing a mountain, the gain in elevation may be, at first, imperceptible. Over time, however, you pause for breath and look around only to discover the dramatic panoramic view you've earned through persistent effort. Like climbing, initially, the differences brought about by your efforts may be subtle, even imperceptible to the untrained eye, but you'll feel the changes inside. Over time, the effects are dramatic. Eventually you will have morphed yourself into a world-class Climber.

The research on neurophysiology, or the workings of the brain, has contributed to how these techniques are arranged—their structure or framework. The LEAD sequence and Stoppers! have evolved over more than ten years of research and tests with professionals, athletes, managers, students, and leaders. I honed these techniques with the invaluable input of dozens of experiments on cognitive retraining performed by researchers around the world. I have taught and further improved these techniques through many dozens of programs and interventions within a broad range of organizations and industries. I have witnessed firsthand the powerful and enduring effect they can have on an individual's, team's, and organization's success.

WHERE DO THESE SKILLS COME FROM?

The LEAD sequence and Stoppers! are derived from two types of information—*research* and *real world experience*. They are adapted from the work of several influential researchers rooted in traditional cognitive psychology. One of the major breakthroughs in this field is the realization that an individual need not relive and endlessly process all the pains of his or her past in order to experience dramatic improvements in psychological health and hardiness.

The research supporting the use of the LEAD sequence and Stoppers! dates back nearly 35 years to Albert Ellis' ABC model. This rational-emotive model of behavior is based on the notion that it is one's *beliefs* about events rather than the events themselves that generate reactions and feelings. Ellis paved the way for several follow-up studies, including those of Aaron Beck, founder of Cognitive Therapy.

Beck's model, which emphasized the need to challenge or dispute negative beliefs about oneself, the present situation, and the future, provided additional theoretical support for the development of these techniques.

Explanatory style or attributional retraining grew out of Beck's work. It is a therapeutic approach that helps people recognize, assess, and dispute their reactions to life's events. It has also been successfully used as part of cognitive therapy for helping depressive adults.

These disputation techniques make a person keenly aware of, and thus able to deal with, formerly subconscious reactions. Learning to dispute, and thus alter, these reactions can result in enduring change through reprogramming one's responses. Attributional retraining has been used in a variety of settings and on a variety of populations.

For example, Raymond Perry and Kurt Penner of the University of Manitoba have demonstrated the effectiveness of such techniques on their students. Those who received attributional retraining boosted their academic performance in comparison to those who received no training. Those who perceived low control (low AQ) benefited the most from the retraining.

In an expanding series of studies funded by a number of grants, Lisa Jaycox and her team from the University of Pennsylvania, including Seligman, have created dramatic results in preventing depression and behavioral problems in teenagers by using cognitive retraining techniques similar to those you are about to learn.

Unlike most training which loses its impact over time, one of the more powerful findings from these studies has been that the effect of cognitive disputation skills seems to take on a life of its own, expanding and growing long after the training.

Suzanne Oullette of the City University of New York and her colleague, psychologist Salvadore Maddi, developed hardiness training based on their studies with Illinois Bell. Two of their techniques are *situation restructuring*, which requires analyzing

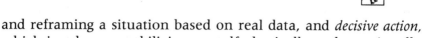

and reframing a situation based on real data, and *decisive action*, which involves remobilizing oneself physically and emotionally through action.

In an effort to provide you with the most proven, effective, and scientifically substantiated skills, I have, over the course of several years, reached inside this research and pulled out and honed the best of the best. You will be trained in what I have found to be the most effective practices in permanently improving your AQ and your success.

HOW AND WHY LEAD WORKS

Cognitive and behavior techniques such as LEAD are effective because they seem to physically alter the wiring in the brain. In 1995, UCLA researchers treated with cognitive therapy patients who had obsessive-compulsive disorder (OCD). Their symptoms included incessant handwashing out of an irrational fear of germs. The scientists took "before" and "after" Positron Emissions Technology (PET) scans, which provide a graphic picture of the brain's activity. Over time they were able to detect that cognitive therapy acutally helped to alter the functioning of the brain, reducing the OCD activity and structure. Purely psychological strategies resulted in significant biochemical and physical changes in the brain.

If cognitive techniques can alter the brains of people with OCD, imagine what they can do for you! As Dr. Louis Baxter, a pharmacologist at UCLA and the University of Alabama, put it when describing the relationship of thought and brain function, " . . . to separate the brain from the mind at a deep level doesn't make much sense." Your patterns of thought alter the physiology of your brain. Using the LEAD sequence will help you condition your brain to withstand and handle any adversity.

The evidence suggests that the LEAD sequence has a chemical effect on the brain. It strengthens your sense of control through greater *ownership* and the commitment to *act*. Physiologically, your brain responds to this heightened sense of control by flooding your body with healthy levels of nerotransmitters that positively influence your immune functions and overall health.

The field of psychoneuroimmunology has provided many leading-edge findings in recent years. Among these is the growing realization that there are strong links between your emotions and the hormones released under stress, or while experiencing certain psychological states, such as panic, pessimism, sadness, unremitting tension, and helplessness. Those who catastrophize, are therefore more likely to suffer these emotions and their physiological fall-out. Tools, such as Stoppers! and the LEAD sequence, prevent catastrophizing and such destructive emotional states. The result is greater emotional and physical resilience in response to the daily stresses of life.

Conversely, lower AQ people experience a more enduring and damaging form of stress. Among the many neurotransmitters, catacholamines (norepinephrine and epinephrine), cortisol, prolactin, along with the natural opiates beta endorphin and enkephalin are all released when you experience stress. Henry Dreher, author of *The Immune Power Personality,* points out that such chronically high levels of stress hormones can weaken your immune cells. As a result, your immune system becomes suppressed.

The same effect is created by endorphins. According to Dr. Yehuda Shavit, a UCLA psychologist, moderate levels of opiod peptides such as endorphins have a positive influence on the level of disease-fighting natural killer cells in your blood. Endorphins in proper balance reduce your experience of severe pain, and boost your immune system. This balance is influenced by your perception of control. If too high or too low, however, endorphins can weaken immune functions. When catacholamine levels drop too low, as when helpless and depressed (loss of control), endorphins elevate to a higher than optimal level. Your body senses this and suppresses your immune system in response. This is how a low AQ and the accompanying lack of perceived control can wear upon one's energy, vitality, health, and fortitude.

It makes sense, therefore, that a high AQ, would bolster your immune functions, pumping health-inducing hormones such as appropriate levels of catacholamines, corticosteroids, along with other neurotransmitters, throughout your body. Your brain reflects the difference between a low and a high AQ by the chemicals it emits. These chemicals pervade your entire body. AQ, therefore, affects you at the cellular level!

Perhaps the most documented improvement as a result of cognitive therapy or enhanced control is the rise in T-cells, a critical component of your immune system. The research cited in Chapter 2 on hardiness, learned optimism, and locus of control—constructs related to AQ—and psychoneuroimmunology is but the tip of the mind-body iceberg. Our understanding of the intimately intertwined relationship between emotions, thoughts, AQ, and your physiology is growing everyday. These bodywide changes are brought about by your *response* to a situation.

According to Dreher, people who respond to life's events with commitment and control—as taught directly through the LEAD sequence—enjoy thriving immune functions.

AQ permeates your body.

CLIMBING SKILLS

What would you do if, while visiting a mental hospital, a patient tore down the hall, running straight for you. While staring in your face, he then declared, "Look around you. The world is falling apart, and it's all your fault! You are a worthless person. Nothing you do will ever make a difference, so why even try? Things can only get worse and worse, so why bother?"

Would you immediately think, "Well, you *are* right. Everything you say is true"? No! Most likely you would think, "Geez! This guy is completely out of his mind." Never for a moment would you even consider taking his words to heart! Yet, when these or similar words come from *within you*, they slip by unquestioned, free to wreak havoc on your energy, motivation, effectiveness, and success.

Your usual response to adversity normally goes unquestioned. Because it is habitual and subconscious, you may be totally *unaware* of it. It only makes sense that you wouldn't notice or challenge it.

Think of it as if you are the owner of your own exclusive club, with a private suite in the *basal ganglia*, or subconscious region of your brain. Only *your* messages are able to slip by security unnoticed and enter the private suite. Anyone else's would be checked or questioned by the security guard strategically posted between your conscious and subconscious. Depending on how much you trust the messenger, some messages would be strip searched before being allowed to pass!

Because people tend to let their own destructive messages slide, Martin Seligman, Aaron Beck, myself, and others have developed and tested techniques to help you *dispute* your destructive responses to life's events. Several years ago, I developed and tested my own series of disputation techniques that have proven highly effective in helping people create enduring improvements in their AQs and how they respond to adversity. I call these techniques LEAD (see Figure 6–1).

FIGURE 6–1   The LEAD Sequence

L = Listen to your adversity response.
- Was it a high or low AQ response?
- On which dimensions was it highest or lowest?

E = Explore all origins and your ownership of the result.
O_r • What are the possible origins of this adversity?
- Given these origins, what portion was my fault?
- What, specifically, could I have done better?
O_w • What aspects of the results should I own?
- Which shouldn't I own?

A = Analyze the evidence.
- What evidence is there that I have *no* control?
- What evidence is there that the adversity *has* to reach into other areas of my life?
- What evidence is there that the adversity *must* last any longer than necessary?

D = Do something!
- What additional information do I need?
- What could I do to gain even a little control over this situation?
- What could I do to limit the reach of this adversity?
- What could I do to limit how long the adversity endures in its current state?

The LEAD sequence is based on the notion that we can alter our success by changing our habits of thought. Change is created by disputing old patterns and consciously forming new ones.

LEADing Yourself to a Higher AQ

Why dispute your responses? Because that's how you're going to raise your AQ. Results occur with diligent use of the LEAD sequence.

There are four simple steps involved in assessing and disputing your adversity response and raising your AQ. You will begin by using the LEAD sequence on yourself. In Chapter 8, I will show you how to use this powerful set of skills on others. But for now, embed The LEAD sequence in your mind.

L = Listen to Your Response to Adversity

L = Listening to your response is the pivotal step in transforming your AQ from a lifelong, subconscious, habitual pattern to a high-powered tool for personal improvement and long-term effectiveness.

Developing the Senses of a Climber

You sleep through your alarm, you're out of toothpaste, the Cheerios are stale, an anticipated Express Mail delivery doesn't arrive, and an important conference call is canceled. By 9:45 A.M. adversity has struck five times. Usually, these events, being fairly normal, might have gone unnoticed. But, since you want to hone and improve your response to adversity, you must be able to *spot* the moment adversity hits.

It's like being able to predict the path of a hurricane long before it comes ashore. It is only once you see the storm, that you can minimize the destruction. If you are unaware of its immanent arrival, the damage can be catastrophic!

The first skill you must acquire, therefore, is the ability to immediately sense when adversity is happening. Without this atunement, none of the other skills will work. Fortunately, *change can immediately take place if you notice the moment adversity strikes.* Just as a forest ranger can smell fire long before it gets out of control, and a police officer might note dangerous activities on the street long before ordinary citizens do, so can you learn to smell adversity before it reaches catastrophic proportions.

The Adversity Lens

Have you ever noticed how, when you buy a new car, you suddenly recognize every vehicle similar to yours on the road? Overnight you have subconsciously cued your brain to spot a certain make and model. What's interesting is that you have the ability to detect this even when you least expect to. If you program your brain with enough *intensity,* there will be a powerful spark of realization when you see that car, even if it interrupts intense conversation.

Imagine what you could do if you programmed your brain in much the same way to notice something *really* important like adversity! This powerful ability to place your brain on alert will assist you to quickly develop the senses of a Climber.

What if I told you that every time you spot potential adversity in your life and shout "Adversity!" I will pay you $10,000? Suddenly, your response to adversity becomes like a game. Without waiting for adversity to hit with full force, you now actively scan the horizon for the first sign of it, ready to cash in. You wake up with a stiff neck, the kind that makes your ears ring. You shout "Adversity! " and the cash register goes off! You open the front door to discover it's raining outside; the morning paper is soaked. You take a shower, only to discover that you are out of soap and there are no clean towels. You head off to work and encounter an accident on the way that causes a ten-minute delay. A mile before your exit, a person angrily cuts you off. As a result of the delay, you arrive at work five minutes late for a meeting. As you walk in the door, you discover that an important client has reported a problem that demands your immediate attention—one more item in an already over-loaded schedule. To top things off, your assistant calls in sick, so you've got to pick up some of the slack. Adversity, adversity, adversity.

Events with the potential to negatively affect you and which would have gone by undetected suddenly appear on your radar screen with blinking red lights! You might be bathing your child, filling out expense reports, or talking on the phone, and the moment adversity hits, BOOM! You notice it. There is no need to dwell on what has occurred, a moment is long enough. Once you've programmed your brain, placing it on constant alert, each potentially adverse event will enter your consciousness just long enough to adjust your response, even in the midst of a busy day.

Develop a Nose for Adversity

The quickly formed habit of noticing other cars like yours serves a purpose, enabling you to compare your car to others, validating your choice, and feeling the pride of ownership that comes from seeing other vehicles like yours tooling down the road.

Noticing each adverse event also has it's payoff. Noticing adversity allows you to gauge and *strengthen* your response. However, you can hardly afford the mental energy of scrutinizing every event and asking, "Is this adversity?" Fortunately, over time the habit becomes increasingly efficient, fading into the background of your brain. There the habit, like a smoke alarm, is triggered *automatically,* requiring minimal energy and conscious thought.

The conscious process of forming a habit requires much more blood and oxygen to the brain than is demanded once the habit is embedded in your subconscious. Be it learning a new language, swinging a golf-club, or improving how you respond to adversity, this is the way in which your brain rewards you for repetition. Your awareness of adversity brings it and your response to it out to the conscious layer of your brain, your cerebral cortex. It is only in the conscious region that your AQ can be changed. For a while, therefore, it will be extremely useful to notice even the small, relatively minor adversities. You may be surprised by how skilled you become at smelling adversity when it hits and how frequently it actually strikes!

Sound the Alarm!

Another technique you can use to imprint the moment that you detect adversity is to sound an alarm in your head every time it hits. Research in the field of neurolinguistic programming suggests that the louder, bigger, and more intense a noise and/or image, the more powerful the imprint it makes in your brain. The stronger the imprint, the more effective it will be. Leslie Cameron-Bandler and her colleagues explain in their book, *The Emprint Method,* that volume, size, and force influence the strength of the imprint.

I imagine the horn used to scramble the pilots at an air base while under attack. My computer crashes in the middle of writing this paragraph, and immediately the scramble alarm screams in my mind, "Awoooooogah! Awoooooogah! Adversity! Adversity!" This silly response offers two immediate benefits. First, it's funny. The more ridiculous the sound you choose, the better. I know a guy who imagines the sound of the gears grinding on his Porsche. Laughter alters your inner state, predisposing you to a more constructive response to adversity.

The second benefit is that it makes you pause and take note of adversity the moment it hits. You have neatly interrupted your *subconscious* response by bringing it clearly into your *conscious* thinking. You are suddenly acutely aware of the problem.

Use whatever alarm you prefer. Here are a few tips for picking the best one:

- *Make your alarm LOUD!* The greater the volume with which you respond, the more intense the result. Whispering, "oh uh" is not the same as screaming "OH MY GOD!" even in the privacy of your mind.

- *The sillier, the better.* Demonstrate your alarm right now by shouting it out, just this once (unless you are reading this book on a crowded airplane). It should make you laugh every time you say it.

- *Add a forceful or stupid gesture!* The one that goes with my alarm is two hands up, one on either side of my head, with my fingers spreading out with each "Awoooooogah!" and closing in between. I *know* how ridiculous this is by the peals of laughter that erupt every time I demonstrate this finely honed technique to a roomful of people attending my program. You may choose something less demonstrative, such as pounding your fist in your palm.

As soon as you have the imprint in your brain, you are ready to use this technique every time adversity hits. Adversity will never slip by unnoticed again! This technique will gradually sink into the background noise of your day, making an appearance when it really counts. Because it takes only a second or two, it will not detract from the natural progression of your activities, except by making you keenly aware of the defining moments—when you respond to adversity.

Gauging Your Response

Once you acknowledge the powerful role even minor adversity plays in your life, you can learn to be more aware of the *quality and nature* of your response. As Dr. Mark Nuwer, Head of Neurophysiology at UCLA Medical Center explained, the *intensity* of an experience can influence the speed of your learning. "When you touch a hot stove, the pain creates an instant, intense alarm in the brain." That alarm signals your cerebral cortex, the conscious region, to make you aware of your choice! The next time you're in the vicinity of a hot stove, you are likely to be keenly aware of it and avoid it.

The same is true for adversity. Having a low AQ is like touching a hot stove. You can only get burned! So, as you fully understand that *how* you respond to adversity will affect *all* aspects of your success, you will give that critical moment when adversity strikes the same importance and intensity as you might give to a raise, a grade, the results of a blood test, or a letter from the IRS. By being keenly aware of when adversity strikes, you can instigate instant change in how you handle the moment.

Once you consciously detect adversity, the next step is to immediately gauge whether you had a low or high AQ response. On which CO_2RE dimensions were your response noticeably high or low?

Your ability to quickly and spontaneously discern an overall low or high AQ response is essential to raising your AQ. With very little practice, you will master this skill. The slightly greater challenge comes in being able to readily gauge your response by each CO_2RE *dimension*. This refinement is useful, but not essential. By

AQ Detection Skills—Stage One

Analyzing others' behavior is an easy way to become acutely aware of your own. Test your ability to spot low versus high AQ responses in others by putting a plus sign (+) for high AQ or a minus sign (−) for low AQ in the blank next to the each of the following responses.

1. Event: Jim, a coworker, evaluates Mark lower than expected on his performance.

     Mark's Response: Well, this is disappointing! It could ruin my chances of getting that pay increase. How will I ever explain this to Sarah? She'll be crushed. I'll obviously have to speak to Jim to learn more about his perceptions and to make *sure* this doesn't happen again. I should have seen this coming.

     _____

2. Event: The funding for Karen's major project is slashed.

     Karen's Response: Every time we get close to doing something important, some idiot comes along and cuts funding. I can't believe this! The whole department is falling apart. I won't allow this. It's time to get the message out about what we're doing!

     _____

3. Event: Margie's best friend forgets her birthday.

     Margie's Response: I'm sure Barbara was busy. It's a wonder I remember my own birthday! There goes the big day, right down the drain. It will be a long time before we get to talk again. Oh well, there's nothing I can do about it now.

     _____

4. Event:

Hal's daughter is caught smoking at school.

Hal's Response:

Oh my God! I can't believe she would ruin her life this way. I can't help but believe that if I'd been a better parent, she wouldn't be in this mess. I'm not going to come down on her. We share the accountability for what happened today. It's never too late to learn from your mistakes. I cannot accept this. It's clearly time she and I had a real talk.

_____

5. Event:

Frank is not invited to an important meeting at work.

Frank's Response:

Well, that's interesting! I'm sure there must be a reason. Not that it's my call anyway! Come to think of it, however, this could have serious implications. If I'm shut out now, I can only imagine what will happen when the big decisions are made!
I should have known. They'll just have to deal with the consequences.

_____

AQ Detection Skills—Stage Two: Analyzing the CO_2RE

Now, place a plus sign (+) or a minus sign (−) next to the each of the CO_2RE dimensions of the following responses to adversity to indicate whether the response on each dimension is positive or negative.

C = Control O_2 = Origin and Ownership   R = Reach   E = Endurance

1. Event:

Jim, a coworker, evaluates Mark lower than expected on his performance.

Response:

_____

C = I'll obviously have to speak to Jim to learn more about his perceptions and to make *sure* this doesn't happen again.

(Continued)

————————	O_2 = I should have seen this coming.
————————	R = This could ruin my chances of getting that pay increase. How will I ever explain this to Sarah? She'll be crushed.
————————	E = I'll obviously have to speak to Jim to learn more about his perceptions and to make sure this doesn't happen again.

2. Event:

    The funding for Karen's major project is slashed.

  Response:

————————	C = I won't allow this.
————————	O_2 = Every time we get close to doing something important, some idiot comes along and cuts funding. Oh well, it's not my job!
————————	R= I can't believe this! The whole department is falling apart.
————————	E= It's time to get the message out about what we're doing!

3. Event:

    Margie's best friend forgets her birthday.

  Response:

————————	C = Oh well, there's nothing I can do about it now.
————————	O_2 = I'm sure Barbara was busy. It's a wonder I remember my own birthday! It's my job to find out what happened.
————————	R = There goes the big day, right down the drain.
————————	E = It will be a long time before we get to talk again.

4. Event: Hal's daughter is caught smoking at school.

   Response:

_____   C = Well, I cannot accept this. It's clearly time she and I had a real talk.

_____ O_2 = I can't help but believe that, if I'd been a better parent, she wouldn't be in this mess. I'm not going to come down on her. We share the accountability for what happened today.

_____   R = Oh my God! I can't believe she would ruin her life this way.

_____   E = It's never too late to learn from your mistakes.

5. Event: Frank is not invited to an important meeting at work.

   Response:

_____   C = Not that it's my call anyway!

_____ O_2 = I should have known. They'll just have to deal with the consequences.

_____   R = Come to think of it, however, this could have serious implications.

_____   E = If I'm shut out now, I can only imagine what will happen when the big decisions are made!

Answers:

Stage One: 1. − or + (½ −, ½ +),   2. − or + (½ + and ½ −), 3. −, 4.+, 5. −.

Stage Two:	C	O	R	E
1.	+	−	−	+
2.	+	−	−	+
3.	−	+	−	−
4.	+	O_r− , O_w+ (moderate)	−	+
5.	−	−	−	−

sensing the dimensional highs and lows, you will, over time, develop the Climber's instinct— automatically responding to all magnitudes of adversity with strength and determination.

Chances are you are now able to detect the difference between low and high AQ responses to adversity. With a little thought, you are probably able to separate out these responses by dimension. With practice, your awareness skills will continue to become sharper and more natural until you have truly developed the intuitive senses of the Climber and can readily spot your response. Try these skills on your own adversity.

AQ Detection Skills—Personal Application: Stage One

1. Write down an example of adversity you had to face over the past two weeks.

   _____

   _____

   _____

   _____

   _____

2. Write down what you might have said in response to the adversity.

   _____

   _____

   _____

   _____

   _____

3. Fill in the following information about your response. Notice that not all responses include all four CO_2RE dimensions.

   _____ Was your response high or low?

Personal Application—Stage Two: Taking Apart Your CO_2RE

C = Control O_2 = Origin and Ownership   R = Reach   E = Endurance

1. On which dimensions did you respond high or low?

    _____ C

    _____ O_2

    _____ R

    _____ E

2. Knowing what you know and that you can control your responses, if you were to respond to the same event today, what might you say?

    _____

    _____

    _____

    _____

    _____

3. As you look at this new response, on which dimensions did you respond high or low?

    _____ C

    _____ O_2

    _____ R

    _____ E

4. How does this CO_2RE compare with that of your earlier response?

    _____

    _____

    _____

    _____

Your Response, Your Choice

If you would like extra practice, go back to the Adversity Response Profile in Chapter 4. As you look at these examples of adversity, how would you want to respond now, recognizing that your response to the adversity is now a *choice?*

Pick two consecutive events from the Adversity Response Profile. Write the numbers you circled for that event below. Next to those numbers, write how you would respond to that event *now.*

C = Control   O$_2$ = Origin and Ownership   R = Reach   E = Endurance

Event #		Responses		New Responses
_____	C	_____	C	_____
	O$_2$	_____	O$_2$	_____
	R	_____	R	_____
	E	_____	E	_____

Event #		Responses		New Responses
_____	C	_____	C	_____
	O$_2$	_____	O$_2$	_____
	R	_____	R	_____
	E	_____	E	_____

Notice that just by being *aware* of your response and the difference between a healthy and a weak CO$_2$RE, you were able to consciously alter and improve your response to an adverse event.

Reinforce the Good, Question the Bad

When you received a report card, were you more likely to react strongly to a D or an A? When your work performance is being evaluated, how often do you breeze past the good news in a rush to find out what you did wrong? We often focus on the *negatives* of our performance, and let the positives slip by, as if they were simply assumed.

One of my clients, a partner in an international management consulting firm, discovered that in his office, people at all levels remembered far more negative than positive feedback in their performance appraisals, even when the evaluations were carefully balanced!

Let's face it. Negative criticism sticks, especially when we are the ones criticizing ourselves! However, this tendency to focus on the negatives can be damaging, since we often miss opportunities to reinforce essential, positive tendencies, especially in our AQs.

If your response to adversity is in line with a higher AQ, you can gain significant long-term value by pausing and validating the positive aspects of your response. Pick out those CO_2RE dimensions on which you responded most constructively. Silently recognize yourself. George, a client in the field of education says he catches these moments and thinks, "Yes, good. Keep climbing!"

Such mental reinforcement can strengthen the positive aspects of your response and the pathways you have formed. So, notice your productive patterns and let them seep in and take hold.

E = Explore All Origins and Your Ownership of the Result

I recently conducted an AQ program for Coopers & Lybrand, a Big Six accounting firm. Everything was going smoothly until about two hours before I was set to begin. That's when adversity hit in the form of another equipment problem. I got a call from a computer technician. "I understand you need a computer monitor," he said. "I'm not sure I can get you what you want, but . . ."

"I'm sorry, there seems to be some mistake," I replied. "I don't need a monitor. I need a video projector to show my multimedia on a large screen."

"Oh!" The technician responded with an audible sigh of relief. "Someone obviously blew it. I mean, hey, that's not really my area! You'll have to speak to Horace. He handles that stuff." The technician hung up without giving me Horace's number or connecting the call, let alone personally seeing the situation through to resolution.

At this moment my alarm went off. "Ahwooogah! Ahwooogah! Adversity! Adversity!" I instantly checked my response. "There has *got* to be a way!" I told myself. "This situation demands some creativity and persistence. I know I can resolve this in time for the program. Even if I don't, the program can still succeed."

Fortified with a strong adversity response and determination, I urgently called my client only to repeatedly run into her voice mail. She apparently was away from her desk, so I decided to handle the situation myself. After several attempts, I got in touch with a man in maintenance . . . the elusive Horace. "Oh, well, that equipment wasn't reserved in the original order for this room!" he exclaimed upon hearing my dilemma.

"Yes, I understand, but given the fact that the program is in less than two hours, what can you and I do to make this work?" I was attempting to motivate Horace toward a little creative problem solving.

"Well, . . . " Horace stalled. Then he uttered those fatal words with well-oiled precision, "There's really nothing I can do. The projector is installed in room four, and you are in room five. Besides, I get off work in ten minutes. You'll have to speak to Angel. She coordinates the rooms."

This time I jumped in before getting another dial tone without a phone number. After several more calls and several more "It's-not-my-job" and "I-don't-think-that-will-work" responses I finally pulled together an unlikely combination of kind-hearted secretaries, managers, and supervisors who were willing to drop what they were doing to change the rooms. A simple glitch nearly ruined the client's plan for the program simply because no one was willing to *own the result* of the adversity. And that, ironically, created even more adversity.

The moment you accept ownership of the result, you immediately enlarge your perceived sense of control over the event, empowering yourself to act, and breaking the potential cycle of helplessness and hopelessness. *Ownership* is a call to action.

The importance of the second step in the LEAD sequence, E=Exploring the origin and your ownership of the adversity, comes down to a single question: *How likely are you to take action to resolve a situation for which you accept blame but feel no ownership?* Your answer, "Not very likely!" For example, had the technician, Horace or anyone else accepted blame without accountability, the situation would have remained untenable. Even if Horace had said, "Well, I guess I failed to provide the correct set-up. It's all my fault. But, it's too late now, and besides, I'm outta here in ten minutes," I still would have been left in a lurch.

Similarly, if you don't own the problem of water usage during a local drought, why would you suffer the necessary inconveniences of shorter showers and a brown lawn? If you blame yourself for, but don't own any part of a financial downturn in your company, how likely are you to throw your energy and any extra hours behind finding a solution? If your team fails to come through on a major project, will you disengage, disowning the failure? Some modicum of ownership, not blame, is *essential* for you to learn from or solve any problem, as well as recover from any adversity, regardless of its size.

This second step in the LEAD sequence is where Climbers really learn from adversity and hone their future strategy. This step has two complementary components: Origin and Ownership.

Origin

You will recall origin involves accepting appropriate blame for causing the event—no more, no less. However, there are two kinds of blame, *productive* and *unproductive*. Taking responsibility for that portion of the adversity that you have caused and learning from your behavior is productive blame. Pummeling yourself with unnecessary criticism is unproductive, if not highly damaging blame.

Accepting appropriate blame strengthens your integrity and credibility. This requires honestly exploring what, if any, role you played in *causing* the adversity. The origin component of the E step in the LEAD sequence involves asking three questions:

- What are the possible origins of this adversity?
- Given these origins, what portion was my fault?
- What, specifically, could I have done differently or better?

Ownership

You will also recall that ownership involves taking an honest and *constructive* look at what aspects of the result you should own. Owning the result means holding yourself accountable for doing *something* to deal with and improve, if not resolve, the situation caused by the adversity even if you didn't cause it. Owning the result does not mean you must accept unnecessary blame for causing the event. It simply means you take on the responsibility for resolution or action.

The ownership component of the E step in the LEAD sequence requires that you ask one question:

- What portion or aspects of the results should I own?

Applying L = Listen and E = Explore—A Case Example

Let's assume your hard drive crashes. If your AQ was quite low, your immediate response might be, "Oh my God! I'm dead. Everything is lost. I've never been very smart with computers. Now, we'll never get this project done on time. I guess we can kiss this client goodbye."

How can you improve your response and raise your AQ? Begin by applying the initial step of the LEAD sequence—L = Listen to the response—and you readily detect a lower AQ. Next, perform the second step, E = Explore all origins and your ownership of the result.

You ask the three origin questions, in order:

- What are the possible origins of this adversity?
- Given these origins, what portion was my fault?
- What, specifically, could I have done better?

List in your mind or on paper all the possible origins for the adversity. The question does not ask for the *likely* origins, but the *possible* origins. This is intentional. Since you are at least partially at fault, there is a tendency to ignore other possible origins, thus, blowing your role out of proportion and burdening yourself with unproductive blame.

So, *what are the possible origins* for a hard drive crash? It may have been caused by any of a number of factors—a manufacturing flaw, a software glitch, a power surge, static electricity, a system error, low humidity, or an evil curse from the techno-gods.

Given these origins, what portion is my fault? You might want to blame yourself for the entire event. "It happened, therefore, it's my fault." Perhaps, what you are really trying to say is you are *accountable* for what happened, even if you didn't *cause* the mishap. But, we're getting ahead of ourselves. As you consider the possible origins, how many have anything to do with you, even remotely? Maybe you didn't supply a static mat, schedule a maintenance check, or update the system software, so maybe you are partially at fault. What portion of the blame is yours? Let's say your best guess is 30 percent for not scheduling a maintenance check.

What, specifically, could I have done differently or better? Even though it is, at most, 30 percent your fault, there are a number of actions you could have taken to reduce the probability of your hard drive crashing. Given the clarity of hindsight, you might have conducted a maintenance check, run a system upgrade, or bought a static mat. So you learn and move on, a wiser person for the experience.

This simple process of looking back and learning from your behavior is the engine of the entire notion of continuous improvement. Your ability to continually improve all facets of your self is essential to your Ascent. The workplace demands that you relentlessly upgrade your skills, and the mountain requires that you improve as you go.

What portion or aspects of the results should I own? Although you may not be to blame for the crash, you may feel highly accountable for the outcome—for the fallout from the crash. You cannot operate your machine, thus no documents can be accessed. If you own this outcome, you accept responsibility for doing something about your frozen computer.

Owning the result does not require you to personally take the time to recover the lost data and learn from the adversity. Owning the result simply means you will personally see to it that someone will take the necessary actions. Certainly, you are accountable for making sure the computer is operational and any lost data is recovered in a timely manner. *How* you choose to do it is not critical.

Burdening yourself with undue blame and disowning the results of an adverse event *do nothing* to strengthen your sense of control. However, the moment you accept *appropriate* blame, decide to learn from your actions, and take ownership of some portion of the outcome, you begin to regain some control and propel yourself toward taking action. This enables you to get past this adversity and continue on your Ascent.

A Qualifier on Reach

If you tend to enlarge or even catastrophize bad events, you'll want to be sure to own only the *known,* and not the *possible* result of the adversity. In the above scenario, for example, you might immediately assume that a crashed hard drive means everything is lost, the project is ruined, and your job is surely in jeopardy. The *known* part of the adversity is simply a crashed hard drive and a frozen computer. That's it. The rest is assumed. By owning only those portions of the adversity that are known or confirmed, you will limit the fallout and avoid being overwhelmed. It is easier to own a mishap than it is a disaster! The fact is, in this, as in many situations, you will need more information.

People with lower AQs often assume the worst until, and if, they learn more. People with higher AQs assume the best, until proven wrong and actively seek the information needed to know where they stand. In Chapter 7, you'll learn more techniques to keep you from catastrophizing negative events.

A = Analyze the Evidence

A = Analyze the Evidence involves a simple questioning process in which you examine, dispute, and eventually derail the destructive aspects of your response. The following LEAD questions are carefully worded, and are meant to be answered in the form in which they are presented:

- What *evidence* is there that I have *no* control?
- What *evidence* is there that the adversity *has* to reach into other areas of my life?

- What *evidence* is there that the adversity *must* last any longer than necessary?

Stop and notice the effect of the key italicized words in these questions. While there may be evidence that you have *limited* control, that the adversity *could* reach into other areas of your life, and that it *might* endure a very long time, the evidence that you have *no* control, that the adversity *has* to reach and *must* endure is much more difficult to find.

Abraham Lincoln once said, "Argue for your limitations and they are yours." Arguing for a loss of control, possible ruination, and enduring fallout is as fruitless as arguing for the *possible* crash of a plane, the *potential* collapse of the world economy, and your inability to have been *born* rich. Meaningful progress can only be made through exploring the limitations of the adversity, not *your* limitations to improve the situation.

A Case of Reach

Go back to the example of your crashed hard drive. An extreme response might be, "Oh no! Everything's ruined! The entire project zapped in a single moment. I'll never get back what I've lost. Besides, if it could happen once, it could happen twice. There's no use even trying. I gave it my best shot, and I blew it. I guess I can kiss that promotion and my son's college fund goodbye." This response reeks of defeatism, catastrophizing, and helplessness.

In the case of this or even less extreme responses, you could ask yourself the three evidence-related questions:

What evidence is there that I have no control? The answer is "none." There is no *evidence*. While it's theoretically possible that you have no control, there is no *evidence* that such helplessness exists in this case. The only fact is that the hard drive crashed, freezing your computer. That's it! Everything else is conjecture.

Why *assume* the worst? Certainly there is no reason to accept a complete lack of control until it is proven! If you went to the doctor with a headache, would you assume it was a brain tumor before you saw the results of your tests? In most situations, it doesn't pay to assume the worst until evidence supports it. Why jump to conclusions, especially when those conclusions can hurt you? So, without more information, you cannot assume you have no control.

Can you imagine a situation in which you literally have no control? Earlier, I mentioned how Vicktor Frankl, Nazi concentration camp survivor, prominent psychologist, and author of *Man's Search for Meaning*, found that, even in the most unimaginably horrific conditions, he had the ultimate control—control over how he *reacted* to any given situation. This lesson, popularized by Stephen Covey in his bestseller *Seven Habits of Highly Effective People*, points out that the critical decision occurs between the stimulus (adversity) and the response (your AQ). It is at this level that each of us, *always*, has control.

It can be so tempting to play victim and give up that control. If things happen *to* you, and you are merely a puppet of the system or a piece of driftwood floating down the river of life, then you need not accept responsibility or have any expectations of yourself. There is no doubt that, at least in appearance, Quitting or Camping are *easier* than Climbing. It is in the long run that one must pay the price or reap the rewards of one's decisions. I know of no decision more tragic than to quit.

You see the sad results of this decision daily: a high school senior who scores poorly on his aptitude tests and gives up on a college education; a friend rejected in the job search stops trying to advance her career; a coworker gets unfavorable feedback on a performance review and decides to resign rather than get tough; a frustrated child angrily lashes out at his mother who permanently distances herself at the time when her love is most important; a woman stops putting effort into her marriage when her husband ignores her desperate attempt to communicate about their relationship. Quitting is pervasive and insidious.

You must honestly confront any assumption of helplessness, when, in fact, *you always have at least some level of control*. Helplessness may appear to be an easier, attractive alternative to accepting control, and with it some implied degree of responsibility. If you're helpless then you are free of responsibility, people may feel sorry for you, and someone else has to take action. But, such a choice may prove devastating. Given the option, in that moment of reaction, between helplessness and control, it is always best to err on the side of control.

What evidence is there that the adversity has to reach into other areas of your life? People with lower AQs often argue for what's called "the domino effect," which implies that one bad event will inevitably cause another and another. It's easy to see how this response could quickly make you feel overwhelmed. You cannot afford such a direct blow to your sense of hope. In the process of disputing your response, you must, therefore, separate your assumptions from what you know.

The truth is, while the adversity *could* reach other areas of your life, there is no evidence that it *has* to! So again, despite your best efforts to catastrophize, the answer to this question is "none."

What evidence is there that the adversity must last any longer than necessary? There are always reasons the adversity might endure, but, rarely, is there evidence that the adversity *must* endure, without improvement. Even the world environment, which represents adversity of global proportions, could continue on its current, dire course but does not *have* to. So, as with the first two, the answer to the third question is "None."

This is great news! You have just separated assumptions from fact, and the fact does not, as of yet, support your response to this adversity! At minimum, you need more information. Seeking that information is, in itself, a positive action, moving you toward learning and improvement.

Evidence in the Face of Mega-Adversity

When Captain Scott O'Grady's plane was shot down over hostile territory in Bosnia, he knew he was in serious trouble. He was facing mega-adversity. His response to this adversity might have been, "It's all over. I'm shot down over hostile territory, and they're sure to find me. Once they do, they'll probably torture and kill me. I guess I'll never see my family again. I might as well give up now." At first glance, there might appear to be plenty of evidence to support such a response. But, take a closer look!

Evidence the Situation *Might* Be Out of His Control	Evidence It Had to Be Out of His Control
▪ Shot down.	None!
▪ He was alone.	
▪ The enemy was all around.	
▪ Limited food and water.	
▪ The enemy was actively searching for him.	
▪ No obvious hope for escape!	

Even in this desperate situation, Scott O'Grady found and created evidence of control. He had already survived the shooting, he possessed some supplies, he had survival training, his gear included a signaling device, and he had found a place to hide. Had O'Grady mentally built a case for helplessness based on assumptions, do you think he would have signaled incessantly for help, wrung out and drunk the sweat from his own socks, never have given up hope, let alone ever been rescued? Probably not. Captain O'Grady's ability to separate the facts from any negative assumptions probably saved his life.

There are other situations, such as a loved one being diagnosed with a terminal or debilitating illness or your losing a limb, where there is evidence that the adversity *will* endure, and *will* significantly reach into other areas of your life. Try as you might, chances are you cannot prevent a person you love from dying from terminal cancer. But, you can dramatically affect how he or she lives with the disease and how you eventually deal with the loss.

Newsweek magazine tells of the courage with which Cardinal Joseph Bernardin, Archbishop of Chicago, faced his final months of life. Despite his pain and weakness, the cardinal was surprisingly productive in his final week. He completed a report on archdiocesean affairs for the Vatican, signed off on a manuscript for a book, *The Gift of Peace*, reviewed his will, and made arrangements for his mother's care. He dispatched letters, including one to the United States Supreme Court requesting the justices reject arguments for physician-assisted suicide, fearing such a ruling would reduce the value of an imperfect life. Another letter was his final Christmas card to his priests and friends.

Rather than giving up when he received his terminal diagnosis, Cardinal Bernardin made a public promise to use whatever time was left "in a way that will be of benefit to the priests and people I have been called to serve." This courageous Climber stayed true to his ascent until his final moment. In so doing, he left a lesson and a legacy about living and dying with dignity from which all could benefit.

Likewise, you cannot recover a lost limb. It is gone forever. Such losses may permanently alter parts of your life. But, you can control to what degree and how long they limit you. At first glance, however, the adversity of losing an arm may appear to be out of your control, far reaching, and likely to last forever.

Part of the Adversity That *Might* Be Out of Your Control	Part of the Adversity That *Has* to Be Out of Your Control
■ I lost my arm. ■ It takes two arms to eat, dress, drive, shop, swim, etc. ■ Some people respond awkwardly to people with missing limbs. ■ My clothes will fit differently.	■ I lost my arm.

Part of the Adversity That *Might* Be Far Reaching	Part of the Adversity That *Has* to Be Far Reaching
■ People with missing limbs cannot do the same things as people with limbs. ■ It takes two hands to drive a car. ■ It takes two hands to eat, dress myself, etc. ■ Some people might laugh or be repulsed. ■ I can't go kayaking. ■ I can't learn the guitar. ■ My partner might leave me.	None!

Part of the Adversity That *Might* Endure a Long Time	Part of the Adversity That *Has* to Endure a Long Time
■ I'll never have my own arm. ■ I'll never be able to drive a normal car. ■ I'll never be able to eat, dress myself, etc. the same way I once could. ■ People will always laugh or be repulsed. ■ I'll never be able to go kayaking. ■ I can't learn the guitar. ■ No one will ever want me. ■ People will always stare at me.	■ I'll never have my own arm.

You can never get back your arm. It is lost, and you have no control over getting it back. In that sense, the adversity is out of your control and long lasting. But, the story does not end there. Far from it!

Notice that with the exception of losing the arm, every aspect of the *fallout* from this severe adversity is negotiable! The list of functions that must be lost or given up is purely based on assumption, not reality. The fact is, people with one arm can climb mountains, paddle kayaks, play the violin, eat, dress, and drive. Some perform at levels considered exceptional for people with two arms!

Consider Jim Abbott, a boy born with one hand. His dream was to play major league baseball, a fantasy for any kid, considered by most to be a pipe dream for Jim. How did Jim respond to the ongoing adversity of having one hand and being ridiculed by his classmates? He adjusted, he adapted. Rather than give up his ascent, he rerouted his climb to go around this overhang.

Jim developed a quick change technique that he used to switch his glove on and off his hand so he could catch and quickly throw. He honed his physical condition, becoming an Olympic champion in the hurdles. He relentlessly stuck to his dream, and became not just a fielder, but a highly respected major league *pitcher* for the California Angels.

Jim had plenty of *reasons* to quit. Instead, he persevered.

As you can see, even when the setback is life-altering, your ability to control what you can, limit the reach of the adversity to the situation at hand, and minimize how long it endures will be the definitive factor in how quickly and to what degree you will recover from these tremendous challenges.

The knowledge that the adversity does not *have* to be out of your control, reach other areas of your life, or endure any longer than necessary is, in itself, dramatically freeing.

D = Do Something!

Many self-improvement and performance-enhancement programs begin by instructing you to take action. Taking action is dynamic, powerful, and sexy. However, the problem with trying to immediately resolve adversity with action is that, quite often, the person hit by the adversity is not *ready* for action.

Even a less than optimal response can steal the vital energy needed to act with relentless conviction. If your AQ indicates that the problem is out of your control, will negatively impact other areas of your life, and/or will endure far into the future, you may not even *consider* action. As Martin Seligman's and others' research has made clear, those who suffer from even mild cases of learned helplessness—the belief that what they do does not matter—are less likely to dig in and to do what it takes to resolve the situation. Why would you take action when you perceive that anything you do would be fruitless, if not demoralizing?

Conversely, the hyped-up command for you to take action *before* you understand how you're wired, could be fruitless, if not damaging.

Imagine if, on the night Candace Lightner lost her child to a drunk driver, she had been told, "You've got to take action!" Her first response might have been to hurt the other driver, or worse! Instead, she took the time to grieve her tragic loss, and when she was ready, chose a much more constructive course of action. Based on her resolve to help other parents avoid the unbearable pain she had suffered, Candace started MADD, Mothers Against Drunk Drivers. By starting this group, Candace helped lobby for and implement legislation that significantly tightened the laws against drunk driving, saving countless lives and immeasurable suffering.

A Case for Action

The LEAD sequence is a valuable tool for helping you respond to the adversity as constructively as possible and moving toward constructive action, *when you are ready*.

The first three steps in the LEAD sequence clear the mental space and fill the emotional fuel tanks required to consider, focus upon, and finally take meaningful action.

And, like the previous steps, taking action requires some carefully crafted questions. The six you will want to ask yourself are:

1. What additional information do I need? How am I going to get it?
2. What could I do to gain even a little control over this situation?
3. What could I do to limit the reach of this adversity?
4. What could I do to limit how long the adversity endures in its current state?
5. Which of these actions will I take first?
6. Exactly when will I take this action? What day, what time?

As we revisit our example of your hard drive crash, you can imagine several actions you could immediately take to better the situation. The six questions help you naturally group your actions to make sure that every dimension of your AQ has been addressed, and the avalanche caused by a destructive adversity response has been permanently cleared.

APPLYING THE LEAD SEQUENCE

Return to the situation of the crashed hard drive. Let's assume that you completed the first three steps of the LEAD sequence. You

L=Listened to your response and discovered it was somewhat low. You then E=Explored the origin and your ownership and discovered that you were overblaming yourself and falling short of owning the outcome of the crash. Next, you A=Analyzed the evidence and discovered that there was little if any evidence to support your low AQ conclusions.

Your next step is to D=Do Something! Begin by listing what you could do to better the situation. Take a moment to consider and mentally list your responses to the above questions. Use a pad of paper and a pencil to see the list you generate.

What additional information did you need? Wouldn't you want to know what, if any, data was lost, before you assumed it was all gone? If you can retrieve the data, wouldn't you want to know the cost and time involved in recovering it? There is some truth to the adage, "Information is power." Information gives you the ability to react to known realities rather than vague, destructive suppositions.

There are also many actions that would boost your sense of control. What did you come up with? Any actions you wrote down are likely to elevate your perceived control. Taking action, in itself, boosts perceived control. What about limiting the reach? Did you decide to do whatever it takes to recreate any lost data? Were there people you wanted to contact to mitigate the fallout from this potentially serious setback? These same actions you took to limit the reach might also limit how long the adversity endures. You may have also chosen to call a data recovery specialist or some team mates to determine when the last back-up was performed.

When Lists Aren't Enough: The Funnel Approach

A mere list of actions can be dangerous. It may relieve you just enough that you stop the process of bettering the adverse situation in its tracks. The problem is, once you've made a list, you have still *done* nothing to improve the situation. It's like buying an organizer to make your life less chaotic. The organizer won't reduce the chaos unless you *use* it. But it might make you feel good about yourself for a little while. We're not out to create the illusion of effectiveness, we want enduring improvements!

In the case of the crashed hard drive, after making your list of actions, what happens when you turn on your computer and it is still frozen? You have a great list, but nothing has changed! You can fill your backpack with all the best gear, but the climb does not begin until you take your first step.

You will notice that the exercise on page 160 didn't end with you simply listing actions. I asked you to *pick one action* to take first. I then asked you to *pinpoint a day and time* when you would take that action. These final steps naturally funnel your thinking from a broad spectrum of options down to a specific, planned commitment to move ahead.

Using such a funnel approach (Figure 6–2), you will move from a list to committing to a specific action and time. This guides you to take that first critical step, which in this case, might be relatively easy. If you've lost your biggest customer, suffered the death

FIGURE 6–2　The Funnel Approach

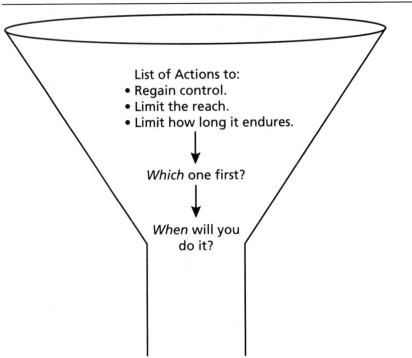

of a loved one, or been downsized, taking that first step can be as hard as climbing through an ice storm, but it is no less important.

Action is the thrust forward, the difference between thought and movement. Without it, nothing happens!

The actions you have listed transcend the boundaries of your individual CO_2RE dimensions, enhancing more than one dimension at once. Actions which enhance control might also limit reach. And those that curtail reach are likely to limit endurance, thus bolstering your sense of control.

LEADING YOURSELF THROUGH MAJOR SETBACKS

Whether or not you've ever suffered mega-adversity, you have probably had moments when you have felt so bad that you were simply not *ready* to think about or do anything. You certainly don't have to experience complete financial bankruptcy, lose your entire family in a car crash, or be diagnosed with lymphoma to feel genuine loss or defeat. We all have those moments where the wind is taken out of our sails, and depending on the severity of the setback or loss, these may last for days or weeks. Even the most highly effective people occasionally feel emotionally drained or defeated. Sometimes we simply need to allow ourselves to feel despair, even grief. Recall Candace Lightener, founder of MADD. Grieving was an essential part of her healing process so she could resume her ascent with a newfound sense of purpose.

So, yes, weep, gnash your teeth, scream, moan, and bellow. Get it out! Grieving is a natural and essential part of healing our hearts, letting go, and moving on. The grieving process should not be circumvented. Nor should grieving be confused with a low AQ.

Using the LEAD sequence during such a time may, therefore, seem counter-intuitive, even absurd! Why would you use a technique to dispute your own bad feelings in face of a major loss? Why would you do anything to sidestep or postpone your grief?

In my experience, however, there is constructive as well as destructive grief. When suffering a major setback, many people get firmly lodged in the dark corners of their souls, as if caught in a negative neural loop, unable to shake loose when it is time to do so.

Others simply become partially, even wholly incapacitated by despair. You can use the LEAD sequence to avoid letting these feelings get out of control. Only you can say when it is best to use the LEAD sequence to guide yourself out of loss or put a lid on the bottomless pit of desolation. My experience, however, is that the LEAD sequence can be a powerful tool for dislodging yourself from despair at a time when other interventions may have failed.

Martin Seligman and his colleagues have made a compelling case that learned helplessness is a major cause of depression. Certainly a state of helplessness would render one prone to depression. Loss of control is a common cause of depression. The LEAD sequence is an effective way of restoring control, and thus preventing depression by LEADing a person to create options and take action.

Lisa Jaycox and Jane Gillham from the University of Pennsylvania, and their team used similar techniques to *prevent* depression in teenagers with dramatic results. While not a cure for depression, the LEAD sequence can help protect you from feeling helpless and may prevent you from despair, as well as from taking one of the Four Dangerous Forks in the Trail described in Chapter 2.

Avoiding the Victimhood Trap: No Whiners Allowed!

Another brand of despair comes from feeling like a victim. Victimhood is a powerful, often luring trap. It commonly results from suffering adversities over which you perceive little control and have little ownership. One dramatically overweight person might develop the mental discipline to exercise regularly and follow a healthful diet, while another might simply fall victim to his genetics. When asked about his poor health, the latter might say, "Hey, my mom was fat. I guess I just got dealt a bad hand. There's nothing I can do about it."

My response is, "You're right, at least not with that mentality!"

Consider Jeff, a neighbor of mine. At 6 foot 2 inches tall and 457 pounds, Jeff is morbidly obese. You might say that he is genetically predisposed to obesity, with his parents' combined weight being in excess of 700 pounds. Yet, Jeff has refused to be a victim of fate. He avidly pursues one of the few exercises he can. He walks. He walks and walks and walks. Every day, as I drive around town, I see him walking to or from work, the store, or errands. No matter what the weather, he keeps walking, miles and miles and miles. "Just because I'm large doesn't mean I can't have a life!" exclaims Jeff, who, at last count, had lost 54 pounds.

Even when a loved one is diagnosed with a terminal disease, there are those who are nonetheless vigilant—comforting the patient, getting him the best care available, pulling together the information he requires to make the most informed decisions, and providing the love needed to make the impending death as bearable as can be. Others simply give up. The first response promotes hardiness and long-term peace of mind through playing a significant role in helping another person deal with extraordinary hardship. It engenders hope. The other response, while understandable, makes one a prime candidate for depression, illness, and despair.

Helpless assumptions create a hopeless reality. The LEAD sequence takes you from the adversity to action. No matter what your misfortune, there is *always* something you can do to gain some control, make things a little better, or survive the worst of it.

THE OVERHANG

You look skyward toward the peak, and there is an overhang in your path. What to do? Do you walk away, or do you somehow reach inside and put forth the effort and ingenuity to go over or around it?

This moment in this book is your overhang. Take a good hard look at it. You have a book in your hand, a hand that has held many books before. You are presented with a tool, a scientifically grounded sequence for permanently rewiring how you respond to adversity, leading to a long list of life-changing benefits. Like the first time you used a toothbrush or turned on a computer, the tool before you appears awkward, and unnatural. There are so many reasons to walk away.

To get past the overhang, you can benefit from adopting the beginner's mind, best exemplified by how a baby learns to walk. She will simply stand up, try, and fall down. Then she'll do it over and over again. She might get frustrated or angry when she falls, but she never gets discouraged and says, "See, I told you I can't walk. Walking is impossible!" *Babies don't attend walking seminars.* Babies have an innate ability to work past the awkward stage of learning something new. *So do you.* Like walking, using the LEAD sequence requires conscious effort, determinedly deviating from the path of least resistance and changing your thinking and behavior. It also involves uncertainty and fear.

> *Our greatest fear is not that we will discover that we are inadequate, but that we will discover that we are powerful beyond measure.*
> Nelson Mandela

We are not so much afraid of what we won't become, but of what we could be. What "could be" lies on the other side of the overhang. Once you've cleared it, the ascent becomes easier for awhile. Similarly, after you learn the LEAD sequence, rewiring yourself to use it as subconsciously and naturally as you put one foot in front of the other, you'll wonder why anyone *wouldn't* use it. For now, it looms as an added demand upon your mind and energy.

Imagine, for even a moment, the power you could unleash if you allowed yourself to fully, actively tap the wellspring of potential which lies largely dormant inside of you. To pump its rich bounty into your life, you must clear the overhang, and use the LEAD sequence, forever changing and improving what you do when the defining moment of adversity arrives.

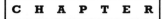

STOP! Catastrophizing

Of all the virtues we can learn, no trait is more useful, more essential for survival and more likely to improve the quality of life than the ability to transform adversity into an enjoyable challenge.
Mihalyi Csikszentmihaly

"Oh no," Steve thought. "What did I do wrong? And my day started off so well!" Frantically, he pressed the "4" on his phone to replay the message on his voice mail. He could hear his pulse in his ears as the system paused before starting. He was breathing hard.

"Steve. This is Tom. I just got back from meeting with Sue Waynewright over at Belcorp. I realize you and I haven't been in touch. I think it's time we had a talk. Call Lisa and see if we can't set something up for this week. Thanks."

Steve set down the receiver and slumped in his chair. His plans would just have to wait. This was serious. "Why would Tom call me? This is bad. Very, very bad," he muttered under his breath.

Steve leapt out of his chair and began to pace his 12 by 14 home office. "This can only mean one thing. Something went terribly wrong." He paced faster. "It must be something about the final report, because everything was going so well. Or *was* it? Maybe there *are* some major holes!" Steve stopped dead in his tracks.

"That's it! Sue showed Tom what we did, and they found some shoddy work! Oh *no!* And this was my baby. I can just imagine what Tom will say." Steve began to absentmindedly rub his temples. "Heads will roll, and mine will be the first to go." He continued to vividly imagine the impending scenario. He could see the disappointment on Tom's face and hear it in his voice. He could visualize Tom firing him. He knew just how he would say it. He could hear every word.

As he paced, Steve played Tom's message over and over in his mind. "I think it's time you and I had a talk." Each time he played it, the message became more and more ominous. "I think it's time you and I had a *talk.*"

Within a couple of minutes, Steve was convinced his career was destroyed and his life in a shambles. He loosened his tie and slumped into his chair. He had planned to stop by the office on his way to attend an executive lunch meeting, but now all he wanted to do was hide. Besides, Sue Waynewright might be at the meeting, and Steve couldn't bear to look her in the eye. Not *now.*

At that moment, Steve's wife, Jill, poked her head in the door. "Hey, sweetheart, do you have a minute before you go?" Steve just looked at her, thinking, "if she only knew."

"What is it, babe?" he asked lifelessly. Do I tell her? he wondered. No! I can't disappoint her like that. This is my fault. I'm not going to drag her through the mud.

Jill looked at him curiously. "Is everything all right, sweetheart? You look kind of funny," she said, walking toward him with concern.

Steve sprang out of his seat prepared to give his best performance, at least under the circumstances. "Fine, babe. What's up?"

Jill eyed Steve suspiciously, unconvinced. "I was rearranging the family room, and I got stuck. There's a big desk I can't move by myself. Can you give me a hand?"

"No problem, where is the beast?" Steve brushed by, avoiding eye-contact with his wife.

He spent the next fifteen minutes helping Jill move furniture, some of it quite heavy. "What do you think?" she asked. "Should we put that old family portrait on that wall or over *there?*" Jill pointed to a large, freshly painted wall.

"Let's put it over there, where everyone can see it." Steve replied. He got out the ladder and hung the picture. For a short while his mind was totally on the task at hand.

When they were through, Jill came up to Steve, and gave him a hug. "Thanks, sweetie. I know how busy you are." She gave Steve a peck on the cheek. "Say, when I came in, you looked—I don't know—kind of worried. *Is* everything okay?" This time she was inches from his face.

Steve paused. Finally, he sighed. Somehow things didn't seem quite as serious as they did thirty minutes earlier. Steve felt a little lighter. "I got a call from Tom . . . " and he proceeded to tell Jill about the call.

WILDFIRE IN THE MIND

According to cognitive psychologists, of the wide array of responses to adversity, the one that can be most debilitating is *catastrophizing*. People catastrophize when they turn everyday inconveniences into major setbacks and those setbacks into disasters. Catastrophizing often involves destructive rumination over bad events. The more one mulls the event over in one's mind, the more ominous it becomes, and the more serious and likely the consequences appear. This rumination represents some of the most damaging connections you can make. Even more catastrophizing can be damaging and demoralizing. You don't have to experience a nervous breakdown to feel drained and anxious.

The more Steve worried about the phone call and its possible implications, the worse he felt, and the more critical the situation became. The only thing that had changed was his *response*. The phone call remained constant. Even so, Steve was on a course to treat it like a disaster, thus creating one.

Catastrophizing relates to the third CO_2RE dimension, *Reach* and occurs when you allow the impact of an event to spread, like wildfire, destroying other parts of your precious life.

Take the simple example of receiving a late notice for your electric bill. A high AQ response would be to limit the reach to the event at hand. A late notice is merely a late notice, nothing more.

You might check your record, call the utility company, arrange to pay, or consider some other method of clearing up the matter immediately.

A more extreme low AQ response would be to catastrophize the event, allowing it to stampede through other aspects of your life. "Oh my God! They're going to turn off the lights. Obviously, this is just the beginning. If we can't pay our electric bill, how will we ever pay our mortgage? We're in over our heads and heading straight for bankruptcy!" This is an example of someone taking a single event and turning it into a major ordeal.

Catastrophizing takes a small burn in one area of our lives and fans the flame, allowing an easily manageable adversity to grow into an uncontrollable conflagration that cuts across boundaries and consumes everything in its path. What's the first thing fire-fighters must do when there is a wildfire? Through a variety of techniques, including digging trenches and setting backfires, they contain the blaze, preventing its perilous spread. You must do the same when you catastrophize. You must stop the spread.

In your brain, catastrophizing is like any other response to adversity. You are merely following a subconscious neurological groove, a pathway made more efficient and discernible from repeated use. To halt this pattern, you must interrupt or stop it dead in its path. You may create this neurological interrupt by using any of the following eight techniques, called *Stoppers!* (Figure 7–1).

These techniques fall under two categories—*Distracters* and *Reframers*. All are effective methods for interrupting destructive neural pathways, pulling you out of a tailspin as you respond to adversity.

You will find that these techniques are best learned by *doing* them. Any of the Stoppers! can help you escape mild or severe catastrophizing. Use them to quicken your recovery from and reduce the fallout of adversity.

Distracters

Distracters are designed to help you immediately interrupt your destructive response and potentially alter your emotional and physical state.

FIGURE 7-1   Techniques to Avoid Catastrophizing

Stoppers!

Distracters

- Slam your palm on a hard surface, shout "Stop!"
- Focus intently on an unrelated object.
- Place a rubber band on your wrist and snap out of it!
- Distract yourself with an unrelated activity.
- Alter your state with exercise.

Reframers

- Refocus on your purpose. *"Why* am I doing this?"
- Get small.
- Help someone else.

Stop! The Reach

Place your hand about eighteen inches above your desk or away from a wall. Make sure there is nothing between your hand and the surface. The next time you read the word "NOW!" on this page slam your hand against the desk or wall and yell "Stop!" Remember the louder you yell and the harder you slam, the deeper the imprint in your brain. Your hand should be in position.

I don't want you to imagine the smell of fresh baked bread right out of the oven. Don't even think about that warm, sweet, homey scent of the loaf as it is popped out of the pan, all steamy. Try not to let yourself picture slathering on some sweet creamery butter and seeing it melt right into the soft center of the bread. NOW! (Slam your hand and yell *"Stop!"*)

At this point your hand should be smarting! Chances are you were following the image of fresh baked bread with melted butter, but the moment you shouted "Stop!" and slammed your hand, the pain and the sound sent a loud signal to your brain, creating a neurological interruption. It immediately halted the pathway you were following.

This technique can be applied to your AQ. It works best in private situations (opening an audit notice from the IRS) or in interpersonal situations where you literally want to startle the other person and/or stop the downward slide of their response.

The other day I was caught in traffic with a friend who had attended my AQ program. The flashing highway sign reported, "Accident ahead. 30 minute delay." Chris immediately began to catastrophize, "Oh no, we're going to miss our flight. I'll never get to LA in time!" Then Chris paused, slamming his hand on his steering wheel. "Stop!" he shouted. I laughed out loud.

"Hey it works!" he said, calming down and settling in for the ride. He called the office and took care of a few things including arranging a back-up plan in case we did, indeed, miss our flight.

Focus on an Unrelated Object

Focusing on an unrelated object is a bit quieter and less dramatic and is, thus, better suited to public situations like meetings, classes, and crowded places. This Stopper! is more subtle. Pick up a pen or a pencil. Take the next thirty seconds right now to stare at this object, and try to find at least one detail you hadn't noticed before. Look at the wording, the coloring, the shape, the size, and so on.

Chances are you were readily able to spot something new about your pen or pencil. By focusing intently on an unrelated object, you are distracting your brain, preventing it from catastrophizing. This technique is both silent and flexible. You can use it anywhere!

Imagine coming home from an evening out and there's a message from a friend on your machine demanding, "Call me right away!" You attempt to return the call, but her line is busy. Instantly you begin to catastrophize, "Oh, no! I hope everything's okay. What if she got in a car accident, or even worse?. . . ." and off you go. You pick up the tape dispenser next to the phone and begin to intently examine it for some noticeable detail. You spot the brand name of the tape, the dimensions of the roll, where the dispenser was manufactured, and the fact that it's missing one rubber bumper from its base. You've silently, abruptly interrupted what could have been a long string of catastrophic thoughts. You've regained control before the spark turned into a wildfire. You are now prepared to LEAD yourself through adversity.

Snap Out of It!

Slip a rubber band over your wrist and turn your arm so the inside is facing upwards. Now, give the rubber band a good six- to ten-inch stretch and let go! Snap! Your wrist may sting. While I hesitate to cause you even the slightest pain, this simple technique is an effective device for interrupting dangerous rumination over bad events. Just in case you think it is silly, look who else uses this technique:

- In basketball, high school senior-turned-pro, Kevin Garnett of the Minnesota Timberwolves was recently asked on national television about the rubber band on his wrist. "Every time my thinking gets out of control, thwack! I give myself a good snap. I use it a lot at the free throw line."
- Charles Barkley, basketball star with the Houston Rockets, All Star player, and three-time member of the U.S. Dream Team uses the rubber band to "help keep things in their place."

Through the AQ programs, thousands of executives, sales professionals, parents, leaders, students, and educators wear rubber bands neatly displayed next to their watches or bracelets. Tim Lintner, a doctoral student in international education at UCLA has developed a color-coded system in which each color is designated for a specific magnitude of adversity. "Red is the most serious. Blue is fairly minor," Tim explains. "I've gotten to the point where just *looking* at the rubber bands (which he wears tightly wrapped on his watchband) is a valuable reminder and device for regrouping my response." Tim and his wife Lisa have faced their share of adversity. Lisa recently lost her father to a heart attack. Starting Tim's doctoral program meant moving to Los Angeles, Lisa getting a new job, and living in a smaller place. Due to funding cuts, Lisa has lost her job, which is made all the more serious by the addition of their first child, Emily, with whom they share their tiny one-bedroom condo. In addition to completing his coursework and writing research papers, Tim has been the primary caregiver. He recently called for some new rubber bands.

This technique is not new. It has been successfully used by a wide range of businesses and programs where habit-breaking is essential, such as weight loss programs, and alcohol and drug recovery. It works because:

1. It is a simple, direct, interruption of the destructive patterns in your brain.
2. It is a visual reminder of the need to stop catastrophizing and reroute your response.

This technique can be used in a wide range of situations both private and public. You'll find that you can get good at surreptitiously giving yourself a hearty snap in the middle of a team meeting or a dinner conversation. Besides, if someone spots you snapping your rubber band, what better chance to explain and help a friend? So wear yours in good health! And if you find yourself dwelling unnecessarily on some misfortune, snap yourself out of it!

Positive Distractions

Joan, my son's high school principal, sat across the aisle by herself. We decided that the fact that she was wearing a hat and sunglasses inside a movie theater indicated that she wanted to be left alone. Yet, it seemed curious that this normally gregarious woman would be alone at a blockbuster action adventure movie.

After the movie, Joan passed me in the aisle. "Wasn't that something!" she exclaimed.

"I'm still catching my breath," I replied, returning her smile. "So, you always go to these sleepy little romantic comedies by yourself?" I inquired facetiously, my curiosity getting the best of me.

"Hey, this is *therapy!*" she explained. "Every time I think I'm in over my head, I just come to one of these. The noisier and wilder the better."

Sometimes, it is extremely effective to intentionally distract yourself from the adversity at hand. This allows you to avoid catastrophizing and buys you an essential "time out" from the situation so you can come at it when you are emotionally and mentally stronger. Postponing your response allows you to collect yourself, consider your response, and tackle the adversity head on.

There are a number of ways to avoid catastrophizing through distraction. Rather than ruminating, listen to loud music. Go to a comedy club or rent a silly video, anything that makes you laugh. Do like Joan and watch an action adventure movie. All of these activities can not only interrupt your pattern, they can dramatically alter your mental and physical state!

Catastrophizing suppresses your immune functions releasing performance depleting chemicals in the form of unhealthy levels of neurotransmitters, such as the catacholamines and corticosteroids. The emotional wildfire is manifested in your bloodstream and throughout the cells of your body. This only makes sense.

You can feel the changes in your body as you experience the emotions and excitement of a movie. You tense, relax, laugh at, and respond to what you're watching. Distractions not only avert your response, *they alter your physiology.*

These are moments where a stupid television show, a juicy novel, or a hobby can prove productive. The list of potential distractions is endless. Besides, letting the adversity play over and over in your mind is not always best. Distractions are a powerful tool for stopping this destructive pattern in its tracks and putting you back on yours.

It is important to distinguish, however, between intentional, productive distractions and the kind of mind-numbing junk TV that can become an addictive escape or time waster. Like chocolate chip cookies, these distractions can be highly therapeutic when used at just the right time, but highly destructive when consumed indiscriminately.

Alter Your State with Exercise

As you ruminate or catastrophize, you are getting pulled into a mental pattern that depletes your energy and vitality. Nothing can demoralize you faster than getting fixated on everything that can go wrong. All you want to do is vegetate, while your mind mulls the problem over and over again. It becomes a vicious cycle of sitting and ruminating, ruminating and sitting.

Sometimes we need to break free of the adversity and come at it with fresh energy. The most effective way to renew your energy is through exercise. Pull yourself out of that chair and walk, run, ride, row—whatever works for you. Flooding your brain with endorphins can only help. To reach this benefit, most people need only twenty minutes of sustained aerobic activity.

The physical and emotional benefits of releasing tension through physical exertion are innumerable. To name a few:

- You feel better about yourself.
- You alter the neurotransmitters in your brain, boosting your immune system and releasing healthy, performance-enhancing chemicals.
- You are more likely to restore a sense of calm.
- Tension is released through the act of using and temporarily exhausting your muscles.

Reframers

Reframers are devices to help you Stop! catastrophizing by putting your adversity into perspective. Catastrophizing is inherently a self-indulgent process. Your focus becomes intense and inward, warping your perspective and creating the temporary reality that only you exist. Reframers help renew your perspective with a sense of balance, allowing you to see beyond yourself and view the adversity in a new light.

What's Your Purpose?

One particularly effective Stopper! consists of reminding yourself of your original reason or purpose for being involved in the situation from which the adversity arose. This technique is best used when you sense you have lost your view of the big picture. You know when these moments hit. You find yourself obsessed with minutiae. You can't stop thinking about that phone call, that meeting, that letter, or that conversation. You go over and over the details and how they affect you, the damage you are convinced they will inevitably cause. You react selfishly rather than considering the greater good.

I have worked with many change teams, including those involved in reengineering, developing strategic growth, or rightsizing their companies. This painful process is often drawn out and made worse by the added hours and emotional burden of playing a role in cutting coworkers' jobs.

As with any adversity, reengineering team members sometimes catastrophize. If they participate on the team they cut jobs, maybe those of close friends! If they refuse, they put their own jobs in jeopardy. They work late hours and weekends, and have little time with their loved ones, sometimes for months on end! Frannie's case was typical.

> *Frannie was in shambles. "This place is going down fast," she complained. "Everyone is scared to death. And they're all watching me, waiting to see who I'll recommend lose their job after years of loyal service. To make matters worse, I never get time with Jim. For all I know he's having an affair! I never see my children. I caught Brian in the garage with his friend the other day doing God knows what! Maybe they're doing drugs. I keep gaining weight. I'll never get to ride my new bike. I just drink coffee, sit in meetings, cut some jobs, come home late, crawl into bed, and do it all over again. But hey, there's nothing I can do about it. I suppose I'm lucky to have a job!"*

Getting to your purpose begins with asking "why?" Why did you choose this job, this company, this location, this situation? If you keep asking yourself why, you eventually get to a core value. For Frannie, the answer was, "My husband and I wanted to live in a beautiful place where our kids could feel safe and go to excellent school."

So I asked Frannie, "Why does this matter to you so much?"

"These are only the most important things in our lives!" She exclaimed passionately.

"Are these same reasons still valid?"

"Absolutely!" she responded.

I paused for effect.

"So your reasons for taking this job were and still are very intense and personal to you. How does it make you feel knowing that you are living according to your core values after all of these years?"

Fran smiled. "Great!" she enthused. "I don't think that many people can say that these days."

"So how do you feel about being a part of this reengineering team now that you remember why you are doing this job."

This time Frannie paused. "Well, it's tough, but I can deal with it for a while longer. It can't last forever, and I realize that I'm still on track." By reigniting her sense of purpose, Frannie turned a catastrophe into a classic high AQ response! She *is* back on track and ready to continue her ascent.

You'll find that by asking yourself these same kinds of questions you can rediscover your own purpose. The German philosopher Friedrich Nietzsche once said, "A person with a strong enough *why* can bear almost any *how*." Recalling your *why* puts the *hows* into perspective.

Get Small

When we ruminate, two things can happen—we can distort the problem until in our minds it's overwhelming and impossible to overcome, or we can get intensely focused on ourselves and how the situation affects us. In either case, *when we catastrophize, we lose perspective.* One technique for regaining perspective and reframing the adversity is to *get small.*

Getting small involves consciously putting yourself in a situation where you are dwarfed by what surrounds you. I use the mountains. To me, there is nothing like standing at the base of a 14,000-foot peak to put my little woes into perspective. Others like to walk on the beach. Some gaze at stars. There is something about staring at the boundless ocean or the sky that makes you realize how insignificant your problems are, in the grand scheme of the universe.

In any case, going to a different setting is an effective way to interrupt your response. Sometimes sitting at an airport or some other location crowded with stressed-out people can be very therapeutic. Sit somewhere with a great view of the maddening crowds. Sip your fruit juice (caffeine and alcohol aren't good while catastrophizing), and watch others go by. Look at their faces. If possible, listen to their words. *Everyone* faces adversity, and somehow, we all get through it.

You may have a special place where things become more serene and complete. You may wish to create one. It may be as simple as listening to a great opera, Broadway musical, or symphony. The grandeur and genius of the music can make you feel small. Great art galleries can have the same effect.

Getting small is an effective method for regaining perspective on your problems and getting outside your head by realizing there is a world out there that somehow continues to functions despite the current disaster.

Help Someone Else

Without a doubt, one of the most powerful tools for putting your problems instantly into perspective is to help someone with problems bigger than your own. Go to a nursing home and help an 87-year-old woman who has no family, can't eat solid food, can barely comb her hair, is told when to urinate, and yet remembers who she used to be and what she used to be able to do.

Volunteer for the Special Olympics and witness the beauty and the miracle of people with more limitations than you may ever know giving their all.

Put in a few hours at the local food bank. It doesn't take long to appreciate your good fortune and how small your challenges might be. Serve dinner to people who have no place to live, no shower, and no dignity. It makes those late hours at work, that missed promotion, that argument with your significant other, or that pulled hamstring look pretty minor.

There is nothing quite like another person's misfortunes to put our own into humble perspective. Do-good activities not only distract you from your own rumination, they create a host of positive physiological and psychological effects, elevating your spirit and immunological hardiness.

STOPPERS! AND LEAD

Use these eight Stoppers! in conjunction with the LEAD sequence. When you listen to your response, employ Stoppers! at the first sign of unnecessary rumination or catastrophizing. This will prevent the dangerous spread of the adversity into those areas of your life that need to remain strong and intact. As a result, your ability to spring back from setbacks and LEAD yourself to a higher AQ will be greatly enhanced.

Think of the LEAD sequence and Stoppers! as a way to condition yourself for the climb ahead. As with any conditioning, you can expect some immediate benefits. You will notice a change in the way you view and respond to adversity. However, the most powerful and meaningful change occurs over time. Soon your ability to sense adversity, listen to your response, explore your ownership, analyze the evidence, and take decisive action will weatherproof you against day-to-day adversity. You will change the way in which you listen to yourself and others. Even mega-adversities will lose much of their clout, temporarily slowing your ascent, but not stopping it.

Learning to use these skills yourself is the first major application of AQ. But what do you do when your employees whine, your spouse catastrophizes, a friend ruminates, or a team member becomes downtrodden by adversity? How do you meaningfully help these people without getting trapped in a destructive cycle of codependence and victimhood? Chapter 8 provides you with this second essential use of AQ—helping others respond to adversity more constructively so they can continue their ascents as well.

C H A P T E R

Improving Others' AQs and
Their Ability to Ascend

*Life is truly known only to those who suffer, lose, endure adversity
and stumble from defeat to defeat.*

Ryszard Kapuscinski, Polish Journalist

As you become more adept at LEADing yourself to a higher AQ,
you will notice others in your life who can also benefit from this
fundamental strategy. Chances are you've had friends or loved ones
who have suffered unnecessarily from life's slings and arrows. You
can learn how to help them strategize and avoid the trap of victimhood and endless whining.

In business, people with low AQs can sap team morale, momentum, productivity, and performance. Listening as a coaching,
parental, and leadership tool provides some benefits, but does not
guarantee that meaningful change will occur. You must go *beyond
listening* to LEAD coworkers and followers to a higher AQ, thereby
guiding them toward more effective action.

This chapter will provide you the opportunity to gently guide
children's AQ development, enhancing their accountability and

sense of control when faced with adversity. Inoculate the children in your life against helplessness and depression by LEADing them to a higher AQ.

LEADING A FRIEND

Samantha is an old friend of our family. She is a petite, youngish, 43-year-old woman who takes pride in her looks. She enjoys staying current in her tastes and hanging out with her daughter's friends.

One day, looking for a friend to talk to, Samantha knocked at our door. She was uncharacteristically disheveled. She wore no make-up and her hair hung limply. As she sat down, Samantha tried to appear upbeat, but her eyes said it all. There was a hollowness in her expression, an anemic apathy where joy used to dance. Hope and vitality had been replaced by desperation and lifelessness. Who could blame Samantha for feeling horrible?

She had spent the last seven years of her life dedicated to creating a marriage, while her husband, Tim, became increasingly verbally and emotionally abusive. His Dr. Jekyll and Mr. Hyde-like cycles of charismatic love and venomous, scathing anger escalated and had taken a severe toll on Samantha and her children. All three, Joe, Ryan, and Lisa now 17, 20, and 23, respectively, were from Samantha's first marriage, but they considered Tim to be their "real dad." He bought them lots of presents, usually to win their loyalty or to make up for his tirades. Over time, Samantha, her children, and her friends realized that Tim's charm was a dangerous, calculated facade. In reality, he was an interpersonal black hole, sucking the energy from the people who passed too close. Samantha and her children were disillusioned and emotionally ravaged.

In response to the abuse, Joe, Ryan, and Lisa were becoming progressively more troubled. Despite Samantha's vigilance, the kids were clearly acting out against Tim's "evil side," the dysfunction of the marriage, and their perception of their mother's misplaced loyalties. Joe got into drugs and dropped out of high school, Lisa had become dangerously promiscuous, and Ryan had unexpectedly become a father while still a teenager. Joe was sure to follow.

The day Samantha stopped by to talk, she had hit rock bottom. Despite her weeks of therapy, it was clear she needed a friend who had known her and Tim since the beginning. The accumulated pain of divorcing Tim, going back to school, and trying to save her children, was more than Samantha could bear. To top things off, she had run Tim's chiropractic office salary-free so he could focus his energy on his patients. Samantha would now have to find a new career.

The LEAD Sequence in Action

Since, for the preceding several weeks, Samantha had been through much of the grieving process over the loss of her marriage and the disturbing behavior of her children, I decided this was a good time to use the LEAD sequence to help her deal with her adversity.

L = Listen to the Adversity Response

I began by listening (L) to Samantha's response to her accumulated adversity. As much as her words revealed, it was Samantha's face, posture, and the lifeless tone in her voice that conveyed her state. "It's just unbearable," Samantha explained, her voice devoid of expression. "My whole life is ruined. I mean, look at this; I've lost my dream of a perfect marriage. My children are going down the tubes, I'm 43 years old, and I'm supposed to start from scratch and look for a new job." Samantha sighed. She continued with little expression.

"Come on, Paul, people like me don't just go out and find jobs. Let's be real! It's not like I'm marketable compared to what's out there." Samantha sighed again. "I've lost everything. I've tried to be a good mother and make things work with Tim, but nothing I do ever makes a difference. You remember years ago, I even got him into therapy, but he just blew it off." I gave my best noncommittal nod. Samantha went on. "I feel worthless. It probably doesn't help that I can't sleep, because I know I should have done something to save the marriage. I should have seen this coming. I just feel so *stupid*." Another sigh, another pause. "Everything's just crumbling around me."

E = Explore the Origins of the Adversity and the Ownership of the Outcome

Immediately my alarm went off. Samantha's adversity response was obviously highly destructive, and, as I thought back on our interactions over the years, I realized that, despite her cheery disposition, she probably had a low AQ. So, I employed the second step in the sequence, one with which women often struggle more than men—explore (E) all origins and ownership.

Heaping the entire loss of a marriage upon herself, as Samantha did, was pretty typical. So, separating my approach into two parts, I decided to start with *origin* first and work on *ownership* second.

Origin—Who's Really at Fault Here? "Samantha," I began, "it sounds as if you're blaming only yourself for this whole mess. Who, or what besides you might have caused the marriage to fail?"

"Tim had to work so hard. When he came home, he was completely drained. It was *my* job to work on the marriage." she replied earnestly.

"Isn't marriage a *partnership?*" I asked. "Do you really believe that one person can make any marriage work, especially one in which a partner is abusive?" Samantha looked up. I pressed on. "Is it really *all* your fault? Who or what else could have caused this marriage to fail?"

"Well, I guess Tim played a *part . . .*"

I slowly peeled back the layers of destructive self-blame which were blinding Samantha from the truth and incapacitating her. By repeating the question, "Yes, but who or what else could have caused this?" I helped her realize that Tim's emotional swings, his refusal to be treated for his emotional instability, his habit of breaking promises, his demanding and intrusive family, his work, and her insecurities about being alone had all contributed to the failure of the marriage.

"Given these multiple causes, what portion of the blame for this divorce is really yours?" I asked.

She looked toward the ceiling, thinking hard. "I guess maybe 40 or 50 percent," she finally admitted.

"Forty to 50 percent," I repeated slowly, for effect. "Hmm. That sure sounds a lot better than 196 percent! But, let's be fair, given

Tim's unwillingness to be treated for his vicious mood swings, do you really believe *anyone* could have made this marriage work?" I hoped to check Samantha's destructive self-blame.

"No, I guess not." she replied, almost smiling with relief.

At this point, Samantha had explored all origins for the adversity and put her role into healthy perspective. It was not my intention to have Samantha disown the bad marriage; I wanted her to *learn* from it. We spent ten to fifteen minutes reflecting on her role and what she could have done differently or better. She came up with a long, insightful list of past mistakes and potential corrections. She realized that she hadn't asked for support from others when she really needed it; hadn't been sufficiently proactive about guarding her health; there had been opportunities for her to protect her children; and she had played into Tim's games early in the relationship by giving up all her power.

I was impressed by her honesty and ability to own her poor decisions. It was clear that Samantha would be less likely to repeat the same mistakes in the future. "Did you ever think you'd learn so much from being married?" I asked rhetorically. Samantha, actually smiled. So, I moved on to ownership.

Ownership—Who's Accountable for Cleaning Up This Mess?

"Let's pause for a moment and think about the results of what has happened," I began. "You mentioned several outcomes, including losing your marriage, your children, your job, and your home. Can you think of any others?"

"None, except not sleeping, having endless headaches, having my digestive system tied in knots, suffering a chronic cold, and not being able to eat." Samantha's emphatic sarcasm showed significantly more energy than when she walked in the door.

"Okay," I pressed on, "that seems like a pretty good list. Let's start with something concrete. Who is responsible for finding you a new job?"

"I am. No one else is going to do it!" Samantha declared, as if being asked if the sun rises every day.

"Who is responsible for repairing your relationships with your children and helping them to get their lives back together?"

"I guess I am," Samantha suggested. "I owe it to them to help them get past this nightmare."

"And, who is responsible for your long-term health and getting rid of those headaches, digestive problems, that cold, and your insomnia?"

"Well, duh!" Samantha shot back smartly, showing her first real signs of life. "*I* am, of course! Don't be silly."

"I just want to understand," I explained, playing it straight. "So you are accountable for your employment, your health, and working on getting things squared away with your kids?"

"That's correct." Samantha went along. "So, where is this leading?" smiling at her unintended pun. I used Samantha's question as a transition into step three of the LEAD sequence.

Dealing with the Rational Brain—*A = Analyze the Evidence*

"You came in here feeling as bad as you can possibly feel. Right?"

"The *worst!*" Samantha exclaimed.

"So, I could just listen to you, validate your feelings, affirm you as a person, and show you that I empathize with how awful you feel. But would that make things any better, besides letting you know I care?"

"Hmm. Well, no, I guess, not really. Actually, I might feel worse! That sometimes happens with my friends." Samantha confirmed my strategy.

"I want to help you improve your situation so you don't feel this way anymore," I explained. "So, *that* is where this is leading." Samantha nodded her approval to continue. So I analyzed (A) the evidence.

"Let's go back to some things you said." I began. "You claimed that there is nothing you can do. That would mean that you have no control." Samantha nodded, her face briefly revisiting her earlier pain. "What evidence is there that you have *no* control?"

"Well, you saw what happened with Tim! I did everything I could to make it work, and the marriage *still* failed. None of my efforts made a difference! It's like all the women who are victimized by husbands that turn into monsters! And you know what?" Samantha didn't wait for my response. "I used to think they were *idiots!*"

"Yes, you obviously felt helpless. Now you're getting out. So, I repeat, what evidence is there that you have no control *now?*"

Samantha was stuck. "Well, . . ." she paused. "None, I guess, not *now*. It's just hard . . ."

"Oh, it *is* hard!" I interrupted, leaning in. "But isn't *hard* different than *impossible?*"

"I see your point," Samantha smiled, somewhat more relaxed.

"So you're saying there is no evidence that you have no control?"

"No, I guess not. *None.*" Samantha confirmed, slapping her thigh for emphasis.

I continued my strategy of analyzing (A) the evidence. "You said 'everything is ruined.' Is there any evidence that everything *has* to be *ruined?*" Again, Samantha tried to list reasons her life might be ruined. Again, I repeated my question. In time, Samantha's reply was, "None." There was no evidence everything *had* to be ruined. She eventually gave the same response when asked, "Is there any evidence that this has to endure for a really long time?" Samantha recognized that, realistically, it would take some time and effort on her part to get hers and her children's lives back on track. But, significant progress toward that goal could be made immediately. There was no evidence for it enduring longer than necessary.

"So," I asked, summarizing, "let me see if I've got this right. This is really at most 50 percent your fault, not 100 percent. There is *no* evidence, whatsoever, that you have no control, that everything is ruined, or that this situation has to last any longer than necessary?"

At this, Samantha thought hard. "No, I guess not." she said, as if something were dawning on her.

"Great! sounds like things are already improving!" I smiled, transitioning to the final step of the LEAD sequence, do (D) something! I reached for a pad of paper and a pen, pausing expectantly.

Taking Action—Do Something!

"So what could you *do* to regain some control?" I asked.

"Oh, I don't know." Samantha stalled. "I guess I could talk to my kids."

"Okay. What would that accomplish?" I asked, guiding her to clarify her thinking.

"It might show me that I can still make a difference in their lives by loving them. That would feel good."

"Great! What else could you do to regain some control?" I jotted down notes as Samantha slowly listed five more actions, including seeing her lawyer.

I continued moving Samantha toward action on limiting the reach of the adversity. "And what could you do to not let this situation get out of hand and ruin everything?" I asked.

"I guess I could get to work on finding a job and a place to live . . ."

"What could you do to get started?" I pressed for specificity.

"I could get my resume together, get customer recommendations, tell people I am job-hunting, and start looking at apartments . . ." Samantha offered slowly. I continued to write as she gradually brainstormed actions.

"And what could you do to make sure this doesn't last any longer than necessary?" Samantha listed more actions, including expediting the divorce and having dinner with her kids.

Funneling into Commitment. I moved in to apply the finishing touch. "So, Samantha, you've told me that this is, at best 50 percent your fault, that you are accountable for getting a new job, a new home and repairing things with your kids over time, and that there is no evidence that you have no control or that this situation has to ruin your life or last any longer than necessary. Right?"

Samantha nodded.

"You then listed," I counted ceremoniously, "twelve actions you can take to make things better. Which one will you commit to taking first?" I turned the list for her to see her own words.

Samantha reviewed the list, and said, "I'm going to take Joe, Ryan, and Lisa out for dinner first. They are my *top* priority." She stood up straight, looking determined and alive. "I can't *wait* to start to rebuild our relationship!" she declared excitedly, clapping her hands.

"Okay! *When* are you going to take them out?" I didn't want to let her off the hook.

"Tonight! Okay?" She smiled.

"Great! Would you like to use my phone?" I asked as I handed it to her. She grabbed it, laughing.

"This is amazing!" she exclaimed, "I walked in here in utter desperation, and within less time than it takes for me to put on my makeup you've got me laughing, ready to call my kids. I swear, I never thought I'd laugh again!"

THE GUTS OF LEADING OTHERS

Perhaps one of the most powerful aspects of the LEAD sequence is its universality. It can be used with virtually *anyone* who possesses the ability to reason. You will want to develop it as a tool to help your coworkers, friends, loved ones, customers, students, and followers. As in Samantha's case, you can customize the LEAD sequence to the people, responses, and the situation at hand.

Although this may *appear* to be a lengthy and involved process, it actually moves quickly, taking 5 to 20 minutes—far less time than is required for a person to complain about their woes. And, the process is simple. My conversation with Samantha can be boiled down to a handful of essential questions and a few follow-ups:

- Who or what might have caused this to happen?
- What or who else?
- Given this list, how much of it is your fault?
- What are the outcomes or results of this situation?
- Which ones do you own?
- You said [insert client's words]. What evidence is there that you have no control, that this has to ruin everything, or that it has to endure any longer than necessary?
- What could you do to regain control, limit the damage, reduce how long it endures?
- Which action do you want to commit to first?

By asking a closely related version of these questions, you will guide others to objectively analyze, dispute, and take action to improve their situations. From there you will customize the process to your style, the needs of the other person, and the specifics of the situation.

Let's assume, for example, that the individual you wish to help believes the situation is within her control, but will ruin everything and last forever. Obviously, you will not ask her, "What evidence is there that this is completely out of your control?" since she never said it was. You will quickly learn to focus on those aspects of the LEAD sequence which best fit the response to adversity.

Ask, Don't Tell

If you had a powerful new piece of information or skill that you knew would help someone you cared about, how would you let him know? What if you knew that, in order for it to help him, he would have to be able to really *get it?* Would you simply sit him down and explain it, or would you want to demonstrate it and let him try it out?

Although your common sense might say it is best to help a person experience a new skill, you might, in reality be greatly tempted to explain. In our zeal to impart new knowledge, we often forget our objective is to have others *learn* the information, rather than hear about it. In the case of the LEAD sequence, it is best discovered and experienced than simply explained.

So, the next time a close friend responds destructively to adversity, you might be tempted, armed with this new knowledge, to sit him down and say something like, "Okay, you're responding to adversity destructively right now, and I know how to help you. First, you've got to listen to your response, which was negative. Next, explore all causes," at which point you list them out for him. "So, as you can see, you're only 25 percent responsible, at best, for what happened and here is what you did wrong. But, you are accountable for the results [which you list]. Next, you need to analyze the evidence. There is no evidence that this is out of your control, *has* to ruin your life, or *has* to endure. So, next, you have to list actions and pick the one you want to take. Got it?"

Most people hate being told what to do. By telling your friend how to run his life, you have done nothing to enhance his learning, or to equip him for future adversity. At best, you've increased his dependency on you for advice! At worst, he feels stupid for not following what you just said.

So, a major part of the LEAD strategy is to *ask, not tell.* Notice that my entire conversation with Samantha was a *questioning* process. All I did was ask questions, which guided her quick and easy discovery and practice of the skill. Whenever you use the LEAD sequence, act as a *guide* not an expert.

When Listening Isn't Enough

Listening has its place and its value. Sometimes we just need someone to listen or to hear ourselves talk. Others' advice can be well-timed and well-received. Listening serves several important functions. It makes one feel validated, affirmed, heard, and cared for. Done right (and that's a heck of a qualifier), listening gives a person the opportunity to air emotions and thoughts in a safe environment. Clearly, this can be helpful healing and nurturing. All of these are reasons why listening is an essential ingredient of human connection.

Unfortunately, the benefits of listening can be limited by a person's AQ. Those with high AQs might use the listener as a sounding board, getting some things off of their chests, while using her insights to help them hone their strategies for action.

Those with lower AQs, however, are prone to appropriating the listener's strength and energy to prop themselves up temporarily. Or they may pull the listener into a cycle of neediness and despair or use self-expression as a way to reconfirm their feelings of low self-worth and powerlessness. This cycle results from their inability to sustain the optimism and strength the listener may have imparted. It's much like pouring water into a sieve. Over time, the listener feels drained or ineffective, while low AQ individuals feel increasingly more hopeless, dependent, and unempowered. They become weakened by their inability to go it on their own.

The moment Samantha came to me with her serious combination of problems I faced a choice—*to listen or to LEAD.* Before developing the LEAD sequence, I probably would have simply listened to Samantha, demonstrating my best, most genuine listening skills—empathizing with her feelings and reflecting my understanding of her problem. If I were successful, I might have given her the safe haven opportunity to open up and really talk things out. She could weep over her loss and desperation, and I could comfort her with my words and a soothing hug. She would thank me for my kindness, and I would thank her for her trust. She would feel better, and our friendship would deepen perceptibly.

By hearing herself talk and having a friend with a sympathetic ear, Samantha might have felt better, realizing things weren't as bad as she first imagined, or, she *might* have felt worse, going deep into her feelings and realizing most of what she cared about had been damaged by her involvement with Tim. Talking about problems is important for your mental and physical health, but it doesn't always make you *feel* better! Samantha could, therefore, feel either relieved *or* more burdened as a result of sharing her emotions. In either case, there is no indication that by simply listening to Samantha the *situation* would have improved, only her outlook, at best.

Avoiding the Advice Trap

If I fell into the classic advice trap, I would tell Samantha to go talk to her kids, or start working up a resume. I'd give her my best "go-gettem" pep talk and make her laugh, convinced that I'd made her feel better. As she drove home, however, Samantha would, due to her low AQ, start ruminating over her adversity once again. Or, she might have faced the reality of coming home to a place that no longer felt like home. All her feelings of being stuck, damaged, and powerless might have resurfaced. The chance that Samantha would have acted on my pep talk would have been quite low especially as time went by. The sense of relief, the seedlings of hope I might have planted for her would have been killed by her low AQ. So where would Samantha go the next time she needed to feel better? She would call me, or another friend prepared to offer *more* advice—creating a unsustainable, lose-lose cycle of false hope and despair. Instead of feeling empowered to act and equipped to take back her life and continue her ascent, Samantha would have, ironically, become more dependent on the help of others.

So how does one hang onto the powerful benefits of listening while avoiding its dangerous downside? The best way is to LEAD the person to a higher AQ. In Samantha's case, the LEAD sequence began with listening, but ended with her commitment to take action. Through the LEAD sequence, Samantha proved *to herself* that there was no evidence to support her destructive conclusions, while she simultaneously strengthened her accountability for the outcomes. In the future, every time she starts to ruminate or slide back toward a low AQ reality, she can return to our conversation and her declaration that no such evidence exists. It is extremely difficult to sustain a belief for which one has proven to oneself that there is no supporting evidence.

Samantha is also equipped with a list of specific actions—*her* list, not mine! These are strategies she devised to improve the situation. I have avoided the advice trap. I know, from some painful experiences, that my best-intentioned advice based on *my* reality may not be a hand-in-glove fit with another's reality, and may likely fail. She is much more likely to follow her *own* ideas.

So, as a result of using the LEAD sequence, Samantha *and* her situation have changed. She feels listened to, cared for, relieved, and empowered to act. Her relationship with her children has already improved through the simple act of calling them for a dinner date. Things are looking up, and forward momentum has been established out of what seemed to be a hopeless situation.

RETHINKING THE ROLE OF LEADER

Being an effective leader has traditionally required a person to master a broad list of competencies. Among these, leaders inspire, influence, create vision, guide, coach, serve, value diversity, strategize, live by example, take risks, drive change, mediate, communicate, show purpose, work with passion, and constantly renew themselves and others. Now, add to this list the ability to LEAD others through adversity. Put another way, leaders must coach their followers to deal with adversity more constructively. *This enlarges their capacity to follow.* Leaders face adversity every day, taking risks, creating a sense of team, guiding others through a minefield of uncertainty, juggling their own needs and the needs of others, or simply being under the constant scrutiny of and serving as an example for their followers.

The conditions under which a leader must lead are also adverse. The "if it ain't broke, break it" approach to running an organization and the "what have you done for me lately" pressures from outside stakeholders make leading an increasingly precarious art.

To demonstrate the importance of the relationship between AQ and leadership, imagine a low AQ leader. At best, he might be brilliant at creating a compelling vision, strategizing, and inspiring others. But, what use are these skills if the leader is incapable of persevering through adversity? If he has a low AQ, all of his skills become fair weather abilities, useful as long as the conditions are perfect and the path is smooth. Would you follow such a leader any sooner than you would board a plane which is ill-equipped to handle turbulence? When are the conditions ever perfect? Like the plane, the moment adversity strikes, the low AQ leader weakens, even fragments, becoming demoralized, dispirited, and disillusioned. In this sense, "leadership" and "low AQ" are mutually exclusive terms.

Flip the equation. Imagine a leader with moderate skills in visioning, risk taking, driving change, and motivating others. She also has a high AQ. By definition, she thrives on adversity, persevering where our low AQ leader gives up. Where she sees unsurmountable overhangs, our high AQ leader sees challenges worthy of even greater effort, creativity, and resources. What she lacks in polish and precision she makes up for in tenacity. In this sense, "leadership" and "high AQ" are synonymous.

LEADING A COLLEAGUE

Martha is a dedicated leader, with a compelling, unifying vision for helping educational institutions reinvent themselves for the future. As a former Superintendent of Schools, a professor of education, and university administrator, Martha has some clout and credibility. Currently, she heads a leadership development center at a major university. Her programs and expertise have been well-received by the educational community—her target market. When consulting for Martha, I learned that, unfortunately, she faces some major obstacles.

Due to the severe financial constraints handed down by the state government, most of the surrounding school systems were struggling with serious budget cuts. In the past, these teachers and administrators had hired Martha to conduct a variety of workshops and interventions, generating much of Martha's revenue. Now, these school systems felt forced to retrench, rather than think about the future. Ironically, the budget cuts were all the more reason to work urgently to reinvent the way schools educated their students. Nonetheless, Martha was realistically concerned over losing whatever momentum she had been able to establish, thus far.

As if to confirm her fears, during one of our meetings, Martha received an unexpected visit from Sharon, a superintendent representing one of the largest districts in the region. Sharon was clearly upset, so Martha introduced me briefly as her consultant and ushered Sharon into the office and shut the door. I was able to witness, firsthand, as Martha used the LEAD sequence as a natural leadership skill in helping Sharon cope with the budget cuts.

Sharon nodded toward me, and asked, "Is he okay?"

"Rest assured, anything you say in front of Dr. Stoltz is completely confidential."

Sharon trusted Martha's word and started right in as I listened quietly. "Martha, what are we going to do?" she asked desperately. "I mean, I just don't get it. Just as we're about to make some really important changes, our budget gets cut. Honestly, these legislators must be speaking out of both sides of their mouths. First, they value education, a week later they cut our funding! This is insane!"

"Yes, it *is* a challenge," Martha began, but Sharon was on a roll.

"Do you realize, our whole school system could crumble? We'll lose our best teachers, we'll lose more programs, and we'll never get the computer equipment we need. How can we upgrade our curriculum? I came here to help things *improve,* not lead this place back into the Stone Age! I just can't believe this. Honestly, our society must be going down the tubes! No matter how hard I try, this kind of thing always happens. . . . " Sharon was going on and on, catastrophizing the vote into an all-consuming disaster.

"Stop!" Martha commanded, while slamming her desk. Sharon was instantly silenced, stunned by Martha's abrupt gesture. Martha continued smoothly, in sharp contrast to her action. "Wait a second. Before we make this any worse than it already is, let's start at the beginning, with the vote. . . . " With this statement, Martha immediately derailed Sharon's catastrophizing, and began the process of looking at the problem.

Had Martha done what most of the educators around her were prone to do in the face of a budget cut over which they perceived no control, she would have commiserated with Sharon, and she would have held forth about the "backward thinking bureaucrats" and how helpless they were to do anything about it. They could have bonded by complaining and agonizing over their uncertain futures, their powerlessness to create change, and the sheer injustice of it all. This kind of support would have been expected and understandable, if not typical.

However, Martha was one of the original participants in the AQ Program for Educators. As a leader, she immediately recognized Sharon's low AQ response. She knew, from past experience, that, left unchecked, Sharon's response was likely to spread like a virus, infecting the school faculties, administrators, and students. Martha recognized the need to LEAD Sharon out of her destructive response pattern, into a higher, more constructive, proactive mind set. To begin, Martha had intuitively completed the first step of the LEAD sequence by, listening (L) to Sharon's response.

Martha took the second step, having customized the LEAD sequence to her own style over time. By listening to Sharon's response, Martha sensed she was blaming the legislators entirely for what had occurred. In addition, Sharon was showing no indication of owning the results of the cuts. She preferred to play victim, a mere puppet being moved about by the financial and political strings of the state legislature. So Martha decided to explore (E) all origins and Sharon's ownership of the outcomes.

"So what do you think *really* caused this budget cut, Sharon?" Martha began.

"Well, those shortsighted bureaucrats in the state capital, of course!" Sharon replied, as if being forced to restate the obvious.

Martha continued to explore. "Oh, I know it was their decision, but why do you think they made this decision, when they chose to increase funding on prisons, road construction, and other needs?"

"It's all about political expediency. You know, they change with the wind, voting for what they think the public wants."

"Go on," Martha urged.

"Well, I guess it's no surprise, the public doesn't value education," Sharon declared.

"And why is that?" Martha asked.

"Because they're stupid!" Sharon whined.

"Oh, come on now Sharon," Martha said calmly. "What's the *real* reason?"

"Because they don't see the value. They don't realize what we have to offer and what a good job we do with what we have," Sharon admitted.

"And why don't you think they *see* the value?" Martha persisted.

"Well, I guess it's because they only hear the bad stuff, not the good. The media presents a distorted image of who we are and what we do."

"Go on," Martha repeated.

"I guess what you're driving at is the budget got cut because the public does not understand what we're trying to do."

Martha persisted. "These are all good reasons, Sharon, but *why* doesn't the public know about what we're trying to do?"

Sharon paused. "Because we don't *let* them know!" she exclaimed.

"Ahhh," Martha said, as if to confirm Sharon's thinking.

As a leader, Martha was effectively using the LEAD sequence to guide Sharon toward learning from her mistakes, realizing some control, and taking some ownership for the result of the vote. In this way, Martha helped Sharon improve her thinking, accountability, and proactivity.

Martha continued her guided dialogue with Sharon. "So, what, if any, role did, or could you have played in this vote?"

"I think I see where this is going," Sharon confided, sitting up a little straighter. "As a leader of one of the largest school districts,

I helped this vote take place by being too passive about communicating our ideas, progress, and benefits to the taxpayer. I really just sat around and waited for this to happen. Even when I saw it coming, I didn't try to fight it, or balance the perceptions of the legislators."

At this point, Martha worked with Sharon to help her look back on the vote and learn from her behavior. Within a few minutes, Sharon had listed several actions she could have taken to help prevent the vote from occurring. Sufficiently convinced that Sharon no longer felt helpless and now saw her own role in the vote, Martha moved on to helping Sharon come to grips with the aspects of the budget cut she must own. She wanted to help Sharon stop complaining and start working toward solutions.

"Even though our information is incomplete at this point, what, specifically, do you think will be the fallout of the vote?" Martha inquired.

"Hmmm." Sharon paused. "I guess we can assume the computer funding is cut, that teacher raises are out of the question, and that the mentoring program will have to go. Freshman athletics may be on the chopping block, as well."

"Okay, " Martha nodded her approval. "Even though you didn't *cause* the vote, which of these things you mentioned as potential fallout are your responsibility? Which ones do you, as a leader, *own?*"

Sharon went on to describe how she felt complete ownership of the mentoring program and computer funding, both of which were her ideas. The other items were community issues toward which she could guide a resolution, but not demand one.

As a leader, it was important to Martha that she do more than help Sharon convince herself that this was not a crisis and there was much that could be done to minimize the damage and prevent such votes in the future. If Martha left matters there, Sharon might catastrophize the next setback, depending on her to, once again, help walk her through her destructive reaction. Martha wanted Sharon to learn that her adversity response, including catastrophizing was ineffective, and unworthy of repeating. She needed to help Sharon replace her current adversity response with a higher AQ approach. She accomplished this not by using her authority to *tell*, but to ask. She acted as a guide, not an expert.

"Before we go any further," Martha began, "let me see if I've got this straight. You said, if I recall correctly, that this vote would mean that the whole school system will crumble, you'll lose all your best teachers, and your school system is bound for the Stone Age. Do you believe these things will happen?"

"Well," Sharon paused, reflecting, "I guess not. I mean not *necessarily*. But, they *could*, if the budget cuts stick!"

"When challenges arise," Martha offered, "I find it useful to separate fact from fiction. Let's go with what we *know*, rather than what we might *assume*. Obviously this vote represents a financial setback for your entire school district. But, do you *know* for a fact that your district will crumble, the computers are doomed, and the Stone Age is around the corner?" Martha asked, smiling. "Or, are you *assuming* these consequences?" Martha waited, while Sharon gathered her thoughts.

"I am assuming those things, of course. But you must admit, Martha, it's only a matter of time before we see these kinds of consequences."

"Do you really believe that? Are these consequences our fate or are they preventable?"

Again Sharon paused. "I guess they're preventable, but that wouldn't be easy, given the way things are going . . ."

Martha took advantage of Sharon's insights to transition into action. "So, if I understand you correctly, there is no evidence that suggests these horrible things—loss of teachers, ruined programs, loss of computers—*have* to happen. You're just saying they could, if nothing is done to prevent them. Is that fair?" Sharon nodded.

"What could you *do* to prevent these horrible consequences? For example, what could you do to keep the computer program alive?"

Sharon shifted in her seat, sitting up even straighter now. "I guess I could seek outside funding. . . . Maybe I could form a strategic alliance with some businesses, kind of like what you did when your funding was cut!"

Martha moved toward a white board located on the far wall of her office and began to jot down Sharon's ideas. "Go on," she suggested as she gestured with the marker, "Go on."

Within several minutes, Sharon had dictated a board full of ideas to counteract all of the consequences she had feared most. Martha continued the process, stepping back from the board. "Wow!" she exclaimed as she looked things over. "You've got quite a list here! But sometimes a long list like this can become unmanageable. I always find it useful to prioritize. Take a minute," she said, handing Sharon the marker, "and prioritize these actions in order of which one you will take first, second, and so on. But, let me suggest," Martha added firmly, "that you not put a number next to any action you are unwilling to commit to taking."

Sharon grabbed the marker, and thoughtfully numbered all but two of the actions. "Those I need to delegate to John. He has a particular interest in teacher compensation issues," Sharon explained, referring to her assistant superintendent.

"What do you want to do with this list?" Martha asked, testing Sharon's commitment.

"Do you mind if I write these down?" Sharon asked. "I'd like them to be the focus of my next staff meeting. We've got a lot to accomplish before next school year, and we need to get cracking."

Calling a special staff meeting was the item which Sharon listed as number one on the board.

"When do you think you will call the meeting?" Martha asked.

"Today! Now! Right away!" Sharon declared vehemently. "There's no time to waste!"

"I need to pick up my mail," Martha explained, heading for the door. "Feel free to use my phone. I'll be back in a couple of minutes to wrap up this conversation." With that, Martha walked away, and Sharon grabbed the phone to begin the scheduling process for her meeting.

When Martha returned, she sat on the end of her desk, pausing, looking Sharon directly in the eye. "How would you describe what happened here, over the course of our conversation?"

"I guess I was pretty upset when I came in," Sharon responded thoughtfully. "I felt as though the walls were closing in on me. You helped me see where I went wrong and what I can do to make the best of the situation. Hah! I already put the wheels in motion for the meeting!"

"That's wonderful," Martha smiled. "But I want to point something out to you, and that is the *way* you got out of disaster mode and into action mode. Remember when I yelled 'Stop!'?"

"Yes, . . . yes, I do."

"I did that for a reason. You were catastrophizing over this vote. That does no one any good. I wanted to get you on track, so I interrupted that approach."

"It sure worked! You surprised the heck out of me!"

"Then I simply helped you prove to yourself that you were jumping to a lot of damaging, unfounded conclusions, based on limited information. You were basing those conclusions on *assumptions,* bad ones I might add, rather than what you *knew* to be the facts."

"Yes, and your system made the whole situation a lot more manageable. It put things into perspective!"

"You're right. Did you notice that there really was no evidence to support your initial claims of total ruin and destruction?" Martha continued the lesson. "Also, that, initially, you chose to blame the legislators and the public for the vote. The problem is, by blaming them entirely, you could miss the opportunity to learn from your *own* inaction, so you could be a more effective leader in the future, when the next challenge comes along, and it will!"

"Probably sooner than later!" Sharon agreed.

"Right! So, while you didn't cause the vote, you realized what you could have done to prevent it."

"Rather than being a victim, I became a participant." Sharon added, "I guess I had underestimated my own control over the situation, giving all the power to the lawmakers."

"Excellent," Martha praised Sharon for her insights, lack of defensiveness, and ability to learn from her own behavior.

"In conclusion," Martha said, "I have a few final questions."

"Shoot."

"How did you feel when you came in here?"

"Well, pretty awful. Desperate, like someone else had control over my destiny. I felt kind of helpless to do much about it. I was in real turmoil."

"And how do you think that state of mind might have affected your ability to lead your district?"

"Hmm. It really would have been pointless to lead," Sharon agreed. "I would have probably brought down my whole team. They would have been demoralized for months!"

"Yes, and how do you feel now?" Sharon paused, smiling, then turned serious.

"I feel strong. I feel as though I'm ready for battle rather than to be torn apart. I also feel a deep urgency to get going. I can't wait to prepare for this meeting!"

"Good," Martha affirmed. "And how will these feelings affect your ability to lead?"

"Oh, there's no doubt. I'll be able to help others deal with this challenge. It will be hard for them to harp on the downside and whine, like they usually do. I think I can propel us toward action," Sharon concluded as she resolutely brushed her hair from her brow.

THE TEFLON KID: LEADING YOUR CHILD TOWARD ACCOUNTABILITY

LEAD is especially valuable for helping to establish accountability within children. Many people consider raising teenagers to be a difficult task. My wife, Ronda, and I find it to be a constant source of amusement and learning. The other day our son received his Scholastic Aptitude Test (SAT) results in the mail. Holding the dreaded envelope, he had a sick look on his face, as if he already knew what was inside.

Like many parents, Ronda and I have always made it clear to our boys that we value education as a way to strengthen their knowledge, broaden their options in life, and enhance the contributions they can make over a lifetime. We also believe that aptitude tests are fraught with shortcomings as a way of assessing a child's potential in life, measuring, at best, two of the seven or eight main forms of intelligence. I have found AQ to be a superior predictor of success. In fact, Dr. Martin Seligman's work from the University of Pennsylvania revealed that students who had constructive adversity responses outperformed the predictions made by their SATs and grade point average, while those with destructive response patterns fell short of those same predictions. These differences became particularly obvious when they faced the adversity of mid-term exams. Students with moderate aptitudes who persevere will outperform high aptitude, low AQ students, almost every time. Other studies have demonstrated similar results.

Nonetheless, we have made it clear to our boys that taking aptitude tests is important and simply part of the game one must play if one decides to go to college. So, we knew our son was about to face one of life's difficult lessons. Despite the many resources, encouragement, and reminders we provided to help him prepare for the SAT, he simply chose not to take it seriously. This was a particularly big mistake, because, although bright, our son is the kind of child who needs to study diligently to do well on tests. In his mind, however, having glanced over a few sample tests nearly a year before the actual exam was sure to be sufficient preparation.

His moment of truth arrived when he opened the envelope and saw how poorly he had performed. But what was most interesting was his *response*. One of the endlessly amusing aspects of having teenagers is their creative attempts to influence their parents' thinking. In our son's mind, if he could get us to feel sorry for him, as if this were a reflection of a permanent condition such as stupidity, then he might gain sympathy instead of facing the harsh reality of the limited options he was in danger of creating by deciding not to study.

His first strategy was confusion. "I don't *get* this," he said with a genuinely lost expression on his youthful face. "I just don't understand what these mean."

So, we went along. "What does the form *say* it means? What do the little numbers indicate?" I asked with equal innocence.

So, he continued with his strategy of pretending that he had just lost his entire frontal lobe. "Geez! I don't know! I'm really confused." We waited, observing. "I guess it says I got these scores. I'm not sure." He looked at us expectantly. So we played along some more, watching him delay the inevitable. He was now visibly sweating.

Eventually Chase "realized" the meaning of his scores and percentiles. He figured out they were, in fact, dismal, and well below his potential. This was his response to his adversity: "Huh. Well, I remember I was tired that day, and there wasn't enough time to complete all the sections. I swear, the administrator was in a hurry. Everything went way too fast. There was no way I could have finished. Besides, I just don't test well on these kinds of timed exams." Chase's excuses would have been a little more palatable had he not scored nearly twice as high on the PSAT, a trial run for the SAT, a year earlier.

If Chase were allowed to walk away, believing his response, he would have perceived himself to be permanently incapable of taking major exams, and he would have learned little to improve his future performance. But it was essential to Ronda and me that Chase *learn* from this adversity so he could improve his options in the future.

Like so many children, Chase had to recognize his role in causing the adversity and own the outcomes that he had created. While too much self-blame is dangerous, a little can be very productive; otherwise, one becomes another victim-in-the-making. Having listened to his response, we chose to LEAD him to a more accountable, empowered response.

"Chase, you're blaming your low scores on the timing, the administrator, and the exam," I said. "What role do you think *you* might have played in creating these low scores?"

He looked at us and started another frantic attempt to sidestep his role. "Well gee, I, um, well, ya know, I did my best!"

"Did you?"

"Sure."

"Then why do you think you scored twice as high on the PSAT, which is, essentially, the same exam?"

Chase paused, looking down. "I guess, well . . . I guess I studied a *little* harder for that one."

"So does studying make a difference?"

"Yeah, well sure. But, I studied last summer!" Another desperate attempt to avoid reality.

"Do you think you could have done better on this test if you had studied more diligently?"

Chase smiled. He knew he was busted. "Yeah, I suppose so. It couldn't have hurt!"

Now it was time to explore (E) all origins and ownership. "So given the many causes you listed for these low scores, how much of it is really your fault?"

Chase paused, contemplating his answer. "I guess around half. The test was harder and the situation was pretty rough, but I know I could have done better than this!" he exclaimed, holding up the scores.

I tagged off, and Ronda took over. "Okay, that's fair enough, sweetheart. Now, what do you think might happen as a result of these scores? What impact will they have?"

Chase thought hard, his smile vanished. "I guess it makes it harder to get into some of the colleges I applied for." I found his honesty touching.

"It's hard, isn't it?" Ronda asked sympathetically.

Chase's eyes briefly welled up. "Yeah, pretty tough."

"What else do you think might happen as a result of these scores?"

"Well, I guess they might influence other schools and jobs I apply for." More painful honesty, more tears. This is the kind of remorse from which a child can *learn.*

"How important are these things to you, Chase?" I asked, knowing the answer.

"They're *totally* important. It's like majorly difficult to get anywhere without college, and jobs are super hard to get."

"So who's responsible for these outcomes if they occur?" I wanted to drive home the point that accountability precedes action.

Chase looked up, hurt that I would point out what he already felt. "*I* am, Dad. Who else *is* there?" We had reached the bottom. This was as much as it would hurt.

So, I briefly analyzed (A) the evidence as a way of clearing the decks for action. "Hey, buddy," I started, "you mentioned that you don't do well on these tests. Is there really any evidence that says you *have* to perform badly, or is it just challenging?"

Again Chase paused. "I guess it's just that these tests are so *hard* for me. Ryan finished every section. I didn't finish one!"

"So do you think you have to work harder than your friend to do well?"

"Yeah, totally, and it's not fair!"

"Okay, but are there things you do better than Ryan?"

Chase straightened up. "For sure! I am way better at music than he is. And I can make people laugh. Ryan tries hard, but he doesn't do so well." So we settled the point about "fair."

"Is there anything here, any evidence, that you have to do poorly, or below your potential on this kind of exam?"

"Well, no, not really. It's pretty much up to me." Chase was making the transition into do something! (D) very easy.

"So, what could you do to minimize the fallout from these scores?" I asked, pointing at the dreaded sheet.

"*Lots* of stuff." I just love the smell of empowerment. "I could study a lot more than I did," Chase admitted, smiling at his mistakes. "And I could practice so I get used to the timing, and I don't get so intimidated."

And so the conversation went. Chase listed several actions he could take, including making use of the flash cards, software, books, and practice tests we had provided him. He also decided to arrange to retake the test. He would start with taking a practice test, so he could measure his improvement and remain motivated.

At no point did Chase feel I was using some slick technique or magic bullet to manipulate his thinking. I was conversationally using a guide, much like a ruler to draw a straight line, to help him separate his potentially debilitating assumptions from the frustrating, but fixable reality. Chase didn't leave our discussion artificially pumped by my pep talk, and I didn't tell him what to do. I only asked questions, which helped him rethink his approach at a pivotal, formative moment.

Without the LEAD sequence, Chase might have remained convinced that his fate was sealed, dreading the thought of ever taking another test. He might have suffered in self-worth, future motivation, and hope. With the LEAD sequence, Chase was able to experience *genuine empowerment* by making conscious decisions to take action. This helped him spring back from this temporary defeat. He learned a technique for avoiding the common pitfalls of adversity, and dove into studying for the next SAT with newfound discipline and ownership.

THE HIDDEN BENEFITS OF LEADING OTHERS

Using the LEAD sequence benefits both the LEADer and the LEADee. In LEADing Samantha through her despair, I, as LEADer, benefit in several ways. First, I enjoyed the rich rewards of having a positive, meaningful, and enduring impact on Samantha and her situation. I left the interaction feeling like I did far more than patch a wound. I helped stop her *internal* bleeding and helped her begin to heal. I could reflect upon the layers of impact I might have had on Samantha, her children, not to mention her health! I know her immune functions are likely to rebound, her sleep and appetite will be restored, and her motivation to choose action over rumination is mounting.

Although the habit of response to adversity takes place in the brain, by LEADing Samantha, I've helped her repair her *soul*. Control, energy, hope, and a sense of empowerment are essential to and the result of replenishing the life-force within. A high AQ can restore what helplessness crushes.

Martha benefited from LEADing Sharon. Martha did an effective job of making it clear that Sharon was the source of resolution and action. Martha experienced the gratifying result of watching Sharon resolve her own situation, knowing full well that she will be fortified for the next one.

By LEADing Chase, Ronda and I helped our son experience and articulate the contrast between being a victim of a permanent condition, like stupidity, versus viewing the setback as temporary and taking charge of and finding a way to better the circumstance. Climbers have the habit of making the best of a bad situation, not by apathetically accepting their fate, but by actively and tenaciously *changing* the situation wherever and whenever possible. To the climber, prolonged helplessness is *not* an option.

Perhaps the most rewarding aspect of LEADing Chase was watching the realization dawn on his face as he started to own the results of his behavior and hold *himself* accountable for signing up, paying, and studying for the next exam. His sense of ownership fueled an unprecedented sense of discipline and purpose.

In LEADing Samantha, Sharon, and Chase, Martha, Ronda, and I also left a legacy. In accordance with the old Chinese proverb, rather than taking the quick and easy way out by simply putting a meal before them, we've taught our friend, colleague, and child to fish. In the future, when they feel down, or are emotionally hungry, they can feed *themselves*.

In Samantha's case, I also know that, in time, I've increased the chances that she will pass these skills onto her children, helping them innoculate themselves against adversity so they too can move forward and up in their lives, no matter what occurs. I think of having a high AQ as a powerful high altitude condition, where, unlike altitude sickness, you become *strengthened* rather than weakened the higher you go.

In a broader sense, you will benefit in these and other ways when you use the LEAD sequence to help others deal with adversity. You will be giving an enduring gift of love and compassion by helping those whom you care about.

As a manager or leader, you will help instill the climber's instinct in the hearts and minds of your people. You begin to create a climbing culture—a place where self-renewal, perseverance, risk taking, the embrace of change, and continual improvement are nurtured and required. Imagine the joy of leading an energized climbing team rather than a comfort-driven camping squad or a group of apathetic, cynical, energy-depleting quitters!

As a parent and/or friend, you help strengthen and rekindle the spirits of those around you. You provide loved ones with the essential tools to successfully navigate life and live with purpose and passion. Imagine raising a child whose natural instinct is to get tough and creative when faced with the kind of challenge that makes other kids quit trying or cop out. Your child can learn a whole new form of self-esteem, one based on the real rewards and proof of successfully confronting challenge after challenge. What greater gift can you give?

These same benefits can also greatly enhance your community and volunteer organizations. The ability to hardwire your brain to prevail through whatever is thrown at you is as important for a community, culture, organization, and team as it is for individuals. I am sure you can readily picture the difference between an organization based on finding ways to make things work, rather than reasons they cannot—a place which values and rewards the continual effort to move forward and up rather than sideways or, worse yet, backward in retreat.

By LEADing Samantha, Sharon, and Chase, Martha, Ronda and I also benefited by learning through doing. You probably had a moment in elementary school when a classmate in the next row leaned over and said, "Pssst. Hey, do you *get* this stuff?" And, although you weren't sure, you may have answered, "Um, sure, I think so." So the kid, whom you wished to impress, posed the challenge: "Could you show me how to *do* it?" You may have given it your best shot, explaining as you went, stumbling along at first. Then, a strange and mysterious transformation probably occurred. The more you explained, the more you understood! Soon, you couldn't wait to teach the next kid who leaned over to ask for your help. You learned by demonstrating and explaining.

This same phenomenon occurs when you use the LEAD sequence with others. The more you employ it, the better at it you become, not just with others, but within yourself.

The LEADee also benefits. First, she enjoys the immediate relief that comes from shining a light under her bed and proving no monster is lurking in the shadows. She realizes that there is no evidence whatsoever to support her worst fears and conclusions.

This realization provides her with the cognitive safety net, ready to catch and stop her the next time she begins to follow her old wiring. It's like putting up a "Road Closed" sign to prevent people from going down a path filled with precarious potholes and dangerous curves. Samantha, Sharon, and Chase now can stop themselves from pursuing that dangerous fork in their neurological roads.

By taking ownership of the outcomes of her marriage, Samantha feels a compelling responsibility, and with it, a personal imperative to take action and heal the damage. This helps her call forth her much-needed reserves to take on the remaining struggles of getting her life back in order. Sharon experienced similar gains by exercising her responsibility as a leader, rather than becoming a victim.

In all three cases, the LEADee also regains a valuable sense of perspective not just on his or her situation, but on what really matters. By acting upon her commitment to call and meet with her children, Samantha has addressed her top priority, as did Sharon by putting the wheels in motion to pull together her meeting, and Chase by committing to retake the SAT. As a result, each immediately senses positive momentum, if not a light at the end of their respective tunnels of adversity.

Only through the ability to persevere through adversity can empowerment truly be established and sustained. Those you LEAD, whether as a parent, friend, manager, or formal leader, will learn how to interrupt their destructive patterns and take on life's challenges with rediscovered resolve.

By asking a few basic questions, you will quickly learn to customize your approach to the person and circumstances. Over time, the LEAD sequence will become as natural as asking someone about their day. Once you experience the efficiency and effectiveness of this tool, you'll be hooked.

One particularly fascinating, fundamental, and far-reaching application of this technology is the ability to transform not just individuals, but entire organizations. As we explore some of the deeper issues and interdependent systems driving organizational behavior in Chapter 9, you will discover some powerful tools for creating high AQ organizations capable of climbing through any obstacle.

The High AQ Organization

Creating the Climbing Culture

A man does what he must—in spite of personal consequences, in spite of obstacles, and dangers and pressures—and that is the basis of all human morality.

John F. Kennedy

Unlike his usually jovial frame of mind during past company picnics, Al had a sick feeling in his gut as he wandered around the park shaking his people's hands and meeting their friends and families. "Come on Al, this is supposed to be a *happy* event," he told himself as he surveyed the 230-plus employees of Infocom's* regional technical support division, of which he was vice president.

"Well, at least *they* seem to be having fun," he decided, observing the disturbingly carefree expressions on everyone's faces as they cheered over the final, heated match between the top two sand volleyball teams in the company. They were competing for

---

* Although this story is based on actual people and events, Infocom is a fictitious name used here strictly to illustrate a point and is not intended to reflect on any existing company with a similar name.

the coveted Rubber Sun Chicken award—a hilarious tradition born out of a war erupted between two technical support teams over who could pull the best prank with a rubber chicken. Gradually the war subsided and the chicken, now nattily attired with Oakley sunglasses and Massimo surf shorts, became the unofficial mascot awarded to the team with the latest noteworthy accomplishment.

Al tried to join in, throwing out a few good natured cheers. "Hey Kromer, try blocking with your hands instead of your face!" he yelled, and several people laughed. "Hey Terry, pants him on the spike!" More laughter.

But, try as he might, Al just couldn't shake his malaise. Earlier that day, he had stopped by the office to pick up a few items for the company party. He zipped through his e-mail and punched up a message from his friend Mac, a highly respected engineer who happened to be working for one of Infocom's many competitors. The message included a copy of an article describing the anticipated fallout caused by impending legislation that would deregulate the entire telecommunications industry. Mac had, in his usual subtle fashion, highlighted one paragraph of the article. It was that particular paragraph that Al couldn't get out of his mind.

"The entire telecommunications industry will be dropped on its ear by this legislation," the author, a prominent business guru had prognosticated. "The old rules are gone, and so will be the companies still operating under them. The organization that wants to survive is going to have to be hungrier, faster, and more innovative than its competitors in meeting the needs of their respective customers. Look for unknowns to rock the marketplace as they emerge as the new service leaders, while today's leaders get suckered into the complacency-inducing pace of business as usual. Ironically, those who have enjoyed the greatest success in recent years are going to experience the greatest pain." Then came the shocker, "Watch the golden touch of Infocom, the *current* king, become tarnished as they are quickly blindsided by more agile, customer-focused up and comers. Unless Infocom rapidly discovers the painful and disciplined religion of reinventing itself, three years from now its stock won't be worth the paper it's printed on."

"Won't be worth the paper it's printed on." The words stuck in Al's mind. *Had* they lost their touch? Were they operating by outdated rules and on the verge of being blindsided by more nimble competitors? Were they destined to be just another business school case study of success turned into complacency? Al knew big changes were in the works and some players would lose, but he had never thought of Infocom as the Goliath another David might slay. Not until now. Yet, he couldn't shake the queasy feeling that they had somehow lost their edge. The signs were everywhere.

He reflected on Infocom's stellar rise from the chaos induced by the break up of AT&T. He fondly remembered how they had created several highly touted innovations that revolutionized the industry and made them the darlings of Wall Street. In those early days, there was *nothing* the company wouldn't try. They had the entrepreneurial spirit, and their stock price reflected their courage. "Maybe it was because we had so much less to lose!" Al reasoned to himself.

Not that their success had come without its rewards. In its early days, Infocom operated out of a crudely modified warehouse with its technical, sales, operations, and service people all in one room primitively decorated with used furniture, mismatched chairs, and a makeshift labyrinth of wires connecting phones and computers.

Al and the other members of "The Renegades"(the original Infocom crew) fondly referred to that first building as "the old garage." They tell newer employees stories of how they used space heaters on cold mornings to compensate for the lack of insulation and carpeting.

For a long while, they had no benefits, no perks, no security— *nothing* but an old desk, a phone, a business card, and boundless opportunity. But what Al could remember as if it were yesterday was the *energy* in the place. It was palpable and electrifying. There was this sense of being on an historic expedition. The Renegades were bonded by a powerful sense of purpose—to offer long distance service at affordable rates to every person in the country. They were out to be the good guys of the industry. It was that driving purpose which kept everyone going, working hard and playing hard. Their senses were keenly alert, always poised for the adventure that awaited each new day. The whole place was so *alive!*

Today, Al reflected, Infocom had come a long way from the "old garage." It was hard to believe that in a dozen years they had grown from a handful to more than 50,000 employees worldwide. Unlike the old days, everyone at Infocom enjoyed a generous benefits and compensation package that was the envy of the industry. The old garage had been replaced with successively larger buildings. In fact, Infocom's name now appeared across the top of one of the more prominent skyscrapers in downtown Los Angeles, where it housed its beautifully appointed corporate headquarters replete with tasteful art work and ergonomically correct chairs.

Now, Al recognized, it seemed people were putting a lot more energy into meeting with each other rather than their customers, and *keeping up* with their competitors rather than boldly leading the industry. Ever since they reengineered, people at Infocom had become increasingly focused on self-preservation. Many just gave up even trying to compete, let alone being the best.

Even in the best of times, their do-good purpose had been replaced with talks of market share and profit margins. No one mentioned the purpose anymore. Al wondered if they even *had* a purpose anymore other than profit.

He thought about a conversation he overheard in the food line at the company cafeteria the day before. "So, what made you pick Infocom?" A salesperson was asking someone whom Al sized up as one of the new technical hires.

"Because, let's face it, it's a *great* place to be," the sharply dressed young woman replied enthusiastically. "The people here are so nice, and it's obvious that you have a lot of fun. Besides, it's not, like, too *intense*. You know what I mean?"

She's *right*. We're not "like, too intense." Al realized. How many more are there like her? he wondered, who came here because we're nice, fun, and not too intense? It's ironic, he thought. It was *intensity* that got us here in the first place. Intensity about our *purpose*. Now we're just a "great place to be."

Al snapped out of his reverie and watched his fellow Info-commies (an affectionate team term) as they started to chant, "Chick-en, Chick-en, Chick-en!" preparing to hand over the coveted award to the winning team. Al sadly realized that it had been a long time since he had seen that kind of team intensity at work. As he pictured the young, new hire, he thought, "Maybe we're not intense *enough!*" He pondered what Infocom might do to bring back the entrepreneurial spirit, to remain competitive, and rekindle the excitement, innovativeness, and sense of purpose in the workplace.

THE RIGHT TIME FOR AQ

There are several factors that make the timing ideal for Al and Infocom to learn and apply AQ. These factors include:

- A threat to survival.
- The need to raise the bar on expectations, performance, and productivity.
- A need to rekindle their sense of purpose.
- Heightened competition.
- A pervasive sense of complacency.
- Greater need for creativity and innovation.
- A growing Camper mentality.
- A deep well of untapped potential.
- Limited tenacity.
- Facing greater adversity.
- Doing more with less.

These challenges are common to many organizations like yours that face renewed threats, competitiveness, and adversity. Like Infocom, the survival of most organizations rests on their ability to withstand and overcome continuous and mounting adversity. The greatest source of adversity for most organizations is the constant avalanche of *change*.

AQ AND CHANGE

Figure 9–1 depicts the classic change curve. The curve shows three phases. Phase One is *Endings,* when you depart from and stop doing what is familiar. This can be difficult for some people depending on the magnitude of the change. Larger changes tend to bring more difficult endings.

FIGURE 9-1   The Normal Change Curve

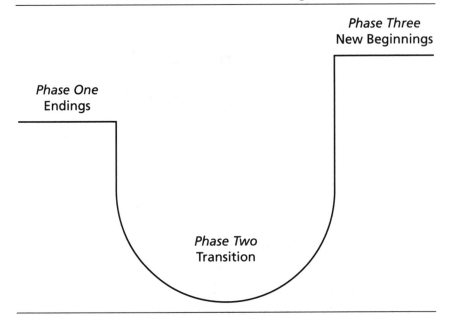

Phase Two is the *Transition* from the old ways to the new. This is the messy, costly, often demoralizing part of change. It is in the transition phase that people lose hope, motivation, and faith that the change can be successful and is worth doing.

Going through the transition phase can be like sailing across the ocean. Long into his journey to the New World, Christopher Columbus faced potential mutiny from a crew of weary sailors who weren't so sure they were going in the right direction. Luckily for Columbus, soon thereafter, someone on the ship spotted land.

Similarly, it is often at the point that change is almost successful that people are ready to give up. *The extra dose of optimistic perseverence is the deciding variable in successfully enduring the transition phase of change.*

Phase Three is *New Beginnings*. For those who are lucky enough to come out on the other side, this phase represents the adoption of new behaviors, systems, strategies, and processes—ways of getting things done. The length and depth of the transition phase, as well as how high the organization comes out on the other side greatly determines people's enthusiasm for the current as well as the next change. If one had to go through hell or if the New Beginnings phase is not a discernable improvement (higher) over the former state, people will resist change with newfound vigor.

Change and Competitive Advantage

Change itself is no longer a source of competitive advantage. True competitive advantage is determined by the *speed, magnitude,* and *direction* with which an organization can change. Speeding up the change cycle is entirely dependent on the readiness of the participants. If the people aren't on board, no amount of speeches and meetings will change a thing.

AQ is the determining variable in speeding up and strengthening change. Figure 9–2 depicts two advantages to creating a high AQ, Climbing culture. First, *a high AQ organization can greatly reduce the depth and width of the transition phase.* This reduces the individual trauma caused by change as well as how long it takes to get to the other side. It would be the equivalent of Christopher Columbus using a hydrofoil to cross the Atlantic. At such speeds, morale and endurance become less of an issue.

The second advantage is that *a high AQ organization can raise the bar on the where it emerges* at the New Beginnings. People who perceive change as possible and something they can influence are going to invest far greater and more sustained energy into the process, increasing their chances of success. A high AQ individual's automatic perception that the transition phase will pass and will not necessarily ruin everything also keeps his or her enthusiasm and energy strong.

High AQ individuals are simply more likely to embrace, drive, and persist through change. *A high AQ response to change also creates the momentum and organizational fortitude necessary to successfully navigate incessant change.*

Eliminating the Transition Phase

Many consultants spend considerable time building up the horrors of the transition phase. While it can be traumatic, *it doesn't have to*

FIGURE 9–2   The High AQ Change Curve

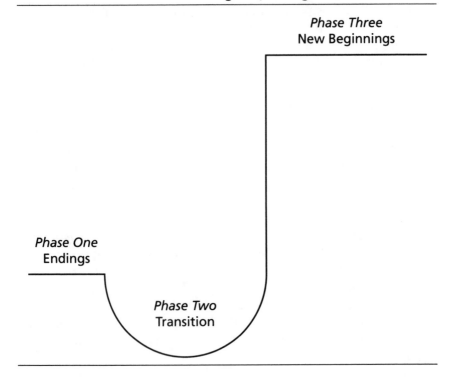

be. My experience is that the synergy that comes from high AQ teams can result in a leap from Endings to New Beginnings for low or moderate magnitude changes. The transition phase is virtually eliminated due to the combined energy, willingness, and persistence of the group.

Navigating change is just one of the many challenges you face as a leader which can be positively influenced by AQ.

CHALLENGES YOU FACE AS A LEADER

Regardless of your position, rank, education, or years at the job, I consider you a leader because you possess the ability to influence others toward mutually desirable ends. In other words, every time you make a positive difference in people's lives or impact the success of your organization, you are a leader.

Today, as a leader, you, like Al, face several questions:

- What does it take to remain competitive in turbulent times?
- What does it take to create and sustain a compelling vision of the future?
- What does it take to recover swiftly from reengineering, downsizing, and restructuring?
- What does it take to win back the hearts and minds of your people?
- How do you align the systems and processes within your organization to foster proactivity, entrepreneurship, and growth?
- How do you get out of the way so creativity can flourish?
- What does it take to reduce the costly downside of change?
- How do you get more people to embrace change right away?
- How do you encourage people to see change through to the end result?
- What does it take to create a cultural hardiness that enables your people to weather incessant change, continuing the Ascent?
- How do you, as a leader, help your organization keep its edge and maintain a healthy intensity?
- How do you create a Climbing culture when you're surrounded by Campers?
- How do you ward off complacency?
- How do you avoid becoming a victim of your own success?
- What does it take to reignite the Climb?

We cannot cover every angle of these complex questions in the pages that follow. However, much ground can be gained by exploring the powerful role AQ can play in answering these questions and in your organization's continuing success.

ORGANIZATIONAL AQ

Just as you can measure an individual's AQ, you can measure your organization's AQ. In my work with organizations, I analyze AQ in terms of:

- The rhetoric of the leader.
- Behavior and language after a setback or change.
- How the organization talks about current challenges and the future.
- The behavior that systems and processes reward and support.
- The degree of alignment between purpose, processes, systems, and behavior (do you walk your talk).
- The metaphors people use to describe their organization.
- The history of dealing with setbacks; stories and sagas; heroes and villains.
- The AQs of influential leaders (compared with others in similar positions and industries).
- The AQs of key teams or other key individuals.

I use a variety of devices for my analysis including:

- Written documents.
- Meetings, videotaped and live.
- Interviews, group and individual.
- The full-length Adversity Response Profile (results from leaders, teams, key individuals).
- The AQ Program as a way of providing language and tools to help an organization self-assess and improve in meaningful ways.

In short, I conduct a cultural audit, assessing the AQ and how the organization withstands adversity. But, unlike a traditional cultural audit, this analysis provides several unique and invaluable pieces of information.

- How well is the organization poised for major change?
- How severe and costly is the fallout likely to be?
- How quickly will people recover?
- How does this organization compare to others attempting similar change?
- What is the organization's CO_2RE profile? What does this imply?
- How can the leaders adjust their strategy and message to increase the effectiveness of the change?
- How is the organization strengthened or weakened (in terms of morale, energy, resilience, performance, and so on) by its AQ?
- Where is the greatest opportunity to improve alignment?
- How well is this organization poised for growth?
- To what degree is the organization fit for the climb?

Examining your organization through the AQ lens provides many insights into its readiness and capacity for adversity. In the process, you can make better use of your precious resources, among them time, money, energy, and *hope*. It is a cost-effective investment in preparing and aligning your organization for the future.

Once you've gathered this information, there are many activities you can undertake to raise your organization's AQ. Later in this chapter, there is a laundry list of 44 actions that will raise your organization's AQ and fortify it and your people for the adversity of competition, uncertainty, and change.

Leaders typically find it revelatory to consider, let alone improve their organization's AQ. As you begin to do so, you will discover that, as indicated in the above questions, AQ plays many important roles in your organization's success.

Taking Inventory

Pause and take an informal inventory of your own organization's AQ. There are many sources you can mine for valuable information.

Where to look:

- *Measure* AQ.
- Ask "old timers."
- Read memos, corporate reports, documents, policy manuals, and so on.
- Ask colleagues.
- Check out the corporate videos, newsletters, annual reports, and so on.
- Ask customers.
- Observe meetings and events.
- Look over the results from organizational surveys.
- Read e-mail and bulletin boards.
- Talk to leaders.
- Ask new hires about their observations.
- Listen to the informal dialogue around the water cooler, copy machine, and lunch room.
- Pay careful attention to how formal messages are crafted.

I find it valuable to write my findings in an AQ journal.

What to Look For

Although not as precise as the full-length Adversity Response Profile, language and behavior can reveal much about your team's and organization's AQ. Listen to your organization's CO_2RE.

- Does the language indicate a sense of control and ownership, or does it communicate that adversity is far-reaching, enduring, and out of control?
- How did people respond to the last change, initiative, or challenge?
- What metaphors does your organization use in describing itself?
- What stories do people tell about past challenges?

- What do leaders say when they face challenges?
- What do your team members do and say when they cope with an impossible deadline, a major change, or a significant demand?
- What are the cultural norms?
- What traditions or customs are in place that dictate what you and your team should do when faced with a seemingly insurmountable challenge?
- What are informal and formal rules for what is and is not an acceptable response to adversity?

A great way to uncover rules is to observe behavior. Then ask the individual why she did what she did. Keep asking why, as each question goes a level deeper, until you hit bottom—the underlying, often unspoken rule for that behavior. Such rules or norms are very influential agents on organizational behavior.

These powerful facets of your organization's culture have an enormous influence on employees' behavior and how they respond to adversity. They provide insight into whether your organization is more likely to quit, camp, or climb.

What to Do with the Information

Once you've collected the data about your organization, you will have a much clearer picture of how and why individuals behave the way they do. This picture serves as a meaningful starting point for addressing a variety of needs and undertaking any number of improvements. These might include:

- Teaching your people about AQ and the Ascent.
- Preparing for creating and sustaining purpose, vision, and values.
- Leadership training/coaching in using AQ to adjust the organizational norms, language, and customs.
- To adjust and strengthen your hiring processes to select Climbers.
- Reenergizing people around their work.

- Integrating the information into a comprehensive change management program.
- As a baseline for a performance management program.
- As a teambuilding device, strengthening the team AQ.
- As a framework for culturewide change.
- To examine diversity issues and balances of power and control.
- As a source for meaningful dialogue among top management and, depending on the level of openness, throughout the ranks of the organization.
- As a starting point in your effort to create a high AQ, change-resilient organization.

You will quickly become adept at spotting high and low AQ indicators throughout all facets of your organization. Every process, document, system, procedure, speech, meeting, and exchange will reveal nuggets of insight. I spot these indicators continually in my clients' organizations.

For years, Deloitte & Touche LLP, a big six accounting firm, used a particularly intense process for selecting who would be promoted to partner within the firm. After initial rounds of nominations, applications, and interviews, final candidates were invited to a selection conference. There they were closely scrutinized for their ability to act and perform as partners. Some of the aspirants would make it, and some would not. The pressure placed upon them was palpable.

Many of the candidates equated the conference to boot camp. They felt under the gun the whole time. The selection committee watched how they ate, talked, presented, interviewed, and worked together as teams.

Partner candidates were placed on teams of 6 to 8 people. The team project required members to work through the night strategizing, gathering data, preparing visual aids and a final report. They had to answer a hypothetical client's needs swiftly, thoroughly, and professionally. Over the course of the event, some people became frustrated, angry, bitter, and withdrawn. Others rose to the challenge with even greater determination and focus. Their final trial was the presentation they gave to the selection committee, which posed as the client.

Midway through the second sleepless night, with two hours remaining until the presentation, a partner from the selection committee entered the room where one of the teams was frantically putting the finishing touches on its presentation. He announced a new piece of information which, if believed, would render useless everything the team had done up to that moment. He then sat back and watched the reaction unfold.

One candidate instantly freaked. "Oh my God! We're ruined! We'll never get this ready in time, and everything we've got is worthless. They just trashed our entire careers!"

Catastrophizing is contagious, so another candidate joined in, throwing his pencil down in disgust: "I can't believe it. We totally blew it. Don't you guys get it? We were supposed to know this a long time ago, but we didn't do our job, so now we're sunk."

Just when the response seemed out of control, Bruce Thompson rose. "Now wait a minute. Up until a few seconds ago, we were feeling pretty good about our presentation. I think it's great! What if they were trying to throw us for a loop, just to see what we'd do? If we freak out, you're right, we are ruined. If we keep our heads, we can make a few minor adjustments and nail this presentation. I say we stick to our guns and show them what we're made of."

Unaware that they were being put to the same test as the others, Bruce's team rallied around his leadership and broke through the adversity. Other teams did not fare as well. One team completely self-destructed. Despite their enormous talent and experience, they were unable to overcome the obstacle placed before them. Bruce (a pseudonym) and many of his teammates were promoted to partner; those who demonstrated a low AQ were not, including the candidate who panicked. The selection committee was testing what they considered to be the most essential partner-level skill of all—the ability to respond to and overcome adversity.

Deloitte & Touche recognized that only those people who were able to persevere, innovate, and remain strong when faced with the relentless onslaught of adversity would succeed. AQ plays the same essential role in any business and institution which hopes to endure and thrive in the current adversity-rich climate.

THE ROLE OF AQ IN ANY ORGANIZATION'S SUCCESS

AQ applies to teams and organizations in the same way it does to individuals. In fact, as with individuals, AQ defines an organization's ability to withstand and climb through adversity, and with it much of its success. It largely influences agility, resilience, and persistence when navigating and creating change. It also impacts an organization's learning, creativity, productivity, performance, longevity, motivation, risk taking, improvement, energy, vitality, stamina, health, and success.

Resilience, Stamina, Persistence

At the bare minimum, people in an organization with a sufficiently high AQ demonstrate the ability to readily surmount obstacles. They are fueled by each new challenge. Individuals persist through uncertain and difficult times, embrace change, and take the necessary risks to further the Ascent. They demonstrate the essential resilience when faced with the setbacks and disappointments which are an inherent part of organizational life.

I discovered this organizational resilience firsthand, when I worked with Deloitte & Touche Tomatsu in Eastern Europe. In contrast to their American counterparts, these professionals face threats, violence, political upheavals, military takeovers, and rampant corruption as a part of their working lives. I listened as they responded to this adversity. "Some companies can't hack it." Peter, a partner in the Moscow office, explained. "They fold up their tents and leave town at the first sign of violence. Not us. We're in it for the long haul. When someone shot at our managing partner, we increased security immediately, but we didn't leave town. He didn't miss a day at the office. . . . We'll make it work. You just have to persist."

It was no surprise when, later that day, I measured everyone's AQ and found these professionals scored, on average, nearly 20 percent higher than their American counterparts. Their AQs played an essential role in jobs which demanded the ability to stick it out.

You may not be literally dodging bullets, but don't you face the magnitude of adversity which warrants exploring the role of AQ in bolstering your organization's resilience and stamina?

Prior to the AQ Program, participants typically receive a quick, confidential questionnaire asking what adversity they are facing in their work. No matter what the industry, the lists are virtually the same. Typical responses include competition, sustained growth, doing more with less, globalization, some recent change initiative (or 2, or 3, or 4), reengineering, diversity issues, performance, communication, uncertainty, and a mounting sense of pressure—in short—*adversity*. Isn't your organization facing many of the same issues as everyone else?

These issues are always there; how people deal with them will determine your organization's resilience, stamina, and persistence, and ultimately, its success.

Creating a Learning Organization

Peter Senge, author of *The Fifth Discipline* and leading expert on learning organizations, defines them as "an organization that is continually expanding its capacity to create its future." Implied in this definition is the ability to gain, grow, and improve as a result of new knowledge. Many top companies have integrated the philosophy and practice of learning organizations in their quest for competitive advantage.

AQ influences your ability to create a learning organization in two ways. First, it impacts the ability of your people to learn. As Carol Dweck and others have shown, given people of equal intelligence, those with higher AQs tend to learn more than those with lower AQs.

Second, it enhances your ability to successfully persist through transformation. The whole concept of being a learning organization is grounded in the notion of continuous improvement, enhancing knowledge, renewal, and frank and open dialogue—all of which bring with them the ability to overcome adversity and sustain hope.

Such transformations do not take place easily. They require great patience and fortitude. When I worked with Motorola, the company was going through the unwieldy process of instituting a worldwide learning loop requiring every employee to provide feedback to the organization four times a year. The loop was designed to improve performance, job fit, employee loyalty, and organizational knowledge. The change process was enormous, involving 120,000 employees in dozens of locations and cultures.

The obstacles were too numerous to list, not the least of which was individual resistance to yet another demand on one's time.

Along the way, there were numerous opportunities and reasons to throw in the towel, or stop short of the company's objective of 100 percent participation. New issues arose, new initiatives vied for Motorola's attention, and everyone was stretched to the limit. Yet Motorola persisted in their goal and has reached virtually complete implementation of this powerful learning initiative.

Motorola has all the signs of a high AQ organization, having demonstrated tremendous resilience and agility for a 30-billion-dollar corporation. Their ability to persist through the skepticism and transition phase of their global change effort earned them the competitive advantage of becoming a learning organization.

Creativity and Innovation

High AQ organizations are more creative. Fueled by the explicit and implicit belief that there must be a way to succeed, the high AQ organization finds methods to do more with less when up against the wall. In Chapter 1, I described how Lee Iacocca refused to throw in the towel on Chrysler and how, through tremendous tenacity and a high AQ, he rescued the company from the brink of bankruptcy.

An instrumental part of that recovery was Chrysler's response, which was to innovate in the face of adversity. They invented the minivan which changed the automotive industry and led to a $1-billion investment in a new, state-of-the-art design facility. Out of that facility has come an unprecedented stream of creative designs which have fueled record revenues. Chrysler's AQ was manifested in its response to adversity: *Innovate or die.*

Each year the Blue Chip Enterprise Award is presented to small businesses which prosper in the face of adversity. In 1996, when the major airlines capped the commissions they pay to travel agents, the agents knew they were in for some rough weather.

As reported in the *Los Angeles Times*, the 1996 winner, Montrose Travel, near Glendale, California, responded in a creative, high AQ fashion. Rather than ruminating over their impending doom, they immediately revised their incentive systems and training for employees to focus their energies on selling and service, rather than administrative chores. They dropped unprofitable accounts, shaved some overhead, and mounted a marketing effort, just as their competitors were starting to respond.

The result was the highest revenues in company history. Joe McClure, Montrose's president summed up his company's high AQ response, "A lot of agencies adopted a woe-is-me attitude" after the airlines instituted the caps. "We looked at it as a growth opportunity." AQ companies get creative when adversity strikes; others lie down and whimper.

Organizational Health

As with an individual, an organization's immune system—its ability to weather challenges without becoming ill—is affected by its AQ. I define organizational health as the ability of its functions, process, systems, and people to sustainably continue working interdependently and with integrity at full capacity. Organizations, as interdependent systems of people, can develop the hardiness to withstand hardship without becoming weak and frail. This applies not just to corporations, but to institutions as well.

While working as a faculty member heading up a new program in organizational communication and change at Northern Arizona University, I experienced the relationship of AQ and organizational health firsthand. The nationwide rash of downsizings had finally hit my university. The taxpayers were in no mood to fund what they perceived as excessive overlap in programs and an underutilized faculty. So, the state legislature delivered a significantly scaled-back budget. As a result, the president of the university announced that we were about to be "rightsized."

Some departments immediately rose to the challenge. They set about improving and establishing the value of their programs. They took a good hard look at their budgets and curricula and came up with viable cuts.

The response among the faculty in my department, however, was largely one of gloom and doom. Despite the urgings of certain young members to work with the president to arrive at a creative solution, the majority's instant response was, "There's no use."

They believed that nothing they could do collaboratively would make a difference.

Convinced that the president had it in for them, the faculty responded by entering the rightsizing forum ceremoniously dressed in black. They sat and brooded near the front of the stage. Departmental meetings quickly became rumination sessions riddled with paranoia—suspicions of spies, covert gatherings, and secret deals.

The following weeks were spent trying to retrench in desperate defense of the department. Budgets were examined and presentations prepared with a pervasive feeling of "Why bother?" or "They're obviously out to get us."

The stress of viewing the adversity as far-reaching, inevitable, out of their control, and enduring was taking its toll on many individuals' health. People suffered from insomnia; many became ill. The adversity was visible on most of my colleagues' faces and in their work. Absenteeism skyrocketed as quickly as did the talk of potential lawsuits to block the rightsizing. A warped game of one-upmanship emerged, in which professors exchanged stories of how badly they felt, how little they slept, or how much they were suffering. The department became progressively ill as well.

Trust was shattered, political coalitions formed, communication became highly dysfunctional, teaching was put on the back burner for many, and students, our customers, became the *real* victims.

Personally, this was an extremely trying time. I was under enormous pressure to join different factions, with the implicit threat of being blacklisted if I did not. As a then-untenured professor, blacklisting would mean professional suicide. Many of the people who were most vocal in their destructive charge against the upper administration were the same individuals who would assess me for tenure. The first challenge emerged when I was instructed to wear black and join the faculty at the rightsizing forum. For me, this was a professional moment of truth. With two young boys and an equally young career, I was keenly aware of the potential consequences of my decision.

The morning of the forum I went for a long walk in the woods. There I revisited my mountain—my purpose in life. Recognizing that my purpose was to help the *students* in a positive, meaningful, and enduring manner, I could not, in good conscience, join the majority. With firm resolve and Ronda's support, I symbolically sat apart from those dressed in black. Their displeasure was readily apparent as I politely ignored their encouragement to join them.

From that moment on, my relationship with the majority of my faculty would never be the same. But my relationship with life and what mattered most grew ever stronger.

With the small minority of other faculty, I kept out of the fray. Not coincidentally, they were some of the top professors in the state. I spent the remainder of my faculty career working to help the students weather adversity—a survival skill for university life.

The majority of the faculty, on the other hand, poured its energy into what they largely perceived as a hopeless battle with adversity. One senior member even became the symbolic martyr of the victimized faculty when he suffered an emotional breakdown in the president's office. He was eventually demoted, resulting in a significant cut in pay.

Despite its doomsday scenarios and enormous suffering, the department was spared from the rightsizing ax. Nonetheless, the low AQ response to the adversity—seeing it as their imminent and permanent destruction—ravaged the effectiveness, productivity, and health of the department. It affected the entire university. The organization's immune system was not strong enough to withstand the hardship it was dealt. This department continues to be referred to as "the cancer of the university" by upper administration.

I think it's important to point out that, due to their low AQ response, the faculty suffered as if they were all going to lose their jobs, unleashing massive stress and uncertainty. Due to their organization's AQ, their immune functions suffered in much the same way their department suffered. Yet, the ill-effects of the adversity were all self-induced. The rightsizing never occurred, but the ripple effect that their *response* caused was tremendous.

Performance and Productivity

Bottom line: High AQ organizations outperform lower AQ organizations. It is often the rhetoric of the leader which guides how its people respond to adversity. The power of rhetoric is perhaps best exemplified in that of Lillian Vernon, pioneer of the Lillian Vernon mail-order catalog business, a $222 million per year company. "Everyone stumbles," says Vernon. "The true test is how well you pick yourself up and move on . . ." Vernon's high AQ approach to the cutthroat catalog business has pervaded her organization, making it a top producer.

In contrast, I did some work for a government agency that responded to each adverse event as if it was the end of the world. When some Washington officials announced Reinventing Government—the major federal cost-cutting initiative, their immediate response was, "Oh boy. Here it comes again. Same old stuff. It's just another way of big brother stealing more power and keeping us in our place. Nothing you can do about it, so you might as well take it."

Again, the consequences of a *response* can be as severe as any adversity. Adopting a stance of victimhood, whining, helplessness, and passivity resulted in the eventual elimination of the agency. They created their own destiny by predicting and acting according to the worst case scenario.

Longevity

An organization's AQ, as influenced by its leader, can have a direct impact on its longevity. It makes sense that only those companies that are able to remain agile, driven, and resilient in the face of adversity can remain.

Take the example of the Federal Employees Credit Union (FECU). As Florence Rogers, CEO of FECU turned to address seven of her top managers, an explosion ripped through the room tossing Rogers hard against the far wall. The entire building collapsed and all in attendance but Rogers plummeted to their deaths. In all, Rogers lost 18 of her 32 employees.

As a survivor of the Oklahoma City bombing—the worst terrorist event in U.S. history, Rogers could have certainly panicked or catastrophized, and with good cause. Seven hours after the bombing, however, Rogers held an emergency meeting of her board of directors. They felt an enormous responsibility to their members.

The examiners warned Rogers that they would instantly lose most of their assets as people pulled their money from the credit union. According to Rogers, that never happened, primarily because she and her remaining employees reacted swiftly to retain their members' trust.

They refused to let the adversity ruin everything nor endure any longer than necessary. Rogers and her people sent out a press release letting people know they would open temporary quarters *within 48 hours*. Their strategy worked. According to Rogers, "Our members were so awed and overjoyed they could use their ATM cards two days later, they wouldn't have left us for anything."

The most difficult part of recovering was hiring replacements for the workers who had been killed in the explosion. "We warned everybody we interviewed that the work would be hard and the conditions adverse." Rogers explains. They sought high AQ workers.

FECU's quick, agile, high AQ response literally enabled it to save itself from the rubble and live on. As a result, FECU grew faster than ever, increasing its assets in 1995 by $3 million.

Clearly, as with individuals, AQ plays a major role in all facets of an organization's success. Given this knowledge, we must consider what prevents an organization from responding as constructively as possible to adversity when it arises. I have discovered that not everyone operates by the same rules, or code.

ROADBLOCKS TO CREATING A
HIGH AQ ORGANIZATION

At a recent AQ program, a CEO of a public utility company stood up in the middle of a discussion and, turning to the whole group, asked, "What do you do when you want to Climb and you've got an organization full of Campers?" His question drew a spirited round of applause and shouts of approval from the room full of leaders.

This is, perhaps, a leader's greatest frustration—trying to lead a climbing expedition, while most people simply want to stay behind in the comfort of the camp.

Campers' Code

Who can blame the Camper? The campground is a safe haven—it offers protection from the harsh, incessant winds of change.

Remember, the greater the adversity, the more people want to camp and the fewer seek to climb. After facing wave after wave of reengineering, restructuring, downsizing, and growth, people want to hide, lie low, and camp out. The incentive to climb has been all but destroyed as organizational purpose becomes clouded or compromised. Even if one survives each new assault, there is no guarantee of future employment or security.

The campground, on the other hand, provides an *illusion* of security. Even in this harsh era of doing ever more with less, the campground is still a relatively comfortable place. Most importantly, one can hang out with other Campers. It is simply easier and deceptively safer to camp than it is to climb.

Justifiably, Campers view life through the Camper's lens, approving and disapproving behavior that either fits or violates their perception of how the world should be. They live according to what I call "the Campers Code."

According to the Campers' Code, it is understood that life should be comfortable, secure, stable, and fun. Ideas and behavior that strengthen the campground are good; those that threaten it are bad. The Campers' Creed is, "The campground is sacred: Preserve it at all costs." Anything that threatens the campground is unwanted, anything that enhances the campground is well-received.

These beliefs and behaviors self-perpetuate. Campers, therefore, tend to affirm, validate, and promote camping behavior. They like to have others around them who also reflect their Creed.

Because they are usually the largest group within an organization, Campers have a strong gravitational pull on its culture. They consciously and unconsciously attempt to align the explicit and implicit rules, norms, assumptions, processes, and pace with their code. They may use any of a variety of techniques to bring campground-threatening change to its knees: going through the motions, giving it lip service, putting energy into other areas, aligning stakeholders against it, and slowing the change process to a crawl. Campers may be subtle and nonconfrontational, gradually killing any new rule, policy, or initiative that threatens the campground.

Without malice, a new but potentially destabilizing growth initiative can be gently ignored, or subtly submarined, but never aggressively pursued. Other initiatives are carried forward, only to a certain extent, but then suddenly and mysteriously lose momentum. You, as leader, become stymied in the process, as each new initiative is given words without life, and no real change takes place. Campers create the self-fulfilling prophecy that the more things change, the more they stay the same. They put a lot of energy into creating a culture consonant with the Campers' Code.

One of my clients invested a great deal of money into crafting a new vision. The top executives went around involving everyone in the process and holding visioning retreats. As the new vision took shape, it became clear that it would demand a newfound sense of focus and a realignment of resources and systems. In other words, *it threatened the campground.* Jobs would change, people would be moved, and many would have to be retrained or seek other employment. So, people participated—they wore the t-shirts and sang the songs. They integrated the new language into their meetings, memos, and presentations. But, when it came time to put the vision into action, the employees ignored it, and no real change occurred.

Even great organizations can get sucked into camping. Today's marketplace is rife with examples of organizations that have lost the edge or are fighting desperately to keep it. Earlier I described how Microsoft, renown as an industry leader, had to quickly scramble to catch up with its smaller competitors in providing Internet services. Its admitted initial complacency regarding the potential of the Internet had forced it to be reactive rather than proactive in claiming market share in that explosive industry. Blinded by its success in developing operating systems, like Windows 95, Microsoft almost missed the Internet bandwagon. It then had to run to catch up. Microsoft's story is far from unique.

In the late 1980s, Oracle Corporation and its founders, Larry Ellison and Robert Miner, could do no wrong. By using IBM's newly developed programming standard, called SQL, or structured query language, Oracle created a new degree of flexibility for its customers. Oracle grew from $1 million in 1980, more than a thousand-fold within a decade to over a billion.

However, despite their initial vision and ability to surmount the adversities of their highly competitive industry, Ellison and Oracle became arrogant, Camping on their successes instead of anticipating the next overhang. Oracle began losing market share and sales to competitors as Digital Equipment Corporations' VAX mainframe computer became less popular and the next round of miniaturization took hold. Oracle's complacence nearly destroyed the company.

Computer giants such as IBM, Digital Equipment, and Apple all have scrapped to recover from devastating losses of market share and drastic cutbacks in their workforces caused by the arrogance and sluggishness often brought on by success. These companies camped and became soft, while others climbed right by them during the storm. Soon they were forced to *Climb or die.* Each of them has renewed its effort to Ascend.

To understand why some organization's camp while others climb, you must consider two opposing facts. First, *inside every Climber lives a Camper.* This applies to individuals as well as organizations. Climbers must, therefore, fight the gravitational pull to rest on their laurels. The lure of stability, comfort, predictability, and calm inside each of us cannot be ignored. The crazier the world gets, the more we seek these qualities in our lives. Ideally, we camp just long enough to refuel for the Ascent ahead. Certainly, we all seek these refuges to varying degrees. Yet when these urges are carried out in an organization, they can ring its death knell. You have probably noticed that the longer you go without exercise, the harder it is to work out. Likewise the longer an organization camps, the harder it becomes to Climb. While it camps, a more agile, determined, higher AQ team of Climbers passes it right by on their way up.

Second, everyone is born with the core human drive to Ascend. In other words, *inside every Camper lives a Climber.* Your job as a leader is to free the Climber inside others so that the critical mass of energy shifts toward the Ascent and a Climbing culture—one based on renewal, continual improvement, purpose, and learning—can emerge. In this way you, the people around you, and your organization can fulfill their potential and ultimately succeed.

When Greatness Is Buried Within

As a college professor, in addition to teaching, I advised students in our department. One day, every student I saw was struggling with a deep sense of uncertainty about his or her future. I would ask each of them, "What do you visualize? What matters to you most?"

Each student answered in exactly the same way. "Well, it's like . . . it's like I just *feel* something *inside* of me sometimes. I mean, I feel like I'm destined to do something *great,* something really *important.* I just don't know what it *is.*" I was taken aback, not so much by the identical nature of their responses, but with the *intensity* with which they spoke. To each of them it was clear that they possessed something special. They felt as though they were given a mantle of greatness.

As a coach and consultant, I see the same private belief of greatness in people from all walks of life. It's just hidden beneath layers of compromise, rationalization, and numbing demands.

We all have that core human drive to Ascend. For some of us, it has just been buried deeper and requires more work to unearth, but unearth it we must. Time is ticking by, and it doesn't care how we live our lives or whether we live it at all. Inside every Camper is a Climber. As a leader you can help people revitalize that sense of greatness inside of them by LEADing them to a higher AQ. You can also provide a high AQ culture which is aligned toward and nurtures their individual and collective Ascents. They benefit, you benefit, and your organization truly benefits.

Getting your people to remember their greatness is but one part of the leadership challenge. The second part is to create organizational processes that serve as stepping stones rather than stumbling blocks along the Ascent.

The Alignment Challenge

In many organizations, the systems and processes that guide behavior are not in alignment with a Climbing culture. I run into many concerned leaders who struggle with how to align their organizations toward the Ascent.

> *Jeff, director of manufacturing, set down his drink and listened while Phil, his coworker and district sales manager poured out his guts. "We've got to find a way," Phil exclaimed. "My people are dying out there. We tell them they're empowered, we tell them they're in control, and then, every time they take a risk or fail, they get shot in the foot for trying!"*

*"What exactly do you mean?" Jeff asked as he took another sip of wine.
"Well," Phil continued, "look at the big local service initiative which we helped launch. Behind all the glitz and fanfare, the whole message is about our people delivering better service and developing better relationships with their customers."*

"Yeah, so?" Jeff asked. "I don't follow."

"Let me try to explain." Phil offered. "We tell our people and our customers that service is everything, right?"

"Right!" Jeff replied.

"Great! So what do we do? We hold back their service orders for weeks in processing, waiting for approvals."

"Weeks?" Jeff asked, a little surprised.

"Weeks!" Phil confirmed. "And these people care! They can't even look their customers in the eye. We tell them to promise, then we prevent them from delivering. How can we expect their best?"

"You've got a point." Jeff replied. "But, at least we take good care of them with our generous compensation system," he added, somewhat defensively.

"Oh sure, people make money here. But, for what?" Phil asked pointedly.

"For performance, of course." Jeff responded.

"Yes, but what kind of performance? Our system is set up so that people are rewarded for two things; not rocking the boat and filling out paper work. They are not rewarded for improving service, offering new ideas, and building relationships—all the things we profess to care about. Trying anything new is nothing short of political suicide!"

"What are you driving at Phil?

"The point is, what we ask for and what we actually reward are two different things. As a result, we're losing good people."

Jeff's eyebrows shot up.

"Oh yes!" Phil responded. "Just last week, Don Giovale, one of my top people, handed in his resignation."

"Not Giovale!" Jeff exclaimed.

"Yes, he's not the first. And if things don't change, he won't be the last. You know what he said?" Phil didn't wait for an answer. "He couldn't do his job. I mean, he gave it to me straight. He told me story after story of ideas he developed which we squashed because they challenged the status quo. He gave example after example of how he was prevented from serving his customers, many of whom he considers his friends." Phil paused, letting the gravity of his words sink in.

"He loved it here, Jeff. He just wasn't allowed to succeed. He told me flat out: We talk a good game, but we're not really willing to change. He felt

that after giving it his all, nothing he could do would make a difference. And, you know what?"

"What?" Jeff asked, already dreading the reply.

"The only difference between Don and the rest of our people is that Don had the guts to leave. You can't hold Giovale down. Everyone else just sits around, helpless to do the job they really want to do, halfheartedly hoping something will change. They've just given up. They know what Don explained—we reward the status quo, not raising the bar."

Jeff let out a deep sigh as Phil concluded, "The fact is, if we want to survive, we've got to prove to people it's still worth it to put forth their best effort. We've got to walk our talk in even the smallest ways. Otherwise, we're history."

Misalignments require both some analysis and the conviction to fix them. Given these two ingredients, tremendous energy can be unleashed as alignment is created or restored.

Companies like Phil and Jeff's frequently encounter misalignments between their goal—to Ascend—and the way they operate.

LIFE AFTER THE SEMINAR: WHAT GOES WRONG?

Let's assume that you invest some money and put your people through the AQ Program. They discover the underlying science, measure their AQs, learn and practice the LEAD sequence and a variety of techniques for raising their AQs so they can weather any storm. They are then provided with a series of follow-up tools to assist them in integrating the new behavior into their lives and their work.

What forces help the important new behavior to take hold or cause it to fail? Although you cannot stop a person from having and demonstrating a high AQ, you or the organization can make it pretty uncomfortable by creating an environment that opposes high AQ behavior. The individual then has two choices: He or she can either give up, which would have devastating consequences, or like Don Giovale he or she can go somewhere else, and you lose a valuable Climber.

What are some of the factors, intentional and unintentional that can hinder or destroy a person's attempt to raise their AQs at work? What must you, as a leader, avoid in your effort to create a Climbing culture? How do leaders discourage the Climb before it even begins? You probably have your own answers; here are twenty-two that I have discerned.

Twenty-Two Ways to Destroy Your Followers' AQs

1. *Always promise more than you can deliver.* Empty promises are excellent motivation crushers. Use them often. There's no better way to dismantle a climbing team than to violate their trust. Trust is an essential ingredient for a team Ascent. Kill trust and you kill the team's Ascent.

2. *Be consistently inconsistent.* Keep your people off guard. Never do what you say, except to throw them off. Change your mind frequently about major issues, especially issues of policy, conduct, and ethical choice. Be unpredictable. Keep your people wondering what will come next. This way they will hesitate before taking action, missing many opportunities.

3. *Remember: There's always a downside to everything.* Be sure to point it out in vivid, lurid detail. Weigh heavily on the impossibilities of a given situation. Be sure to point out every potential or imagined obstacle along the way. If people are still excited, repeat this step as needed.

4. *Model victimhood.* Act depressed, hopeless, and overwhelmed—it's contagious. Others are sure to catch on. Complain relentlessly in passive terms about how things happen *to* you, rather than the other way around. Make it clear that the whole world is against you, and there's nothing you can do about it.

5. *Dodge any incoming bullets from external forces.* Let your people feel the full brunt of adversity. The sooner they are hit, the sooner they will realize there is nothing they can do about it anyway. Be sure your people know that when the going gets tough, you disappear.

6. *Give lip service to accountability and responsibility.* Talk at great length about the virtues of committing to projects and

owning the results of your work. Then, be sure to punish any attempts by people to demonstrate such initiative by heaping more responsibility on them, with no perceptible reward.

7. *Ignore any potential contribution to the team's success.* Real Climbers don't have feelings! Don't weaken them with positive feedback. Never consider their point of view. If in doubt, take complete charge of everything. Do it all yourself. Sure it's more work, but your people will soon learn to passively await your next command.

8. *Help your team see setbacks for what they are—major failures.* In fact, use the word "failure" frequently when describing disappointments of any kind. The sooner the members realize that there is no margin for error, the sooner they will stop taking silly risks and going about half-cocked, acting as if they own the place.

9. *Frame success as a freak accident.* Don't waste time extolling your employees' successes, which are sure to be few and far between. The next thing you know they'll want to take valuable time away from the job to celebrate. Attribute success to fleeting, blind luck. There's no use letting your team get all full of themselves. They'll just want more money.

10. *Torpedo humor at all costs.* There's nothing funny about failure. Humor just burns up valuable time and energy. If people are feeling creative, let them put it into their work. You've got a bottom line to achieve, and there's nothing funny about that.

11. *Sap their strength.* Make your team work long hours with no rejuvenation. It worked on the slaves in Egypt! Be the first at your desk and the last to leave every day. Make it clear that you have no life, and, as far as you're concerned, neither should your employees. If they start getting feisty, invent an urgent deadline that will require long hours and weekends. The harder they work, the more compliant they will become. It will be easier on everyone in the long run.

12. *Crush creativity.* There's no room for frivolity. Wait until some new, young, energetic person enthusiastically offers

an idea at a meeting. Hear her out all the way, then publicly slam her ideas. Make it clear that if you need ideas, you'll ask for them.

13. *Punish all attempts at independence, swiftly and severely.* Publicly humiliate anyone who acts outside your authority.

14. *Dismantle any hope or optimism.* Given the overwhelming adversity everyone must face, it's the only humane thing to do. The sooner your employees learn that there is no hope, the sooner they'll stop being disappointed.

15. *Surround your Climbers with Campers.* Why do all the work yourself? Put your most dangerous maverick in a low AQ team. They'll teach him or her to shape up or ship out.

16. *Set your team up for failure.* Coax them into risks that are sure to bomb. There's no quicker way to knock the legs out from under them than to show them that risks will be swiftly punished.

17. *Reward them for playing by the rules.* Destroy individuality. Rules, policies, and procedures exist for a reason. After all, someone invested a heap of money in that manual! Learn it cover to cover, and use it fully whenever someone tries to act without your authority. Make it clear that, if in doubt, employees should always ask permission.

18. *Construct a rigid, stark, colorless environment.* Rid the workplace of plants, pictures, and other signs of your employees' lives outside of work. Work *is* their life, and the sooner they know that the better. Work is serious business. Make sure the environment reflects your tone.

19. *Uproot enthusiasm before it can grow.* No use fostering false expectations. There's nothing exciting about work.

20. *Press everyone to create a mission and vision, then forget about it.* This is an excellent technique for flushing out any covert pockets of hope from your team. Invest in a vision retreat at a nice location with an expensive consultant, who will, unknowingly, play along. Exhaust your team's best ideas, then ignore them completely.

21. *Provide responsibility with no authority.* Burden your employees with impossible tasks over which they have no

authority to pull together the resources they need to succeed. Let them wallow endlessly in their frustration.

22. *Use "empowerment" as a weapon to get them to do more with less.* Tell your people they are empowered, then heap on the work and deadlines, not the resources. Make it clear that it is their job to do whatever it takes to succeed, with your approval, of course.

This far from comprehensive list contains those habits which crush an individual's or team's hope, energy, motivation, and sense of control. *Which ones have you experienced?* These factors teach the members of an organization that it doesn't pay to exercise autonomy or mastery over their work lives. As a result, the organization receives a mere fraction of the combined potential of its people. Like a comatose patient, it functions, but never benefits from the full use of its faculties.

While there is no magic climbing phone booth in which an organization can instantly transform itself from a mild-mannered Camper to a high-powered Superclimber, there are some basic, common sense practices which, when employed, can dramatically shift the organization's momentum toward the Ascent.

THE CLIMBING ORGANIZATION

The Climbing organization is not just a champion of market share, profitability, shareholder return, or a candidate for the Malcolm Baldrige Award for quality, although these may be the rewards *earned* by an organization which is dedicated to the Ascent. To create a climbing organization you need to consider the mountain— the purpose of your organization. This describes *why* you climb. Your driving principles serve as rules of conduct, describing *how* you climb.

Purpose and Principles

As with individuals, each organization has its mountain to Ascend. Its mountain is defined by its purpose or mission—its reason for being. Individuals often confuse the ends with the means, frequently assuming financial gain is the goal, when, in reality, it can be the reward of a purposeful Ascent. Organizations often suffer from the same confusion.

Most people are not willing to define the best hours of their lives as a journey toward merely financial rewards. Money is important, but we must ask ourselves, money *for what purpose?*

If your organization's purpose is to make money, then it makes no difference what you do or how you do it. Why not sell cocaine or weapons to terrorists? It is your ethical framework which makes such an assertion sound absurd. To guide your moral decision making, you must, therefore, have an implicit or explicit set of core values or driving principles, which, like the Ten Commandments, define *how* you will Ascend along your purpose.

Purpose is often articulated in a mission statement which, far too often, ends up as a nicely framed document on the wall or another project filed away for future reference. The true challenge is to *live* the purpose every day, and that consistency and passion starts with the leader.

So, to get the deepest, most synergistic commitment and dedication from a group of people, there must be a higher, enduring purpose toward which they can commonly strive. Unlike a goal, which is short-term, a mission is never completed, it defines a *purpose*, or journey, not a destination.

Forty-Four Ways to Boost Your Followers' AQs

Let's consider what you can do to nurture high AQ behavior and grow a high AQ culture in your organization, and, in the process, unleash the full potential of your people so they can effectuate its mission. These suggestions fall into the following categories: Purpose, Values, Climate, People, The Message, and Coaching.

Purpose—Why We Are Here

1. *Define the mountain.* Dedicate the time and resources to define your organization's purpose. It should answer the question, "Why do we exist as an organization." Involve everyone. Agree on what matters, then persist, persist,

persist. If you question the value of purpose, imagine spending your life working for an organization without one.

2. *Consistently articulate an uplifting, inspirational, and optimistic vision.* While purpose answers *why* you exist, vision answers *where*—where are you going? A vision represents a compelling, attractive, elevating, ideal future state. Involve everyone in its creation, but take it upon yourself to keep it alive and kicking.

3. *Align all systems to the mountain.* Although it is easier said than done, sniff out and destroy helplessness-inducing systems. Most organizations suffer from some degree of misalignment. This is tantamount to delivering a double message to your people: "We value Climbing, but reward you for Camping." Explore your hiring, compensation, performance appraisal, performance management, training, disciplinary, reward, and communication systems to see how well they enhance or defeat high AQ behavior.

    Like a wheel on a car, a system which is out of alignment can be damaging. At best, it reduces the efficiency. At worst, it steers you off course.

4. *Create a climbing culture that aligns your team's mountain with the organization's.* Everything on this list contributes to a Climbing culture. Make it explicit to your team so new hires and veterans alike know what it takes to be in step with the organization's direction and operation. New hires can self-select based on perceived fit, drawing Climbers and repelling Campers and Quitters. A strong, clearly articulated culture provides a framework for and exerts a powerful influence upon the members' behavior and choices.

5. *Align individual and organizational purposes.* Have and show an authentic interest in your team's success. If trust and communication permit, people may feel comfortable sharing their personal purpose (their mountain) with you. In so doing, they are telling you what matters most to them, and you, as a leader, can help align their purpose with that of the organization. Go out of your way to help this alignment

occur. Nothing engenders greater commitment than a sense of genuine alignment of purpose.

6. *Make success a journey, not a pill.* Reward character over quick-fix solutions. Make it clear that you believe in enduring solutions and strategies by avoiding the temptation to shower your people with quick-fix, magic-bullet solutions. Avoid becoming an active member of the flavor-of-the-month club. Pick what matters, and stick to it. It may not be sexy, but it works.

Values—Strengthening AQ-Related Values

7. *Promise only what you can deliver, then deliver it—no matter what.* Every promise is an opportunity to demonstrate and exercise your integrity. If the conditions change, making it more challenging to fulfill your promise, consider it an opportunity to model the persistence you require of others. The tougher the obstacle, the greater the message and lesson about AQ.

8. *Integrate persistence, resilience, and continuous improvement into your core values.* The next time you revisit your core values as an organization, make it clear that you value resilience, persistence, and the relentless pursuit of your mission.

9. *Model your driving values consistently.* Never compromise on values. Like promises, look for opportunities to demonstrate the driving values. The words have no meaning until action is taken. The greater the dilemma, challenge, or obstacle you must face, the clearer and more memorable the message about the driving value and AQ.

10. *Let empowerment be the result of trust, communication, and genuine commitment.* Demonstrate *and* communicate your trust of others. Let them own their results, and *don't* look over their shoulders. This is hard to do, because sometimes people fail. But, over time, trust will grow *true* empowerment. Show your commitment, your trust, and your purpose to your people. Remember, at the heart of AQ is a sense of control. This control can be expanded by letting your team try and fail, and learning to do it better next time.

Climate—Creating an Environment That Fosters High AQ

11. *Inject humor regularly as a way to keep perspective and health.* Humor communicates an "it's all part of the journey" mentality. It buoys the spirits of the Climbers when their legs begin to tire. Celebrate humor with cartoons, pranks, traditions, and silliness. Above all else, laugh at yourselves.

12. *Reward and model personal balance.* Climbers need to rejuvenate. Be adamant and proactive about team members taking time to replenish their bodies, minds, and souls. Invest the resources of time and money for people to learn, exercise, pray, or whatever works for them. Be an exemplary role model of personal balance and how it enables people to persist in your Ascent.

13. *Foster creativity.* Reroute in the face of avalanches. Creativity is the force that changes the question from "If" to "How." When organizations face adversity, they must rely on their creativity to turn a problem into an opportunity. Whining over doing more with less wastes time and saps energy. Innovation ignites possibilities and hope.

14. *Point out and nurture moments of synergy and collaboration.* People climb in teams. Seek out the moments where one person gives another a leg up. Highlight and reward those moments so the message is clear: "We always answer the call of a fallen teammate."

15. *Construct and maintain an open, lively, synergistic environment.* Remove all obstacles to people communicating and working together. Move the walls, furniture, computers, wires, and anything else that provides an archaic barrier of power or territory. People work well together when they can see and physically interface with one another as much as possible. Involve your telecommuters. Make them feel as if they are present, and pull them into the office for regular events.

16. *Grab any opportunity to grow enthusiasm.* Add to enthusiasm when it cautiously pokes out its head. Express your own authentic enthusiasm every day. It adds to the sense

of energy, fun, and possibility within a team. It's highly contagious!

17. *Live by the self-fulfilling prophecy.* Predicting success enhances success. Predict success where others hedge their bets, then prove everyone else wrong. Show that faith in the future and in what's possible can be instrumental to achieving success. Once proven, communicate the lesson.

18. *Establish support for the ascent.* Make it a norm to discuss challenges, setbacks, and adversity. Revisit the Ascent regularly in your meetings and discussions. Calmly and confidently address the obstacles people are facing, have the team work together to LEAD itself out of any potentially low AQ responses, and strategize meaningful action.

People—Finding and Developing Climbers

19. *Hire and create a high AQ climbing team.* Every job demands the ability to prevail through adversity. Measure and assess an applicant's AQ. It will instantly communicate his or her ability to *use* his or her talent and skills, perform at the full potential, and persist through the hard times. I know many managers who, any day of the week, would rather hire a person with a lukewarm resume and a high AQ than one with a great resume and a low AQ.

   It is cheaper and easier to hire Climbers than to grow them. For this reason, my company offers a tool similar to the Adversity Response Profile to help organizations hire top performers (see Appendix). Through its instantaneous computer printout, you can assess how an applicant responds to adversity at the same time you consider his or her resume, interview skills, and fit within your organization. This tool can be augmented by specially crafted questions and behavioral interviewing techniques.

20. *Find and provide the resources to get the job done.* Figure out what resources are essential to your team's success. Demonstrate creativity and persistence in acquiring them. You won't always prevail, but you will prove the old adage,

"If you don't ask, you don't get." Ideally, over time, you will enable your people to gather their *own* resources.

21. *Demonstrate and clarify team members' individual importance to the whole.* I once joined a rock-climbing team that was going to take on a fairly arduous granite wall. One person on the team was assigned the task of *belay*—he was to hold the rope so people didn't fall and die—something he had never done before. He considered the assignment unglamorous because, despite its importance, it involved mostly sitting and waiting while Climbers prepared and gradually ascended. Out of boredom, he let the rope go. One of my team members fell. Fortunately, he escaped injury, but the message was clear. Let everyone know how much their job contributes to the ascent of the entire team.

22. *Help team members recognize and develop their strengths and minimize their weaknesses.* Climbers are dedicated to continually improving themselves as a way to strengthen their contribution, impact, and Ascent. Provide your people with the tools, feedback, training, and incentives to continually better themselves.

23. *Allow people to run with ideas that do not threaten the survival of others.* Like risks, your team will only learn to generate new ideas if the ones they throw out are taken seriously. Give your team the opportunity to try something outrageous. If it works, great! If it fails, celebrate the effort.

24. *Always ask for input and commitment.* There's a reason that every influential management book of the last decade extols the virtues of participation and involvement. This creates a sense of control, which leads to greater proactivity and high AQ behavior. People with greater perceived control over events tend to persist longer, be more creative, and remain healthier.

25. *Nurture and celebrate mastery.* Competence is about ability, whereas mastery is about perceived control. Teach your team to develop mastery by having them take on challenging, but not impossible, tasks. Then support or "spot" them as they climb. Once they've succeeded, make sure they

pause long enough to let the sense of mastery sink in. Mastery builds on itself, creating an overarching sense of control over one's ability to handle any situation. Such mastery is highly contagious to the entire team and organization.

Message—Strengthening the Meaning of AQ

26. *Glorify past struggles-turned-successes.* Find, bring forth, communicate, and publicize the historic, high AQ turning points in your organization where someone had to prevail over adversity. Every organization that's been in operation for more than a week has a story to tell. Institutionalize the stories and characters by repeating the message through video, newsletters, e-mail, and every other means. It communicates what matters and what is celebrated.

27. *Acknowledge relevant, heartfelt contributions to the ascent.* Look for moments in which team members enact your organization's purpose. Stop the presses, hold the phones, get everyone's attention, and let it be clear: The purpose is what matters most.

28. *Create the stuff of high AQ folklore.* Look for and take on a project that no one believes can be done, and accomplish it faster and better than anyone dreamed possible. It will become the stuff of company folklore, and it will raise the bar for the entire team or organization.

29. *Point out and celebrate high AQ success stories.* Make the Climbers your team's heroes. Make it clear that anyone can be a master Climber by noticing and glorifying the moments in which an individual tries what you've taught them and breaks through adversity. Celebrate the moments that best demonstrate the ability to prevail.

30. *Use the language of the climb.* Make the mountain your icon for success. Teach your people about Climbers, Campers, and Quitters. Provide them with a visual of the mountain as a symbol of the Ascent. This inspirational image is easily remembered and provides fertile ground for their own applications and analogies.

Avoid words like impossible, never, always, can't, un-reachable, inevitable, and have to. Check your own adversity response on a regular basis. Ferret out anything that sounds like a negative CO_2RE. Listen for Control, Origin, and Ownership, Reach, and Endurance.

31. *Prove that the impossible isn't.* Begin on a small scale. A great way to get people to look forward and up, past their per-ceived obstacles, is to pick a seemingly insurmountable challenge and demonstrate how it can be resolved. Ideally, you'll let your team prove this to themselves by coaching and guiding them to their success. Once they break through, there is a tremendous unleashing of energy and excitement. Capture the moment, and use it as a way to prove to your team what *can* be done when they get stuck on what cannot.

Coaching toward a High AQ

32. *Help your employees fight their own battles.* Prepare them for the climb. Provide carefully administered doses of adversity to your people so they prove to themselves their hardiness and their ability to prevail through increasingly tougher challenges.

33. *Establish and enable genuine accountability and responsibility.* Create a clear, unmistakable understanding of these two organizational virtues. As people form commitments, they are responsible for following through and accountable for the results they produce. Nothing can replace the AQ af-firming moment in which they prove to themselves what they are capable of doing.

34. *Ask for and reward appropriate risks—even if they result in belly flops.* Be consistent in your message about rewarding risks that do not threaten the livelihood of your organization, but which are an expected part of the Ascent. Pick a situ-ation in which someone does a really ugly face plant, and make it funny, noticed, and clearly approved of as an at-tempt to Ascend.

35. *Reward your team for results over rules.* Too many rules render people tentative. Like first graders made to sit at their tables for the first time, people hold back in fear of violating some rule. Reward the results your people achieve and communicate that creativity (within ethical bounds), risks, mistakes, even messiness are valued.

36. *Compartmentalize adversity.* A crisis in one area need not destroy others. Verbally separate the dimensions affected by the adversity from those which remain strong. When I backpack in the rain, everything is compartmentalized so that when one area gets wet, others are likely to remain dry. That way, even if my sleeping bag, tent, shoes, and other clothes are soaked, there is always a chance to get into some dry, warm clothes, no matter how bad the storm.

If you have earnings or service problems in one part of your business, be diligent in limiting both the perception of and their actual spread. Prevent them from physically or psychically bleeding into other areas.

37. *Raise the bar to enable your team to jump.* Never settle for less in yourself or others. Strive for higher levels of performance. I visited a doctor once who reeked of tobacco and spent the next 20 minutes extolling the benefits of exercise and a good diet. No credibility. Ask for greatness in yourself first, *then* you can ask for it in others.

38. *Ask your team, "What are the greatest obstacles to your success?"* Help them tear down those impediments. By having people name them, these obstacles come out of the shadows and into the daylight where, like a dragon, they can be slain. Give your team members the power and the tools to kill their dragon and celebrate its death.

39. *Teach people "If you don't ask, you don't get."* Continually ask for the impossible, and eventually you will get it. I have a good friend who makes a habit of checking into fine hotels on his business travel. When registering, he politely asks those at the front desk if he can have the room at half the standard corporate rate since, if he didn't take it, the room would only go empty. He often succeeds. This is high AQ possibility thinking. It can work with vendors, customers, competitors, and each other.

40. *Praise the person, criticize the behavior.* This adage goes far to support high AQ behavior. Behavior is temporary and adjustable, personal faults are more stable, and thus, more likely to endure. As a result, harping on personal faults is more likely to teach someone to quit, whereas feedback on behavior can guide one's development.

41. *No victims, only volunteers!* Eliminate victimhood and whining from the menu of behaviors. Do nothing to reward or nurture whining. It weakens the entire team. If it gets out of hand, pause and give everyone 2 minutes to whine loudly and pathetically. They'll laugh at their childishness and move on to what matters. Use the LEAD sequence to replace whining with meaningful dialogue and substantive action.

42. *Use the LEAD sequence to boost AQ.* Use LEAD with others publicly and privately. Demonstrate its utility to your team by letting them experience and witness its transformative effects on themselves and others. Through consistent use, employees will integrate it into their thinking and interpersonal vocabulary.

43. *Use Stoppers! to erase catastrophizing as an option.* These serve as effective techniques for stopping the fire before it destroys unnecessary acreage. Your team will be grateful for your ability to help them keep a challenge in perspective and avoid wasting valuable time and energy dwelling on the hypothetical downside.

44. *Define, measure, discuss, and nurture AQ.* By teaching your people the concepts, skills, and principles provided in this book, you will establish an essential language and competency for breaking through adversity. I have witnessed numerous instances in which a low AQ, morale-sagging response is immediately addressed with the comment, "Hey, that's low AQ." Once people possess the essential skills and vocabulary, they can readily adjust their behavior *and response.*

AQ AT WORK

At its CO_2RE, AQ is about enlarging control and ownership while reducing destructive self-blame, catastrophizing, and permanence. It is about educating and in many cases *reawakening* your team to a new way of talking, thinking, and behaving in the face of daily challenges, setbacks, and disappointments.

How your team responds to adversity, both individually and in concert, will have far-reaching effects on all facets of your organization's success. By teaching members these skills and aligning your systems and processes to foster their growth, you can create a sustainable, high AQ culture that drives the organization forward and up along its purpose. By using these strategies, you will create an organization that can prevail where others fall short or give up. In so doing, you will reduce the costly downside of change and begin to win back the hearts and minds of those people who suffered most from past initiatives, cutbacks, and reengineering efforts. Ultimately, you will improve performance, productivity, creativity, the ability to embrace change, and your bottom line.

Gary, a marketing manager for Biotech, Inc., knew that his organization's AQ would have a profound impact on its long-term success. After attending the AQ Program, he was anxious to assess his organization's AQ. One Monday morning, he walked into the weekly staff meeting a few minutes early and arranged his papers so he would be poised and ready to take notes on what he heard. Gary greeted people as they filtered into the room.

"Most of you are not yet aware," Rita, regional vice president and Gary's boss, began, "that we are all facing the biggest challenge in Biotech's seventeen-year history." Rita paused, looking around the room, letting her message sink in. "Genetic Innovation just announced that they have received approval for their new, noninvasive cancer therapy." A few people gasped. "This is a direct threat to our biggest and most expensive project. The bottom line is: Either we cut our time to market in half, or we're out of business. It's as simple as that."

"But that's impossible!" Stan from engineering piped in. "We're already pulling long shifts."

"Well, there's no use beating our heads against the wall. We've been beaten fair and square," Liz responded. "I don't know about the rest of you, but I'm going to start updating my resume!" And so the conversation went.

Gary was alarmed by what he witnessed. As he thought back on other meetings and challenges, he realized that people at Biotech had always responded to the big challenges by losing their grip. Just last year they had lost one of their key customers to a competitor, and the place just fell apart. Gary knew that AQ would impact Biotech's survival.

After further analysis, Gary realized that Biotech prided itself on its leading-edge thinking and innovation, but it didn't directly reward innovation anywhere in its compensation plan. This misalignment between Biotech's purpose and the compensation system caused great confusion and the pervasive feeling that people were being given mixed messages.

Gary decided to take charge of the effort to catch up to Genetic Innovation. He asked Rita for a special force to whom he could grant incentives for their ideas and innovation. People were to be rewarded for the quantity and quality of ideas, knowing that some of the craziest ones might bear fruit.

He then laid down a foundation of high AQ language, making it clear that the force's focus was on action and results, not complaining and whining. Even on his toughest days, Gary modeled this new behavior, adding enthusiasm and ideas of his own whenever possible.

Knowing resources were in short supply, Gary took on what appeared to be an impossible task: He went to the CEO and asked for a facility in which they could operate. With budgets as tight as they were, everyone thought Gary was crazy! Yet, he walked out of the CEO's office an hour later with a promise for a new facility and a smile on his face.

Gary then guided the Force to form a clearly defined vision—"To beat Genetic Innovation to market with a superior product." After much discussion, they wrote a set of driving values, which would guide their behavior. They included concepts like fairness, compassion, balance, helping others, honesty, and teamwork. They even defined their terms. Gary's team also nailed down a mission: "To help rid the world of cancer." With a clear, elevating sense of purpose, Gary's team began to form commitments around different parts of the project.

Gary made it clear that, with commitment comes responsibility. People would be held accountable for the outcomes of their efforts, not just the effort itself. Gary then built these changes into the performance appraisal process to create greater alignment between what people were doing and what they were evaluated upon.

Over time, Gary made other changes, too. At one of the Force's first meetings, he introduced the mountain and the tendencies to be a Quitter, Camper, or Climber. The team quickly adopted the language of the Ascent and provided weekly "updates from on high" which served as intrateam progress reports. People were given new levels of input, influence, and control over what they did and how they did it. Gary took advantage of every opportunity to build trust by keeping every promise he made to anyone on the team. He even set an ambitious, seemingly impossible deadline for the initial phase of the project. Few believed it could be met. Gary then made sure the team completed the first phase in plenty of time.

This was a major turning point. Since beating the first deadline, the team started to adopt an attitude of "we can do anything." Gary was pleased to hear the new language coming through. On several occasions, he overheard team members catching each other as they began to respond destructively. "That's low AQ!" became a common device for immediately adjusting one's response.

As each new obstacle arose, people quickly learned to keep it in check, not letting it affect the parts of the project which were still on track. There were occasions, however, in which he had to demonstrate the LEAD sequence during a meeting. Soon, however, people caught on, starting to use the same method for catching and helping each other as they dealt with the nonstop adversity.

Despite the long hours and tremendous pressure, Gary's team was the most energized, innovative, exciting unit in the entire organization. By staying on purpose and operating as a high AQ crack team, Gary's squad was able to halve their time to market and compete directly with Genetic Innovation. They rose to the challenge, becoming a synergistic, innovative, tough, top-performing team.

Rita and Jeff, Biotech's CEO, later rewarded the Force for raising the bar and making the impossible happen with an all-expenses paid weekend to a health spa.

AQ is a fundamental, determining variable in organizational success. It will influence your ability to lead and your followers' capacity to follow. AQ will determine the severity and success of change as well as how well and how quickly your people navigate *incessant* change. In short, AQ represents a true source for organizational health, performance, empowerment, and competitive advantage.

The Climber's Habit

To affect the quality of the day, that is the highest of arts.

Henry David Thoreau

You have three primary reasons to invest the time and energy needed to use and teach the concepts and tools in this book. First, there may, regardless of your current level of success, be certain areas of your life that you would like to strengthen. You now recognize that AQ provides new insights and tools for navigating the adversity you face every day.

The second reason you may choose to invest in integrating these tools into your life is to help others. After completing the preceding chapters, you realize that the LEAD sequence, Stoppers!, and AQ theory can be used to significantly enhance others' quality of life and work. There are probably people in your life who will benefit from what you have learned.

Third, you also recognize how AQ can determine an organization's competitive advantage and its ability to persevere through continuous change.

This ability to persevere begins with you, the individual. However, change is rarely easy. In fact, sometimes it's downright formidable.

WHY MOST LEARNING GOES DOWN THE TUBES: HOWELL'S FIVE LEVELS OF COMPETENCE

While completing my doctorate at the University of Minnesota, I had the honor of working with the senior professor in our department, Dr. William Howell. Described as "the Great White Buffalo," Dr. Howell had accumulated decades of wisdom on the practices of Japanese business leaders, long before it was in vogue to do so. Dr. Howell developed a model that described what happens when we receive new information or try to develop a new skill. This model applies to any new skill, including the LEAD sequence, Stoppers, and the 44 tips provided in the last chapter.

Learning a New Skill: Howell's Five Levels of Competence

You will recall from my interview with Dr. Mark Nuwer, of UCLA Medical Center, that you can change a habit *instantaneously*. By sending a loud alarm to your brain, you can immediately cease the patterns that make up a less-than-optimal AQ, rerouting them with a new, robust, high-AQ response.

Although change can happen instantaneously, the new skills do require practice. Here's why.

Level One: Unconscious Incompetence

Think back to the time when you first learned to drive a new car, preferably a manual transmission. How good were you the first time you got into the car? You may have started out where my younger son did a few months ago. He would ask me, "Dad, can I drive the car?"

To which I would respond, "No, Sean. You may not."

"But,... but *why?*" he would plead.

"There are two reasons. First, you don't have a license. So it's illegal. Second, you don't know *how* to drive."

"Yes I do!" he insisted.

So I gave him the keys, and said, "Fine, why don't you *start* the car."

He took off for the garage. Moments later I heard the car door slam, followed by a loud *Kerchunk!* He had stalled.

Initially, Sean was at a level of learning called *Unconscious Incompetence.* This means he didn't even know he didn't know how to drive.

Level Two: Conscious Incompetence

The moment my son stalled the car, he slammed into Level Two. He became instantly aware that he didn't know *how* to start the car. This is not a very enjoyable or comfortable stage to experience. At this point many people, especially adults, abandon whatever they wanted to learn. They would rather be less skilled and have their egos intact, then risk embarrassment and momentary incompetence.

You may perceive yourself to be at this level with the skills taught in this book. You *know* you're not good at them. But that's no reason to quit, especially when all facets of your success are at stake! Over time, you will, like the teenage driver, progress to Level Three.

Level Three: Conscious Competence

Think back to your own early driving experiences, especially with a manual transmission. You may remember that first stop sign on a hill, with a car six inches behind your rear bumper. You were sweating bullets, but if you really went over the motions in your mind, concentrating intensely on the mechanics of driving, you pulled it off. You then reached a level called *Conscious Competence.* At this level, you can do it, if you really concentrate.

Like Level Two, this level is neither comfortable nor fun. Driving in this stage is tense and forced, demanding your full concentration to avoid an accident.

As you progress to this stage in implementing what I have taught you, you will gain confidence, but limited pleasure. It will be hard to use your new AQ skills, but you will succeed in helping yourself and others deal with adversity.

Fortunately, it becomes easier and easier as you glide into Level Four.

Level Four: Unconscious Competence

If you are like most drivers, you probably do not concentrate on the mechanics of driving. You shift, break, accelerate, and operate all the knobs and buttons without a second thought. You have reached *Unconscious Competence*. At this point driving becomes fun.

The same is true of the LEAD sequence, Stoppers, and the 44 tips provided in the preceding chapter. You will notice substantial rewards as you help yourself and others boost AQ.

To reach this stage takes nothing more or less than practice. It took you days to learn to drive, and months to learn to drive well. Since the tools presented in this book are less demanding than driving, you will, with practice, begin to notice results almost *immediately.*

Level Five: Unconscious Supercompetence

We are exposed to the rare air of Level Five every time we watch the Olympics and see a Carl Lewis run, a Dan Jansen skate, or a "FloJo" jump. These people have gone beyond basic Unconscious Competence to a level of *Supercompetence.* In this stage you are able to do something *superbly* without thinking about it. Over time you may reach this level in helping yourself and others enhance AQ.

What Goes On in the Brain

As you read these five levels, they should sound at least vaguely familiar. They describe the activity that occurs in the brain as you form a habit. You will recall that the more you think or do something, the more subconscious and automatic it becomes. Your brain is ideally equipped to facilitate the migration of the activity from the cerebral cortex (conscious region) to the basal ganglia (subconscious region). In the process, your dendrites (connections) become thicker and more efficient. In essence, Howell's model intuitively describes what happens as you hardwire your brain with new skills.

TWO FACTORS THAT INFLUENCE YOUR SUCCESS

Like the teenage driver, there are two factors that will influence your success. First, is *importance*. The reason the teenager prevails in learning to drive is because it *matters* so much! Driving means independence, popularity, fun, and mobility. How many teenagers have you met who gave up on driving because it was too difficult?

The second factor is *difficulty*. If you think about it, you will realize that driving a car is highly challenging. There are many complex simultaneous actions one must execute while under the life-threatening realities of the road! Yet, almost all of us do it.

The difficulty of LEADing yourself or others to a higher AQ pales in comparison to the mental and physical challenge of driving mom's or dad's car. Difficulty is not, therefore, a genuine barrier to your success.

So, the utility of this book comes down to one simple question: *How important is it to you to strengthen your AQ and your ability to climb through adversity?*

If I've done my job, you should understand that AQ is *critical* to all facets of your success. I have yet to find a more far-reaching, global predictor of success. The benefits should be incentive enough to persevere through Howell's Five Levels of Competence and hardwire your brain with a high AQ.

WHAT YOU CAN EXPECT

As you use the tools and concepts presented in this book, gradually, almost imperceptibly your relationship with life transforms. If you have a less-than-ideal AQ, that relationship evolves from love-hate, where you would actively avoid, fight, and often lose to adversity, to that of a dance. Your new dance reflects the natural rhythm of adversity-response-result, adversity-response-result.

You begin to witness the first inklings of influence over your children's AQ development. This influence will evolve into a life-long legacy of resilience, stamina, persistence, and hardiness—a legacy they are likely to pass on to their own offspring.

You are energized by your newfound serenity in facing each new challenge, and rightfully so. You can see that your people are responding favorably to your demeanor, calling you for advice.

Even so, you, like all Climbers, are human and sometimes get tired from your struggle to Ascend. You'll have moments when you feel down, and when life seems unbearably hard. The difference is that, compared to a person with a lower AQ, such moments are fewer and farther between, posing less of a long-term threat to your emotional, physical, and spiritual strength.

No matter what life throws your way, your recovery from even the most unimaginable adversity is likely to be quicker and more complete than that of a person with a lower AQ. And, with each new challenge comes the living proof that there is little, if anything you cannot withstand and overcome.

Over time, the rewards of raising your AQ and your ability to re-spond to adversity go beyond the immediate improvements in en-ergy, perspective, mental acuity, and stress. They migrate deeper and take the form of improved health, as your immune functions begin to mirror your fortified spirit. You gradually experience en-hanced performance, reflected in greater consistency, focus, persis-tence, and productivity. You feel mentally freer and more creative. You're better able to soak in the details at work and in life.

Then, there are the intangibles. You notice that people respond to you differently—with a newfound respect. They pick up on the subtle, yet powerful, differences in how you handle situations as they unfold. They are inspired by and drawn to your example.

Perhaps the greatest reward is that you start to feel a sense of control over your life. The daily financial, emotional, physical, in-terpersonal, and career-related challenges have somehow lost much of their power to rob you of your vitality. As a result, you ex-perience greater joy. You realize that you had spent many moments in life being satisfied, at best. You now realize that joy is not just for children, but it comes from a sense of mastery over your life and the ability to maintain your emotional and spiritual reserves no matter what is thrown your way.

There is nothing false or rehearsed about your emerging de-meanor. You emit greater authenticity in how you interact with people and navigate life.

Time and time again you witness others suffering tremendous and unnecessary anguish due to the assumptions embedded deep within their AQs and their brains. You are constantly struck by the realization that it is the *response* that shapes their reality far more than the event itself.

STRENGTHEN THE CLIMBER

As you Ascend, the greatest burdens you bear are largely internal. There may be aspects of your past or present that weigh heavily upon your shoulders, weakening you and slowing your progress along your path. Damaged self-worth, psychological traumas, abusive relationships, and chemical imbalances are but a few of the obstacles that must be overcome by millions in their effort to be whole. AQ provides some efficient ideas, but is not meant as a quick fix for these deep inner struggles that many bear every day.

Part of the journey, therefore, is to work incessantly to make yourself as emotionally, physically, and spiritually whole as you can be, not just for yourself, but to enhance the legacy you leave the world.

AQ AND THE GREATER GOOD

Chances are you know someone who has been laid off from his or her job in recent years. The odds indicate that person is either currently unemployed, underemployed, and/or sorely underpaid. There is also a good chance that you know parents who struggle to find time with their children, or children who struggle to find optimism about the future.

As we complete our transition from an industrial to an informational society, we are dealing with one of the greatest social transformations in human history. With such massive transition comes massive adversity. As we, our coworkers, our loved ones, and our fellow humans face this adversity, so much more than our attitude is at stake. Indeed, it is our very survival on the line.

Joel Barker, noted futurist and author of *Paradigms,* presents a model which demonstrates the role of *vision* in kicking up to a higher feedback loop resulting in a continuous cycle between hopefulness and helplessness. He defines a vision as "dreams in action." Barker suggests that a clear, compelling, positive vision of the future can break us free of the cycle of despair. Vision is essential to hope at the personal, organizational, and societal levels (Figure 10–1).

I believe that the element required to form and carry through a positive vision is AQ. A person must be able to see and work past the never-ending avalanche of adversity to escape the helplessness-hopelessness cycle of despair (Figure 10–2). It is this learned propensity to climb that enables an individual to sustain hope in seemingly hopeless times.

AQ is pivotal in all three stages of creating and fulfilling a vision.

FIGURE 10–1   The Role of Vision

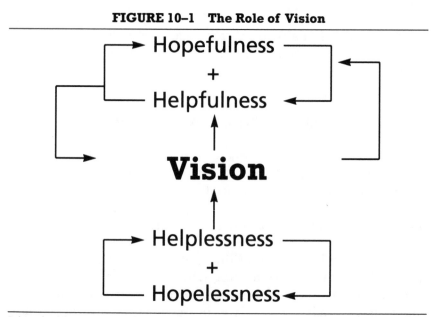

Printed with permission from Joel A. Barker.

FIGURE 10–2   The Role of AQ in Achieving Any Vision

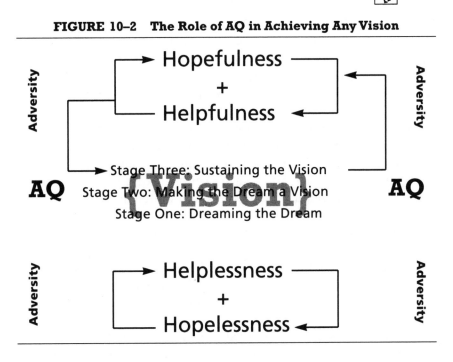

Stage One: Dreaming the Dream

People place limitations on what they allow themselves to imagine. This limits the range of what's possible, before the vision is even formed. Intuitively, we understand that people with higher AQs allow themselves to imagine greater possibilities than do those with lower AQs. *AQ determines what future you allow yourself to even consider.*

Stage Two: Making the Dream the Vision

There is a moment when you consider taking action on a dream, thus turning it into a vision. It is at this moment that some of the possible realities and sacrifices start to sink in.

I recently spoke with Greg Townsman, an engineer who had been laid off from Hughes. He described the helplessness he felt in his job, unable to break free of something he never really enjoyed. In expressing his disenchantment with his career path, he spoke passionately about his original dream of being a doctor. His whole face lit up as he vividly described how and why he had always wanted to help heal young children. He had thought out every phase of his life as a doctor.

When asked what had stopped him from pursuing his dream, Greg described the years of school and sacrifice he would have had to endure. He described how formidable the challenge of medical school appeared to be, and that he simply didn't believe he could make it. He believed it was hopeless to pursue such a path. In retrospect, he explained, those sacrifices would have paled in comparison to the heartache of doing something for which he felt no passion.

Greg had stopped short at Stage Two by letting the realities of the Ascent prevent him from pursuing his true path. By refusing to act on his dream, being a doctor remained *only* a dream, never a true vision.

Greg's low AQ had prevented him from seeing past the adversity of medical school. He had defined his mountain, but denied himself the fulfillment of the Ascent. He perceived the adversity as enduring, far-reaching, and overwhelming. As a result, he spent most of his adult life climbing the wrong mountain.

Stage Three: Sustaining the Vision

The number of people who stay on path to their vision gets smaller as they move through each succeeding stage. Of those with AQs high enough to allow themselves to dream, only a portion will have the fortitude to think past the challenges and take action on their dreams, turning them into visions. Far fewer still will persevere through the drudgery of sustaining the vision.

It is the Climber who is not dissuaded, but is often *fueled* by the adversity of the Ascent. Dreaming is one thing, staying on path is another. *Sustaining* the vision is the most difficult part. Along the way we can be so easily distracted by other, easier paths, or disheartened by the relentless effort required to forge ahead. Only those capable of climbing through adversity see the vision realized.

Clearly, all three stages of creating and fulfilling a vision are greatly influenced by one's AQ. Ultimately, it is the synergistic combination of AQ and vision which allows one to break free of the cycle of despair and live a life filled with hope and purpose.

The true purpose of this work is, therefore, to provide a mechanism to fortify ourselves and those around us to break free of the cycle of despair and begin to reignite the essential element of hope. This is the *essence* of the Ascent. Without it, we face a bleak future, indeed. With it, there are no limits to what we can do. It all begins with you—the individual—and your ability to get past the adversity.

> *Change and growth take place when a person has risked himself and dares to become involved with experimenting with his own life.*
>
> Herbert Otto

In *My Life of Adventure*, 89-year-old Norman Vaughan reflects back on his life as a Climber. He recognizes that the journey never ends regardless of age and limitations.

Although a mountain at the South Pole was named after him for his early explorations, it wasn't until he was 89 that he actually climbed it. He says, as he reflects back on his ascent of Mount Vaughan in Antarctica and on his Ascent in life, "I realized that I hadn't done anything anyone else couldn't do. The only difference is I actually did it."

Even at age 89, Vaughan refused to simply camp, taking on a life of continuous challenge, uncertainty, and adversity. His rewards have been a life of vigor, adventure, dreams, countless setbacks, and ultimately, fulfillment.

In short, like Vaughan, as you raise your AQ, all facets of your life progressively improve despite significant adversity. *As long as you are alive, you can ascend.* Unlike other strategies you may have attempted, you become convinced that AQ is not a quick-fix, but rather an enduring formula built on a fundamental truth that life is hard—but how you handle it *determines your destiny.*

APPENDIX

This appendix is provided for you to share the opportunity to measure AQ with someone you care about. Take this opportunity to have him or her complete this copy of the condensed Adversity Response Profile.

Please do not violate federal copyright law by duplicating, scanning, or photographing this instrument in any way. Additional copies can be obtained by contacting the number shown at the end of this appendix.

Instructions for Completing the Adversity Response Profile

There are 30 events listed. Complete the questions for each event as follows.

1. Vividly imagine each event as if it is happening now, even if it seems unrealistic.
2. For both of the questions following each event, circle a number 1 through 5 that represents your response.

---

1. Your coworkers are not receptive to your ideas.

The reason my coworkers are not receptive to my ideas is something over which I have:

No control	1	2	3	4	5	Complete Control

C—

The reason my coworkers are not receptive to my ideas is something that completely has to do with:

Me	1	2	3	4	5	Other people or factors

O_r—

2. People are unresponsive to your presentation at a meeting.

The reason people are unresponsive to my presentation is something that

Relates to all aspects of my life	1	2	3	4	5	Just relates to this situation

R—

The reason people are unresponsive to my presentation will:

Always exist	1	2	3	4	5	Never exist again

E—

3. You make a lot of money from a major investment.

The reason I am making a lot of money is something that:

Relates to all aspects of my life	1	2	3	4	5	Just relates to this situation

R+

The reason I am making a lot of money will:

Always exist	1	2	3	4	5	Never exist again

E+

4. You and your loved ones seem to be drifting further and further apart.

The reason we seem to be drifting further apart is something that:

Relates to all aspects of my life	1	2	3	4	5	Just relates to this situation

R—

The reason we seem to be drifting further apart will:

Always exist	1	2	3	4	5	Never exist again

E—

5. Someone you respect calls you for advice.

The reason this person called me for advice is something that:

Relates to all aspects of my life	1	2	3	4	5	Just relates to this situation

$R+$

The reason this person called me for advice will:

Always exist	1	2	3	4	5	Never exist again

$E+$

6. You have a heated argument with your spouse (significant other).

The reason we have a heated argument is something over which I have:

No control	1	2	3	4	5	Complete control

$C-$

The outcome of this event is something for which I feel:

Not at all responsible	1	2	3	4	5	Completely responsible

O_w-

7. You are required to relocate in order to keep your job.

The reason I am required to relocate is something that:

Relates to all aspects of my life	1	2	3	4	5	Just relates to this situation

$R-$

The reason I am required to relocate will:

Always exist	1	2	3	4	5	Never exist again

$E-$

8. A valued friend doesn't call on your birthday.

The reason my friend didn't call me is something over which I have:

No control	1	2	3	4	5	Complete control

$C-$

The reason my friend didn't call me is something that completely has to do with:

Me	1	2	3	4	5	Other people or factors

O_r-

(Continued)

9. A close friend becomes seriously ill.

The reason my friend is seriously ill is something over which I have:

No control   1   2   3   4   5   *Complete control*

$C-$

The outcome of this event is something for which I feel:

Not at all responsible   1   2   3   4   5   *Completely responsible*

O_w-

10. You are invited to an important event.

The reason I am being invited is something over which I have:

No control   1   2   3   4   5   *Complete control*

$C+$

The reason I am being invited is someting that completely has to do with:

Me   1   2   3   4   5   *Other people or factors*

O_r+

11. You are turned down for an important assignment.

The reason I am being turned down for this assignment is something that:

Relates to all aspects of my life   1   2   3   4   5   *Just relates to this situation*

$R-$

The reason I am being turned down for this assignment will:

Always exist   1   2   3   4   5   *Never exist again*

$E-$

12. You receive some negative feedback from a valued coworker.

The reason I am receiving negative feedback is something that:

Relates to all aspects of my life   1   2   3   4   5   *Just relates to this situation*

$R-$

The reason I am receiving negative feedback will:

Always exist   1   2   3   4   5   *Never exist again*

$E-$

13. You receive a pay increase.

The reason I am receiving a pay increase is something over which I have:

No control	1	2	3	4	5	Complete control

C+

The reason I am receiving a pay increase is something that completely has do do with:

Me	1	2	3	4	5	Other people or factors

O_r+

14. Someone close to you is diagnosed with cancer.

The reason he or she has cancer is something that:

Relates to all aspects of my life	1	2	3	4	5	Just relates to this situation

R−

The reason he or she has cancer will:

Always exist	1	2	3	4	5	Never exist again

E−

15. Your latest investment strategy backfires.

The reason my strategy is backfiring is something that:

Relates to all aspects of my life	1	2	3	4	5	Just relates to this situation

R−

The reason my strategy is backfiring will:

Always exist	1	2	3	4	5	Never exist again

E−

16. You miss your airplane flight.

The reason I missed my flight is something over which I have:

No control	1	2	3	4	5	Complete control

C−

The reason I missed my flight is something that completely has to do with:

Me	1	2	3	4	5	Other people or factors

$O_r−$

(Continued)

17. You are selected for an important project.

The reason I am being selected for this project is something over which I have:

No control	1	2	3	4	5	Complete control

$C+$

The outcome of this event is something for which I feel:

Not at all responsible	1	2	3	4	5	Completely responsible

O_w+

18. The project you are in charge of fails.

The reason the project is failing is something over which I have:

No control	1	2	3	4	5	Complete control

$C-$

The outcome of this event is something for which I feel:

Not at all responsible	1	2	3	4	5	Completely responsible

O_w-

19. Your employer offers you a 30 percent pay cut to keep your job.

The reason I am asked to take the pay cut is something over which I have:

No control	1	2	3	4	5	Complete control

$C-$

The reason I am asked to take the pay cut is something that completely has to do with:

Me	1	2	3	4	5	Other people or factors

O_r-

20. You receive an unexpected gift on your birthday.

The reason I received this gift is something that:

Relates to all aspects of my life	1	2	3	4	5	Just relates to this situation

$R+$

The reason I received this gift will:

Always exist	1	2	3	4	5	Never exist again

$E+$

21. Your car breaks down on the way to an appointment.

The reason my car broke down is something that:

| *Relates to all aspects of my life* | 1 | 2 | 3 | 4 | 5 | *Just relates to this situation* |

R—

The reason my car broke down will:

| *Always exist* | 1 | 2 | 3 | 4 | 5 | *Never exist again* |

E—

22. Your doctor calls to tell you that your cholesterol level is too high.

The reason my cholesterol is too high is something that:

| *Relates to all aspects of my life* | 1 | 2 | 3 | 4 | 5 | *Just relates to this situation* |

R—

The reason my cholesterol is too high will:

| *Always exist* | 1 | 2 | 3 | 4 | 5 | *Never exist again* |

E—

23. You are chosen to lead a major project.

The reason I am being chosen is something over which I have:

| *No control* | 1 | 2 | 3 | 4 | 5 | *Complete control* |

C+

The reason I am being chosen is something that completely has to do with:

| *Me* | 1 | 2 | 3 | 4 | 5 | *Other people or factors* |

O_r+

24. You place several phone calls to a friend, and not one of them is returned.

The reason my friend did not return my call is something that:

| *Relates to all aspects of my life* | 1 | 2 | 3 | 4 | 5 | *Just relates to this situation* |

R—

The reason my friend did not return my call will:

| *Always exist* | 1 | 2 | 3 | 4 | 5 | *Never exist again* |

E—

(Continued)

25. You are publicly praised for your work.

The reason I am being praised is something that:

Relates to all aspects of my life 1 2 3 4 5 *Just relates to this situation*

R+

The reason I am being praised will:

Always exist 1 2 3 4 5 *Never exist again*

E+

26. At your physical exam, your doctor cautions you on your health.

The reason my doctor is cautioning me is something over which I have:

No control 1 2 3 4 5 *Complete control*

C−

The outcome of this event is something for which I feel:

Not at all responsible 1 2 3 4 5 *Completely responsible*

O_w-

27. Someone you respect pays you a compliment.

The reason I was paid a compliment is something over which I have:

No control 1 2 3 4 5 *Complete control*

C+

The outcome of this event is something for which I feel:

Not at all responsible 1 2 3 4 5 *Completely responsible*

O_w+

28. You receive an unfavorable performance appraisal.

The reason I am receiving this appraisal is something over which I have:

No control 1 2 3 4 5 *Complete control*

C−

The outcome of this event is something for which I feel:

Not at all responsible 1 2 3 4 5 *Completely responsible*

O_w-

29. You do not receive a much-anticipated promotion.

The reason I did not receive a promotion is something over which I have:

| *No control* | 1 | 2 | 3 | 4 | 5 | *Complete control* |

$C-$

The reason I did not receive a promotion is something that completely has to do with:

| *Me* | 1 | 2 | 3 | 4 | 5 | *Other people or factors* |

O_r-

30. You are elected by your peers to head an important committee.

The reason I am being elected is something that:

| *Relates to all aspects of my life* | 1 | 2 | 3 | 4 | 5 | *Just relates to this situation* |

$R+$

The reason I am being elected will:

| *Always exist* | 1 | 2 | 3 | 4 | 5 | *Never exist again* |

$E+$

Scoring:

You will notice a small C, Or, Ow, R, or E next to each question where you circled a response. Some have pluses, others have minuses. Since we are most concerned with your responses to *adversity*, you will only be scoring those answers with minus signs next to them. These are the adverse events.

1. In the worksheet provided, insert your responses in the blanks next to the number for each event.
2. Follow the sequential instructions on the worksheet to calculate your CO_2RE dimensions and your overall AQ.

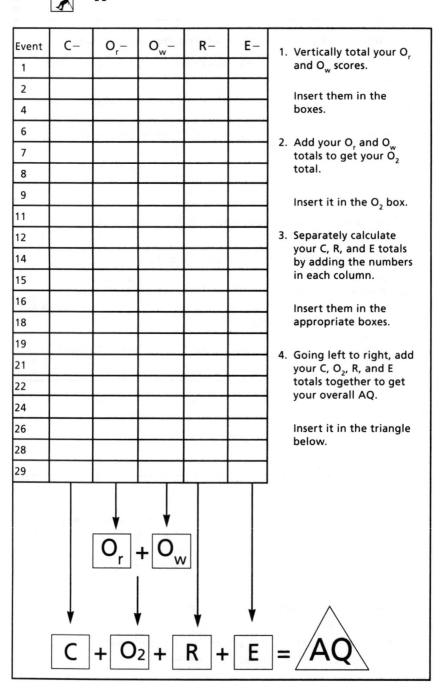

Event	C−	O_r−	O_w−	R−	E−
1					
2					
4					
6					
7					
8					
9					
11					
12					
14					
15					
16					
18					
19					
21					
22					
24					
26					
28					
29					

1. Vertically total your O_r and O_w scores.

   Insert them in the boxes.

2. Add your O_r and O_w totals to get your O_2 total.

   Insert it in the O_2 box.

3. Separately calculate your C, R, and E totals by adding the numbers in each column.

   Insert them in the appropriate boxes.

4. Going left to right, add your C, O_2, R, and E totals together to get your overall AQ.

   Insert it in the triangle below.

$$O_r + O_w$$

$$C + O_2 + R + E = AQ$$

MORE INFORMATION

AQ Programs

As president of PEAK Learning, Inc., Dr. Stoltz offers a wide range of interactive, experiential AQ programs customized to each individual client's needs and audience. PEAK Learning also provides a team of highly skilled program leaders prepared to deliver AQ programs for a wide range of applications.

The Adversity Response Profile™

The full version of the Adversity Response Profile™ is used for a wide range of developmental purposes, including career planning, performance management, sales, team building, leadership development, training, empowerment, managing change, and dealing with adversity. If you desire additional information on this tool, please contact PEAK Learning, Inc. at the numbers shown next.

Consulting

Dr. Paul G. Stoltz has been a consultant and thought leader for a wide range of organizations around the world. Areas of expertise include change management, leadership development, performance management, personal and professional development, communication, athletic performance, team effectiveness, hiring processes, organizational alignment, vision, purpose, values, ethics, life management, and resilience. Dr. Stoltz assists his clients in hiring and developing high AQ people, as well as developing high AQ organizations.

Clients span many industries including health care, electronics, semiconductors, accounting, telecommunications, management consulting, computers, beverages, professional development, public utilities, consumer products, data processing, finance, professional associations, government agencies, and nonprofit organizations.

SPEAKING

Dr. Paul G. Stoltz is a top-ranked national and international speaker. He has presented to more than 100,000 executives, professionals, managers, leaders, salespeople, parents, community members, students, and educators. He frequently speaks on a a variety of issues dealing with AQ at various conferences and events. Related topics include change management, leadership development, performance management, personal and professional development, communication, team effectiveness, hiring processes, organizational alignment, vision, purpose, values, ethics, life management, and resilience.

TO CONTACT DR. STOLTZ OR PEAK LEARNING, INC.

PEAK Learning, Inc. by phone (800) 255-5572 or (520) 527-3333, or by fax (520) 526-3160. Or contact PEAK Learning, Inc. at Four Hundred North Skyview, Flagstaff, Arizona USA 86004.

NOTES

Chapter 1   A New View of Success

4   Jerry Adler and Rod Norland, "High Risk," *Newsweek* (May 27, 1996), pp. 50–57.

6   Martin Seligman, *Learned Optimism* (New York: Knopf, 1990).

11   "Ted had a special talent": Nancy Gibbs, "Tracking Down the Unibomber," *Time* (April 15, 1996), p. 45.

18   "Mr. Edison, you have failed": *The World's 100 Greatest People*, Volume I (New York: Intelligence Learning Systems, 1995).

25   Douglas Lawson, *Give to Live* (La Jolla, CA: Alti Publishing, 1991).

27   "Never Say Die," *Success* (August 1996), p. 38.

32   Twin studies statistics: T. J. Bouchard, Jr., L. Heston, E. Ekert, M. Keys, and S. Resnick, "The Minnesota Study of Twins Reared Apart: Project Description and Sample Results in the Development Domain." In L. Gedda, P. Parisi, and W. Nance (Eds.), *Twin Research 3: Part B. Intelligence, Personality and Development* (New York: Alan R. Liss, Inc., 1981), pp. 227–233. T. J. Bouchard, Jr., D. T. Lykken, M. McGue, N. L. Segal, and A. Tellegen, "Sources of Human Psychological Difference: The Minnesota Study of Twins Reared Apart," *Science, 250*, pp. 223–228.

33   More recent research on twins: Paul Reger, "Anxious? Laid Back? Genes May Play Role," *Arizona Daily Sun* (November 29, 1996), p. 23.

33 "Our genetic blueprint has": David Vanbiema, "Depak Chopra: Emperor of the Soul," *Time* (June 24, 1996), p. 61.

35 Data on children adversity studies from: Carol S. Dweck and Ellen Bush, "Sex Differences in Learned Helplessness: I. Differential Debilitation with Peer and Adult Evaluators," *Developmental Psychology, 12,* pp. 147–156. Carol S. Dweck, William Davidson, Sharon Nelson, and Bradley Enna, "Sex Differences in Learned Helplessness: II. The Contingencies of Evaluative Feedback in the Classroom and III. An Experimental Analysis," *Developmental Psychology, 14,* pp. 268–276.

Chapter 2   The Age of Adversity

40 "The Crisis of Public Order," *Atlantic Monthly* (July 1995), p. 46.

42 Data for nationwide teacher surveys taken from William J. Bennett, *The Index of Leading Cultural Indicators* (New York: Simon & Schuster, 1994), p. 83.

42 "Work Is Hell," *Newsweek* (August 12, 1996).

42 Susan Page, "Angst Makes for Joyless Recovery," *USA Today* (February 20, 1996), p. B1.

49 Adam Rodgers, "Getting Faster by the Second," *Newsweek* (December 9, 1996), p. 148.

Chapter 3   The Science of AQ

55 Christopher Peterson, Steven Maier, and Martin Seligman, *Learned Helplessness* (New York: Oxford University Press, 1993).

56 Viktor E. Frankl, *Man's Search for Meaning* (New York: Washington Square Press, 1984).

64 "Invincible Kids," *US News & World Report* (November 11, 1996), pp. 62–71.

66 Julian Rotter, Jr., "Generalized Expectancies for Internal versus External Control of Reinforcement," *Psychological Monographs, 81*(1, Whole No. 609).

68 Joel Barker, speech, "Paradigms," Seattle, Washington (October 1996).

72 "High Hopes Help Heart Patients Recover, Study Finds," *Minneapolis Tribune* (April 16, 1994), p. 7A.

75 Henry Dreher, *The Immune Power Personality* (New York: Penguin, 1995), pp. 14–15.

75 Lawrence Leshan, *You Can Fight for Your Life!* (New York: M. Evans, 1977).

75 E. J. Langer and J. Rodin, "The Effects of Choice and Enhanced Responsibility for the Aged: A Field Experiment in an Institutional Setting," *Journal of Personality and Social Psychology, 34*, pp. 191–198.

75 "A pioneering British study": S. Greer, T. Morris, and K. W. Pettingale, "Psychological Response to Breast Cancer: Effect and Outcome," *The Lancet, 2*, pp. 785–787. Ten year follow-up reported in S. Greer, K. W. Pettingale, T. Morris, and J. Haybittle, "Mental Attitudes to Cancer: An Additional Prognostic Factor," *The Lancet, 1*, p. 750. Fifteen year follow-up reported in S. Greer, T. Morris, K. W. Pettingale, and J. Haybittle, *The Lancet, 1*, pp. 49–50.

75 Martin Seligman, *Learned Optimism,* (New York: Knopf, 1990), p. 175.

76 "The University": "High Hopes Help Heart Patients Recover, Study Finds," *Minneapolis Tribune* (April 16, 1994), p. 7A.

76 S. E. Locke et al., "Life Change Stress, Psychiatric Symptoms and Natural Killer Cell Activity." *Psychosomatic Medicine, 46*(5), pp. 441–453.

76 Kenny Moore, "The Eternal Example," *Sports Illustrated* (December 21, 1992), p. 21.

76 G. F. Solomon et al., "Prolonged Asymptomatic States in HIV Seropositive Persons with Fewer Than 50 CD4+ T-cells/mm³. Preliminary Psychoimmunologic Findings," *Journal of Acquired Immune Deficiency Syndromes, 6*(10), pp. 1173–1174.

77 Christopher Peterson, Steven Maier, and Martin Seligman, "Optimism and Bypass Surgery," *Learned Helplessness,* (New York: Oxford University Press, 1993).

77 D. C. McClelland, "Some Reflections on the Two Psychologies of Love," *Journal of Personality, 54*, pp. 334–353.

D. C. McClelland. "Motivational factors in health and disease." *American Psychologist, 44*(4), pp. 675–683.

77 J. W. Pennebaker, J. K. Kiecolt-Glaser, and R. Glaser, "Disclosures of Traumas and Immune Functions: Health Implications for Psychotherapy," *Journal of Consulting and Clinical Psychology, 56*, pp. 239–245.

82 Dr. Larry Squire, personal interview, June 1993. Related work: Lawrence Squire, *Memory and Brain* (New York: Oxford University Press, 1987).

Chapter 6   LEAD: Improving Your AQ and Your Ability to Ascend

149 A. Ellis, *Reason and Emotion in Psychotherapy* (Secaucus, NJ: Lyle Stuart, 1962).

150 A. T. Beck, *Cognitive Therapy and the Emotional Disorders* (New York: International University Press, 1976).

150 Raymond P. Perry and Kurt S. Penner, "Enhancing Academic Achievement in College Students through Attribution and Instruction," *Journal of Educational Psychology, 82*, pp. 262–271.

150 Lisa H. Jaycox, Karen J. Reivich, Jane Gillham, and Martin Seligman, "Prevention of Depressive Symptoms in School Children," *Behavioral Research Therapy, 32*, pp. 801–816.

150 S. R. Maddi and S. C. Kobasa, *The Hardy Executive: Health Under Stress* (Homewood, IL: Dow Jones-Irwin, 1984).

151 "As Dr. Louis Baxter": "Neuroscience 1, Philosophy 0," *Psychology Today* (July/August, 1996), p. 18.

152 Henry Dreher, *The Immune Power Personality* (New York: Penguin, 1995) p. 64.

152 Y. Shavit, G. W. Terman, F. C. Martin et al., "Stress Opioid Peptides, the Immune System, and Cancer," *The Journal of Immunology, 135*(2), pp. 834s–837s.

158 Leslie Cameron-Bandler, David Gorden, and Michael Lebean, *The Emprint Method* (New York: Future Pace, 1985).

159 Dr. Mark Nuwer, personal interview, June 1993.

174 Stephen R. Covey, *Seven Habits of Highly Effective People* (New York: Simon & Schuster, 1989).

176 Kenneth L. Woodward and John McCormick, "The Art of Dying Well," *Newsweek* (November 25, 1996), pp. 61–67.

184 Lisa H. Jaycox, Karen J. Reivich, Jane Gillham, and Martin Seligman, "Prevention of Depressive Symptoms in School Children," *Behavioral Research Therapy, 32,* pp. 801–816.

Chapter 8 Improving Others' AQs and Their Ability to Ascend

222 Martin Seligman, *Learned Optimism* (New York: Knopf, 1990), pp. 150–152.

223 "Other Studies have": C. Peterson and L. Barrett, "Explanatory Style and Academic Performance among University Freshmen," *Journal of Personality and Social Psychology, 53,* pp. 603–607.

Chapter 9 The High AQ Organization: Creating the Climbing Culture

247 Peter M. Senge, *The Fifth Discipline* (New York: Currency Doubleday, 1990).

247 C. S. Dweck and B. Licht, "Learned Helplessness and Intellectual Achievement." In J. Garber and M. E. P. Seligman (Eds.), *Human Helplessness* (New York: Academic Press, 1980) pp. 197–221.

251 Information on Lillian Vernon: "Entrepreneurs Who Excel," *Nation's Business* (August 1996), p. 24.

Chapter 10 The Climber's Habit

284 Joel Barker, *Paradigms* (New York: HarperCollins, 1992).

BIBLIOGRAPHY

Abramson, L. Y., Seligman, Martin E. P., and Teasdale, J. (1978). Learned helplessness in humans: Critique and reformulation. *Journal of Abnormal Psychology, 87,* pp. 32–48.

Ader, R. (Ed.) (1981). *Psychoneuroimmunology.* New York: Academic Press.

Ader, R., Felten, D. L., and Cohen, N. (Eds.) (1991). *Psychoneuroimmunology II.* New York: Academic Press.

Arnold, R. M., and Razak, W. N. (1991). Overcoming learned helplessness: Managerial strategies for the 1990's. *Journal of Employment Counseling, 28,* pp. 99–106.

Arvey, R. D., and Bouchard, J. T., Jr. (1994). Genetics, twins, and organizational behavior. In B. A. Staw and L. L. Cummings (Eds.), *Research in organizational behavior, Vol. 16,* pp. 47–82.

Arvey, R. D., McCall, B., Bouchard, T. J., Jr., Taubman, P., and Cavanaugh, M. A. (1994). Genetic influence on job satisfaction and work values. *Personality and Individual Differences, 17,* pp. 21–33.

Bandura, A. (1977). Self-efficacy: Towards a unifying theory of behavioural change. *Psychological Review, 84,* pp. 191–215.

Barker, J. A. (1992). *Paradigms: The business of discovering the future.* New York: HarperCollins.

Beck, A. T. (1967). *Depression: Causes and treatment.* Philadelphia: University of Pennsylvania Press.

Beck, A. T. (1976). *Cognitive therapy and the emotional disorders.* New York: International University Press.

Begley, S. (1995). Gray matters. *Newsweek,* March 27, pp. 48–54.

Benard, B. (1993). Fostering resiliency in kids. *Educational Leadership,* (November), pp. 44–48.

Bonanno, G. A., Davis, P. J., Singer, J. L., and Schwartz, G. E. (1991). The repressor personality and avoidant information processing: A dichotic listening study. *Journal of Research in Personality, 25*(4), pp. 386–401.

Bouchard, T. J., Jr., Heston, L., Ekert, E., Keys, M., and Resnick, S. (1981). The Minnesota study of twins reared apart: Project description and sample results in the development domain. In L. Gedda, P. Parisi, and W. Nance (Eds.), *Twin research 3: Part B. Intelligence, personality and development,* (pp. 227–233), New York: Alan R. Liss.

Bouchard, T. J., Jr., Lykken, D. T., McGue, M., Segal, N. L., and Tellegen, A. (1990). Sources of human psychological difference: The. Minnesota study of twins reared apart. *Science, 250,* pp. 223–228.

Bowers, K. S. (1968). Pain, anxiety, and perceived control. *Journal of Consulting and Clinical Psychology, 32,* pp. 596–602.

Brown, K. A. (1984). Explaining group poor performance: An attributional analysis. *Academy of Management Review, 9,* pp. 54–63.

Bryant, B. K., and Trockel, J. F. (1976). Personal history of psychological stress related to locus of control orientation among college women. *Journal of Consulting and Clinical Psychology, 44,* pp. 266-271.

Burns, M. O., and Seligman, M. E. P. (1989). Explanatory style across the life span: Evidence for stability over 52 years. *Journal of Personality and Social Psychology, 56,* pp. 471–477.

Clapham, S., and Schwenk, C. (1991). Self-serving attributions, managerial cognition, and company performance. *Strategic Management Journal, 12,* pp. 219–229.

Collins, B. E., Martin J. C., Ashmore, R. D., and Ross, L. (1973). Some dimensions of the internal-external metaphor in theories of personality. *Journal of Personality, 41,* pp. 471–492.

Cone, J. D. (1971). Locus of control and desirability. *Journal of Consulting and Clinical Psychology, 36,* p. 449.

Connor, M. J. (1995). Locus of control. *Therapeutic Care and Education,* 4(1), pp. 16–26.

Curtis, K. A. (1992). Altering beliefs about the importance of strategy: An attribution dimension. *Journal of Applied Social Psychology, 22*(20), p. 953.

Deaux, K. (1976). Sex: A perspective on the attribution process. In J. H. Harvey, W. J. Ickes, and R. F. Kidd (Eds.), *New directions in attribution research, Vol 1,* (pp. 335–352), Hillsdale, NJ: Erlbaum.

DeRubeis, R. J., Evans, M. D., Hollon, S. D., Garvey, M. J., Grove, W. M., and Tuason, A. B. (1990). How does cognitive therapy work? Cognitive change and symptom change in cognitive therapy and pharmacotherapy for depression. *Journal of Consulting and Clinical Psychology, 58,* pp. 862–869.

Diener, C. I., and Dweck, C. S. (1978). An analysis of learned helplessness: Continuous changes in performance, strategy, and achievement cognitions following failure. *Journal of Personality and Social Psychology, 36,* pp. 451–462.

Diener, C. I., and Dweck, C. S. (1980). An analysis of learned helplessness: II. The processing of success. *Journal of Personality and Social Psychology, 39,* pp. 940–952.

Dweck, C. S. (1975). The role of expectations and attributions in the alleviation of learned helplessness. *Journal of Personality and Social Psychology, 31,* pp. 674–685.

Dweck, C. S., and Bush E., (1976). Sex differences in learned helplessness: I. Differential debilitation with peer and adult evaluators. *Developmental Psychology, 12,* pp. 147–156.

Dweck, C. S., Davidson, W., Nelson, S., and Enna, B. (1978). Sex differences in learned helplessness: II. The contingencies of evaluative feedback in the classroom and III. An experimental analysis. *Developmental Psychology, 14,* pp. 268–276.

Dweck, C. S., and Goetz, T. E. (1978). Attributions and learned helplessness. In J. H. Harvey, W. Ickes, and R. F. Kidd (Eds.), *New directions in attribution research, Vol. 2,* (pp. 157–179), Hillsdale, NJ: Erlbaum.

Dweck, C. S., and Licht, B. (1980). Learned helplessness and intellectual achievement. In J. Garber and M. E. P. Seligman (Eds.), *Human helplessness,* (pp.197–221), New York: Academic Press.

Dweck, C. S., and Reppucci, N. D. (1973). Learned helplessness and reinforcement responsibility in children. *Journal of Personality and Social Psychology, 25,* pp. 109–116.

Dweck, C. S., and Wortman, C. B. (1982). Learned helplessness, anxiety, and achievement motivation. In H. W. Krohne and L. Laux (Eds.), *Achievement, stress, and anxiety,* (pp. 93–125), New York: Hemisphere.

Elliot, G. C. (1989). Self-serving biases in the face of reality: The effect of task outcome and potential causes on self-other attributions. *Human Relations, 42,* pp. 1015–1032.

Ellis, A. (1962). *Reason and emotion in psychotherapy.* Secaucus, NJ: Lyle Stuart.

Farber, S. L. (1981). *Identical twins reared apart.* New York: Basic Books.

Fawzy, F. I., Kemeny, M. E., et al. (1990). A structured psychiatric intervention for cancer patients. II. Changes over time in immunological measures. *Archives of General Psychiatry, 47,* pp. 729–735.

Flippin, R. (1992). Good Luks: A champion of volunteerism insists helping is healthy. *American Health,* (November).

Fontaine, G. (1974). Social comparison and some determinants of expected personal control and expected performance in a novel task situation. *Journal of Personality and Social Psychology, 29,* pp. 487–496.

Forsyth, D. R., and Kelley, K. N. (1994). Attribution in groups: Estimations of personal contributions to collective endeavors. *Small Group Research, 25,* pp. 367–383.

Garber, J., and Hollon, S. D. (1980). Universal versus personal helplessness in depression: Belief in uncontrollability or incompetence? *Journal of Abnormal Psychology, 89,* pp. 56–66.

Garber, J., Miller, S. M., and Abramson, L .Y. (1980). On the distinction between anxiety states and depression: Percieved control, certainty, and probability of goal attainment. In J. Garber and M. E. P. Seligman (Eds.), *Human helplessness: Theory and applications.* New York: Academic Press.

Garland, H. (1984). Relation of effort-performance expectancy to performance in goal-setting experiments. *Journal of Applied Psychology, 69,* pp. 79–84.

Gillham, J. E., Reivich, K. J., Jaycox, L. H., and Seligman, M. E. P. (1995). Prevention of depressive symptoms in school children: Two-year follow-up. *Psychological Science, 6,* pp. 343–351.

Gist, M. (1987). Self-efficacy: Implications for organizational behavior and human resource management. *Academy of Management Review, 23*(3), pp. 472–485.

Glausiusz, J. (1996). The chemistry of obsession. *Discover,* (June), p. 36.

Green, S. G., and Mitchell, T. R. (1979). Attribution processes in leader member interactions. *Organizational Behavior and Human Performance, 23,* pp. 429–458.

Hanusa, B. H., and Schulz, R. (1977). Attributional mediators of learned helplessness. *Journal of Personality and Social Psychology, 35,* pp. 602–611.

Heimberg, R. G., Klosko, J. S., Dodge, C. S., Shadick, R., et al. (1989). Anxiety disorders, depression, and attributional style: A further test of the specificity of depressive attributions. *Cognitive Therapy and Research, 13,* pp. 21–36.

Heimberg, R. G., Vermilyea, J. A., Dodge, C. S., and Becker, R. E. (1987). Attribution style, depression, and anxiety: An evaluation of the specificity of depressive attributions. Special Issue: Anxiety:

Cognitive factors and the anxiety disorders. *Cognitive Therapy and Research, 11,* pp. 537–550.

Henry, J., and Campbell, C. (1995). A comparison of the validity, predictiveness and consistency of a trait versus situational measure of attributions. In M. J. Martinko (Ed.), *Attribution theory: An organizational perspective,* Delray Beach, FL: St. Lucie Press.

Henry, J., Martinko, M. J., and Pierce, M. A. (1993). Attributional style as a predictor of success in a first computer science course. *Computers in Human Behavior, 9,* pp. 341–352.

Heyman, G. D., Dweck, C. S., and Cain, K. M. (1992). Young children's vulnerability to self-blame and helplessness: Relationship to beliefs about goodness. *Child Development, 63,* pp. 401–415.

Ilgen, D., and Knowlton, W. (1980). Performance attribution effects on feedback from superiors. *Organizational Behavior and Human Performance, 25,* pp. 441–456.

Jamner, L., Schwartz, G. E., and Leigh, H. (1988). The relationship between repressive and defensive coping styles and monocyte, eosinophile, and serum glucose levels: Support for the opioid peptide hypothesis of repression. *Psychosomatic Medicine, 50,* pp. 567–575.

Jaycox, L. H., Reivich, K. J., Gillham, J., and Seligman, M. E. P. (1994). Prevention of depressive symptoms in school children. *Behavioral Research Therapy, 32,* pp. 801–816.

Jensen, M. R. (1987). Psychobiological factors predicting the course of cancer. *Journal of Personality, 55*(2), pp. 317–342.

Kabat-Zinn, J. (1991). *Full catastrophe living: Using the wisdom of your body and mind to face stress, pain, and illness.* New York: Delacorte.

Kabat-Zinn, J. (1994). *Wherever you go, there you are.* New York: Hyperion Books.

Kent, R., and Martinko, M. (1995). The development and evaluation of a scale to measure organizational attributional style. In M. J. Martinko (Ed.), *Attribution theory: An organizational perspective,* Delray Beach, FL: St. Lucie Press.

Klee, S., and Meyer, R. G. (1979). Prevention of learned helplessness in humans. *Journal of Consulting and Clinical Psychology, 47,* pp. 411–412.

Lange, L. G., and Schreiner, G. F. (1994). Immune mechanisms of cardiac disease. *New England Journal of Medicine, 330*(16), pp. 1129–1135.

Lefcourt, H. M., Von Baeyer, C. L., Ware E. E., and Cox, D. J. (1979). The Multidimensional-Multiattributional Causality Scale: The development of a goal specific locus of control scale. *Canadian Journal of Behavioural Science, 11*(4), pp. 286–304.

Levine, G. F. (1977). "Learned helplessness" and the evening news. *Journal of Communication,* (Fall), pp. 100–105.

Lifton, R. J. (1993). *The protean self: Human resilience in an age of fragmentation.* New York: Basic Books.

Locke, E., Frederick, E., Lee, C., and Bobko, P. (1984). The effect of self-efficacy, goals, and task strategies on task performance. *Journal of Applied Psychology, 69,* pp. 241–251.

Luks, A. (1992). *The healing power of doing good.* New York: Fawcett Columbine.

Maddi, S. R., and Kobasa, S. C. (1984). *The hardy executive: Health under stress.* Homewood, IL: Dow Jones-Irwin.

Maier, S. F., and Laundenslauger, M. L. (1988). Inescapable shock, shock controllability, and mitogen-stimulated lymphocyte proliferation. *Brain, Behavior, and Immunity, 2,* pp. 87–91.

Maier, S. F., and Seligamn, M. E. P. (1976). Learned helplessness: Theory and evidence. *Journal of Experimental Psychology: General, 105,* pp. 3–46.

Martinko, M. J., and Gardner, W. L. (1982). Learned helplessness: An alternative explanation for performance deficits. *Academy of Management Review, 7,* pp. 195–204.

McElroy, J. (1982). A typology of attribution leadership research. *Academy of Management Review, 7,* pp. 413–417.

McGue, M., and Bouchard, T. J., Jr. (1989). Genetic and environmental determinants of information processing and special mental abilities: A twin analysis. In R. J. Sternberg (Ed.), *Advances in the psychology of human intelligence, Vol. 5,* (pp. 7–45).

McGue, M., Bouchard, T. J., Jr., Lykken, D. T., and Finkel, D. (1991). On genes, environment, and experience. *Behavior and Brain Sciences, 14,* pp. 400–401.

Mirowsky, J., and Ross, C. E. (1990). Control or defense? Depression and the sense of control over good and bad outcomes. *Journal of Health and Social Behavior, 31,* pp. 71–86.

Nicholls, J. G. (1975). Casual attributions and other achievement-related cognitions: Effects of task outcome, attainment value, and sex. *Journal of Personality and Social Psychology, 31,* pp. 379–389.

Nurmi, J. -E., Onatsu, T., and Haavisto, T. (1995). Underachiever's cognitive behavior strategies—Self-handicapping at school. *Contemporary Education Psychology, 20,* pp. 188–200.

Okun, M. A., Zautra, A. J., and Robinson, S. E. (1976). The effects of choice and enhanced responsibility for the aged: A field experiment in an institutional setting. *Journal of Personality and Social Psychology, 34,* pp. 191–198.

Ornish, D. M., Brown, S. E., Scherwitz, L. W., et al. (1990). Can lifestyle changes reverse coronary atherosclerosis? The lifestyle heart trial. *The Lancet, 336,* pp. 129–133.

Ornstein, R., and Sobel, D. (1988). *The healing brain.* New York: Touchstone Books.

Pennebaker, J. W. (1989). Confession, inhibition, and disease. *Advances in Experimental Psychology, 22,* pp. 212–244.

Pennebaker, J. W. (1990). *Opening up: The healing power of confiding in others.* New York: William Morrow.

Pennebaker, J. W., Barger, S. D., and Tiebout, H. (1989). Disclosure of traumas and health among holocaust survivors. *Psychosomatic Medicine, 51,* pp. 577–589.

Pennebaker, J. W., and Beall, S. (1986). Confronting a traumatic event: Toward an understanding of inhibition and disease. *Journal of Abnormal Psychology, 95,* pp. 274–281.

Perry, R. P., and Penner, K. S. (1990). Enhancing academic achievement in college students through attribution and instruction. *Journal of Educational Psychology, 82,* pp. 262–271.

Peterson, C. (1991). The meaning and measurement of explanatory style. *Psychological Inquiry, 2,* pp. 1–10.

Peterson, C. (1992). Explanatory style. In C. P. Smith (Ed.), *Handbook of thematic content analysis,* (pp. 376–382), New York: Cambridge University Press.

Peterson, C., and Barrett, L. (1987). Explanatory style and academic performance among university freshmen. *Journal of Personality and Social Psychology, 53,* pp. 603–607.

Peterson, C., Maier, S. F., and Seligman, M. E. P. (1993). *Learned helplessness.* New York: Oxford University Press.

Peterson, C., and Seligman, M. E. P. (1984). Casual explanations as a risk factor for depression: Theory and evidence. *Psychological Review, 91,* pp. 347–374.

Peterson, C., Seligman, M. E. P., and Vaillant, G. E. (1988). Pessimistic explanatory style is a risk factor for physical illness: A thirty-five-year longitudinal study. *Journal of Personality and Social Psychology, 55,* pp. 23–27.

Peterson, C., Semmel, A., von Baeyer, C., Abramson, L. Y., Metalsky, G. I., and Seligman, M. E. P. (1982). The Attributional Style Questionnaire. *Cognitive Therapy and Research, 6*(3), pp. 287–300.

Peterson, C., and Ulrey, L. M. (1994). Can explanatory style be scored from TAT protocols? *Personality and Social Psychology Bulletin, 20*(1), pp. 102–106.

Rettew, D., Reivich, K., Seligman, M. E. P., and Seligman, D. (1990). *Professional sports and explanatory style: Predicting performance in the major leagues.* Manuscript submitted for publication.

Riskind, J. H., Castellon, C. S., and Beck, A. T. (1989). Spontaneous casual explanations in unipolar depression and generalized anxiety: Content analysis of dysfunctional-thought diaries. *Cognitive Therapy and Research, 13*(2), pp. 97–108.

Rodin, J., and Langer, E. J. (1977). Long-term effects of a control-relevant intervention with the institutionalized aged. *Journal of Personality and Social Psychology, 35,* pp. 897–902.

Ronis, D., Hanson, R., and O'Leary, V. (1983). Understanding the meaning of achievement attributions: A test of derived locus and stability scores. *Journal of Personality and Social Psychology, 77,* pp. 702–711.

Rotter, J. (1966). Generalized expectations for internal versus external control of reinforcement. *Psychological Monographs, 70*(1).

Rutter, M. (1993). Resilience: Some conceptual considerations. *Journal of Adoloescent Health, 14,* pp. 626–631.

Satterfield, J. M., and Seligman, M. E. P. (1994). Military aggression and risk predicted by explanatory style. *Psychological Science, 5,* pp. 77–82.

Schulman, P., Castellon, C., and Seligman, M. E. P.(1989). Assessing explanatory style: The content analysis of verbatim explanations and the Attributional Style Questionnaire. *Behavior Research and Therapy, 27*(5), pp. 505–512.

Schulman, P., Seligman, M. E. P., and Amsterdam, D. (1987). The Attributional Style Questionnaire is not transparent. *Behavior Research and Therapy, 25,* pp. 391–395.

Schwartz, G. E. (1984). Psychobiology of health: A new synthesis. *Psychology and Health: Master Lecture Series, 3,* pp. 145–195.

Schwartz, G. E. (1988). From behavior therapy to cognitive therapy to systems therapy. In *Paradigms in behavior therapy: Present and promise.* New York: Springer.

Seligman, M. E. P. (1975). *Helplessness: On depression, development and death.* San Francisco: Freeman.

Seligman, M. E.P. (1991). *Learned optimism.* New York: Knopf.

Seligman, M. E. P., Abramson, L. Y., Semmel, A., and von Baeyer, C. (1979). Depressive explanatory style. *Journal of Abnormal Psychology, 88,* pp. 242–247.

Seligman, M. E. P., Castellon, C., Cacciola, J., Schulman, P., Luborsky, L., Ollove, M., and Downing, R. (1988). Explanatory style change during cognitive therapy for unipolar depression. *Journal of Abnormal Psychology, 97,* pp. 1–6.

Seligman, M. E. P., Kaslow, N. J., Alloy, L. B., Peterson, C., Tanenbaum, R. L., and Abramson, L. Y. (1984). Attributional style and depressive symptoms among children. *Journal of Abnormal Psychology, 93,* pp. 235–238.

Seligman, M. E. P., Nolen-Hoeksema, S., Thornton, N., and Thornton, K. M. (1990). Explanatory style as a mechanism of disappointing athletic performance. *Psychological Science, 1,* pp. 143–146.

Seligman, M. E. P., and Schulman, P. (1986). Explanatory style as a predictor of productivity and quitting among life insurance sales agents. *Journal of Personality and Social Psychology, 50,* pp. 832–838.

Sethi, S., and Seligman, M. E. P. (1993). Optimism and fundamentalism. *Pyschological Science, 4*(4), pp. 256–259.

Shavit, Y., Lewis, J., Terman, G., et al. (1984). Opioid peptides mediate the suppressive effect of stress on natural killer cell cytotoxicity. *Science, 223,* pp. 188–190.

Shavit, Y., Terman, G. W., Martin, F. C., et al. (1985). Stress opioid peptides, the immune system, and cancer. *Journal of Immunology, 135*(2), pp. 834s–837s.

Snyder, D. M. (1990). Complementarity and the relation between psychological and neurophysiological phenomena. *Journal of Mind and Behavior, 11,* pp. 219–224.

Solomon, G. F. (1985). The emerging field of psychoneuroimmunology: Hypotheses, supporting evidence, and new directions. *Advances, 2,* pp. 6–19.

Struthers, C. W., Colwill, N. L., and Perry, R. P. (1992). An attribution analysis of decision making in a personnel selection interview. *Journal of Applied Social Psychology, 22*(18), p. 801.

Sweeney, P., Anderson K., and Bailey, S. (1986). Attribution style in depression: A meta-analytic review. *Journal of Personality and Social Psychology, 50*, pp. 974–991.

Taylor, S., and Fiske, S. (1975). Point of view and perceptions of causality. *Journal of Personality and Social Psychology, 32*, pp. 439–445.

Teas, R., and McElroy, J. (1986). Casual attributions and expectancy estimates: A framework for understanding the dynamics of salesforce motivation. *Journal of Marketing, 50*(January), pp. 75–86.

Tellegen, A., Lykken, D. T., Bouchard, T. J., Jr., Wilcox, K. J., Segal, N. L., and Rich, S. (1988). Personality similarity in twins reared apart and together. *Journal of Personality and Social Psychology, 54*, pp. 1031–1039.

Temoshok, L., and Dreher, H. (1992). *The type c connection: The behavioral links to cancer and your health.* New York: Random House.

Tennen, H., and Eller, S. J. (1977). Attributional components of learned helplessness and facilitation. *Journal of Personality and Social Psychology, 35*, pp. 265–271.

Tetlock, P., E., Skitka, L., and Boettger, R. (1989). Social cognitive strategies for coping with accountability: Conformity, complexity, and bolstering. *Journal of Personality and Social Psychology, 57*, pp. 632–640.

Trotter, R. J. (1987). Stop blaming yourself. How you explain unfortunate events to yourself may influence your achievements as well as your health. *Psychology Today,* (February), pp. 31–39.

Urban, M. S., and Witt, L. A. (1989). Self-serving bias in group member attributions of success and failure. *Journal of Social Psychology, 130*(3), pp. 417–418.

Valle, V. A., and Frieze, I. H. (1976). Stability of casual attributions as a mediator in changing expectations for success. *Journal of Personality and Social Psychology, 33*, pp. 579–587.

Visintainer, M. A., Volpicelli, J. R., and Seligman, M. R. (1982). Tumor rejection in rats after inescapable or escapable shock. *Science, 216*, pp. 437–439.

Walling, M. D., and Martineck, T., J. (1995). Learned helplessness: A case study of a middle school student. *Journal of Teaching in Physical Education, 14*, 454–466.

Weiner, B. (1974). *Achievement motivation and attribution theory.* Morristown, NJ: General Learning Process.

Weiner, B. (1985). An attribution theory of achievement motivation and emotion. *Psychological Review, 92*(4), pp. 548–573.

Weiner, B. (1986). *An attribution theory of motivation and emotion.* New York: Springer-Verlag.

Weiner, B. (1993). A theory of perceived responsibility and social motivation. *American Psychologist, 48,* pp. 957–965.

Weiner, B., Frieze, I., Kukla, A., Reed, L., Rest, S., and Rosenbaum, R. S. (1971). Perceiving the causes of success and failure. In E. E. Jones, D. E. Kanouse, H. H. Kelley, R. E. Nisbett, S. Valins, and B. Weiner (Eds.), *Attribution: Perceiving the causes of behavior,* (pp. 95–121). Morristown, NJ: General Learning Press.

Zaccaro, S. J., Peterson C., and Walker, S. (1987). Self-serving attributions for individual and group performance. *Social Psychology Quarterly, 50*(3), pp. 257–263.

Zullow, H. M., Oettingen, G., Peterson, C., and Seligman, M. E. P. (1988). Pessimistic explanatory style in the historical record: CAVing, LBJ, presidential candidates, and East versus West Berlin. *American Psychologist, 43,* pp. 673–682.

Zullow, H. M., and Seligman, M. E. P. (1990). Pessimistic rumination predicts defeat of presidential candidates, 1900 to 1984. *Psychological Inquiry, 1*(1), pp. 52–61.

ACKNOWLEDGMENTS

Adversity fuels greatness.

This book is the product of decades of work by great minds and great people. It was born from a synergistic combination of fundamental truth, driving purpose, scientific research, and practical application. I am grateful to the hundreds of visionary pioneers whose work and dedication helped me answer the question of why and how a person can persevere through adversity—the central question of human effectiveness, soul, and survival.

I am also grateful to the thousands of executives, professionals, students, managers, salespeople, leaders, and clients who saw hope and importance in innoculating people against adversity. Gradually, over many years, I tested and improved this material with their feedback, encouragement, and application.

For the creation of this book and its many applications, I wish to express my most sincere gratitude to:

- Ronda for her encouragement, faith, brilliance, and love. Her example of climbing through adversity inspires all whom she meets—me most of all.
- My sons Chase and Sean for their patience, respect, character, and love. I am inspired by their capacity to reach past the ugliness and embrace the beauty in themselves, others, and life.
- My parents, Gary and Sandra together, for their input, involvement, ideas, concern; for teaching me the relentless pursuit of what matters, and for their active love and support. I thank each for their investment in my future.

- My mother for exceptional intuitiveness, as well as her last minute insights and sharp, heartfelt inspirations.

- My father for empathizing with and growing this entrepreneur.

- My sister, Sabina—a Climber—for clarifying for the world the difference between limitations and challenges.

- My grandparents, Mildred and Nate, for their love of life, and Jack, for teaching me to keep laughing and about the dignity and grace of growing older.

- The countless heroes who overcome adversity every day and awaken the rest of us to what is possible.

- My friends and business colleagues, especially:

- Phil Styrlund for his friendship, relentless encouragement, and for letting me be a part of his never-ending effort to better the world.

- Joel Barker for his exceptional wisdom, purpose, quality, guidance, intellect, and compassion for humankind.

- Steve Burrill, Duane Giannini, Jim Ericson, Dan Dubrava, and Jim Williams—for their friendship, vision, support, kindness, and investment.

- Stephen Stern, Jeff Thompson, Jerry Pepper, and Tim Lintner for their ongoing input, encouragement, involvement, and friendship.

- Tom Schaff for his eagle eye and commitment to do significant work.

- Jim Ericson for his guidance and wisdom.

- Dave Kenney for his talent for using AQ to enhance athletic performance and for investing in win-win, and the future of our planet.

- Anthony Polvere for his general assistance and investigative talent.

- Dick Leider for his exceptional guidance of the soul.

- Ali G. for using AQ to come back from injury and take on the world.

- Jeri Grandy for her impeccable research and number-crunching skills.
- Stephen R. Covey for reawakening our generation to what's important, for bettering the world, for instilling faith, and for living his words.
- Howard Gardner for expanding our notion of intelligence.
- Daniel Goleman for introducing the world to emotional intelligence and for instilling hope in countless parents, educators, and concerned individuals.
- Martin Seligman and Peter Jacobs for having an abundance mentality and for creating meaningful and important knowledge.
- Jim Wade for his early editing of and interest in this book.
- My literary agents, Margaret McBride and Clare Horn, for their well-earned reputation for excellence and for helping me introduce AQ to the world.
- Todd Rossel for introducing AQ to Eastern Europe.
- Susan Golant, editor, for her outstanding editorial assistance, insightfulness intelligence, dedication, compassion for humanity, and the instrumental role she played in creating the final draft of this book up to the last minute.
- Nancy Marcus Land, editor, Publications Development Company of Texas, for taking this book to heart and making it discernably better.
- John Wiley & Sons team—Mike Hamilton, Jim Childs, and Laurie Frank—for their vision, enthusiasm, encouragement, dedication, flexibility, and investment.
- Chuck Cole and Bob Duncan for their guidance in shaping this book and my career.
- You, the reader, for having the courage and tenacity to create a high AQ world and life.
- All Climbers—past, present, and future—whose lives have left and will create the legacy of the Ascent.

INDEX